Specialty of the House

Also by Sandy Lesberg

The Single Chef's Cookbook

Specialty
of the
House by Sandy Lesberg

A collection of recipes from the finest restaurants around the world compiled
with the cooperation of the American Express Card

PRENTICE-HALL, INC.
Englewood Cliffs, N. J.

Specialty of the House by Sandy Lesberg
© 1970 by Sandy Lesberg
All rights reserved. No part of this book may be
reproduced in any form or by any means, except for
the inclusion of brief quotations in a review, without
permission in writing from the publisher.
Library of Congress Catalog Card Number: 70-116532
Printed in the United States of America   T
1SBN   O-13-826560-7
Prentice-Hall International, Inc., London
Prentice-Hall of Australia, Pty. Ltd., Sydney
Prentice-Hall of Canada, Ltd., Toronto
Prentice-Hall of India Private Ltd., New Delhi
Prentice-Hall of Japan, Inc., Tokyo

This book is for Susan,
who is perpetually dessert,
and for my children,
Steve, Margot, David, and Adam,
four very different appetizers—
all sweet

INTRODUCTION For most of us the easiest place to be a genius is in the kitchen. And I suggest that it is a genuinely worthy arena, a place where the combination of concentration and good humor can result in a rewarding experience.

The preparation of gourmet food is within the grasp of every person who possesses a simple life ingredient, the desire to please himself and, perhaps more importantly, to please someone close to him. In a previous book I remarked that next to making love, making a good meal is the friendliest gesture of communication known to man. For some, the making of a meal may come easier.

This does not mean, however, that an untutored person can march into a kitchen for the first time and produce a three-star entrée. Not at all. Not without help. And that's exactly where *Specialty of the House* comes in.

For the first time the great chefs of the world, from the great restaurants of the world, have generously and without reservation, revealed the recipes of their favorite dishes and, for the most part, these are recipes that have never been seen in print before. Even in the case of a dish that is readily recognizable, there is usually a characteristic ingredient or preparation instruction that renders it unique.

Nevertheless, I think you'll discover that all the recipes have one thing in common. There is a basic simplicity. The fundamental truth about cooking is that more can be accomplished with ingenuity and loving attention than with mumbo jumbo.

In preparing the book I reaffirmed the maxim that the more outstanding the restaurant and the more exalted the chef, the less complicated is their approach to food. Anyone with serious intent and a sound sense of taste, together with a practical spirit of adventure, can produce dishes of quality and, with the proper coaching, even of distinction.

In *Specialty of the House*, you will find an impressive group of culinary coaches. What magic there is to the art of fine cooking we can all share through the generosity of the proprietors of these first-class restaurants and the revelations of their chefs. In spite of the emphasis on specialties of the house there is none of the pyrotechnical verbosity that frequently attends the disclosure of rare secrets. In fact, if I were to give the book a subtitle it would be "Gourmet Cooking Without Pretension."

How closely you pay attention to the various elements of each recipe should depend on your own experience. If you're a neophyte I suggest that you follow the directions exactly. On the other hand, if you're the master of a family of well-worn pots and pans, then it's up to you. But one word of caution: most famous chefs are proud men who invariably have a specific reason for performing even the slightest act of cooking in their own prescribed way. So consider well before you make any changes.

The highly professional worldwide organization that supports the American Express Card assisted me in compiling the recipes that make up this book. Their strong and uniquely personal relationship with first-class restaurants around the world afforded me an unprecedented avenue of communication. For the fine recipes that are included in the book I thank them for their cooperation, but I accept full responsibility for any omissions that were necessary.

Good food is one of my passions and in choosing recipes I have invariably been guided by my own particular preferences. The selections in the book are all mine and in many instances, where a chef wished to be identified with his dish, I have happily complied.

Naturally, in soliciting the recipes I couldn't very well specify the categories from which each chef should choose. That would defeat the purpose of the book, which was to allow the chefs to submit their own specialties. As a result, the majority of recipes are entrées, since most chefs consider the entrée their greatest challenge.

A short section of appetizers and soups comes first. Then the main section of entrées, divided into fish, poultry, oriental dishes, meat and vegetables. There is a varied assortment of salads, dressings, eggs and sauces, and finally a section for crêpes, soufflés and desserts. With most of the entrées the chef or proprietor has indicated an appropriate wine.

Here, then, is a collection of the finest dishes in the world which up to now have been found almost exclusively on the menus of the finest restaurants of the world. For the first time you can produce them in your own home.

There are many simple wonders to be worked from these pages. It's time to start.

CONTENTS

SECTION ONE

Appetizers   *Soups*

Appetizers

The Tower
Los Angeles, California
Chef: Henri Ellena

FRESH CRAB MEAT ESCOFFIER WITH
CAVIAR

1/2	cup mayonnaise
1/3	cup minced sour pickles, thoroughly drained
1	tablespoon finely chopped capers, thoroughly drained
1	chopped hard-cooked egg
1	tablespoon French mustard
1	tablespoon chopped parsley
1	tablespoon tarragon
2	tablespoons catsup
	Salt
	Pepper
1	tablespoon Escoffier sauce
8	ounces fresh Maryland lump crab meat
2	ounces Beluga caviar

In the same bowl, mix all ingredients
gently in order not to break the crab
lumps. Fold in two ounces of fresh Beluga caviar.

Serve in chilled supreme glasses, on bed
of leaf lettuce. Decorate with quartered
lemon and branch of parsley.

Serves: 4

Wine: Pouilly-Fumé

Charlie's (Cafe Exceptionale)
Minneapolis, Minnesota
Chef: Al Mahlke

BAKED OYSTERS EXCEPTIONALE

24	oysters in the shell
2	large ripe avocado pears
1	teaspoon grated onion
1	small clove garlic, chopped fine
1	teaspoon lemon juice
1/4	teaspoon salt
4	drops Tabasco sauce
1/2	teaspoon Worcestershire sauce
3	tablespoons Hollandaise sauce
	Butter

Place all ingredients except oysters into a
blender and run at medium speed until
smooth and free of lumps, then spoon
into a pastry bag with a No. 5 star tube
until ready to use.

Open the oysters, leaving the oysters in
the deeper half shell, and place them 6 to
a pan. Pour a few drops of melted butter
on each oyster and place under broiler
and cook only until the edges curl—do
not overcook. Remove from fire and with
pastry bag squeeze enough of the mixture
to cover each oyster with a large rosette.
Bake in 400° oven until heated through,
then brown under broiler.

French garlic bread is a good
accompaniment.

Serves: 4

T. Pittari's
New Orleans, Louisiana

OYSTERS BIENVILLE À LA PITTARI

      Ice cream salt (coarse salt)
1   dozen oysters on half shell
1   bunch shallots, chopped
1   tablespoon butter
1   tablespoon flour
1/2 cup chicken broth
1/2 cup shrimp, chopped
1/3 cup mushrooms, chopped
1   egg yolk
1/3 glass white wine
      Bread crumbs
      Paprika
      Grated cheese

Place ice cream salt in pie plate or layer cake pan. Place oysters on half shell on salt. Bake oysters in 350° oven until partially done—about 6-8 minutes.

Sauce
Fry shallots in butter until brown. Add flour, and heat until brown. Add chicken broth, shrimp and mushrooms. Beat egg yolk with wine and slowly add to sauce, beating rapidly. Season to taste. Simmer 10 to 15 minutes, stirring constantly. Pour sauce over each oyster; cover with bread crumbs, paprika and grated cheese mixed. Place in oven to brown, about 12 minutes.

Serves: 2

La Boufferie
New York, New York

MUSHROOMS À LA GRECQUE

2   cups water
6   tablespoons olive oil
1/3 cup lemon juice
1/2 teaspoon salt
2   tablespoons minced shallots or green onions
6   sprigs parsley
1   small stalk celery
1   sprig fennel or 1/8 teaspoon fennel seed
1   sprig fresh thyme or 1/8 teaspoon dried thyme
12 black peppercorns
6   coriander seeds
1   pound fresh mushrooms, washed and trimmed
      Minced parsley or chopped mixed green herbs

In a 2 1/2-quart enamel or stainless steel saucepan combine water, olive oil, lemon juice, salt and shallots. Make a bouquet garni of the parsley, celery, fennel, thyme, peppercorns, and coriander; secure tightly in cheesecloth and add to saucepan. Cover tightly and simmer 10 minutes. Add mushrooms to hot liquid, making sure liquid covers them. Cover and simmer 10 minutes. Using slotted spoon, remove mushrooms and arrange on serving dish. Boil cooking liquid rapidly until reduced to about 1/3 cup. Add salt, pepper to taste, strain over mushrooms. Cover and chill thoroughly. Sprinkle with minced parsley or chopped mixed green herbs just before serving.

Serves: 4

Steak Casino
New York, New York
Chef: John Rweri

CLAMS CASINO

24	cherrystone clams
1	stalk celery
1	clove garlic
	Pinch pepper
1/4	teaspoon oregano
1/4	cup mixed nuts
1	pimento
1/2	cup bread crumbs
3	tablespoons Parmesan cheese
4	ounces butter or olive oil
1/2	glass white wine (sauterne)
1	sprig parsley

Shuck clams, saving juice and shells. Grind very fine: clams, nuts, pimentos, pepper, celery, parsley and garlic. Put butter or oil in skillet with wine and clam juice. Raise flame for a few minutes to condense liquid. Then add all ingredients, mix thoroughly and simmer for about 10 minutes. Place this combination into empty clam shells. Place in 350° oven until top is brown and a bit crusty. Serve with lemon wedges.

Serves: 4

Wine: Dry white wine

Caribbean Room
Pontchartrain Hotel
New Orleans, Louisiana

CRAB MEAT PUFFS

16	(2-inch) bread rounds
1/2	tablespoon softened butter
4	teaspoons mayonnaise
16	thin tomato slices
1	(6 1/2-ounce) can crab meat
	Salt, pepper, lemon juice

Toast bread rounds on one side and brush with butter, cool. Spread untoasted side with mayonnaise. Top with two teaspoons of crab meat, tomato slice and 1/2 teaspoon mayonnaise. Add few drops of lemon juice. Broil until mayonnaise puffs and starts to brown.

Serves: 8

Caribbean Room
Pontchartrain Hotel
New Orleans, Louisiana

EGGPLANT STUFFED WITH CRAB MEAT

1	cup mixed onions and celery, minced
2	tablespoons oil
1	cup cracker crumbs
1	egg
2	eggplants
1	cup crab meat
	Lemon juice
	Butter
	Salt
	Pepper

Brown onions and celery in 1 tablespoon oil for a few minutes and then add cracker crumbs and brown some more. In a separate pot boil eggplants until soft, then remove pulp from skin, chop pulp and place it in skillet with onions and celery. Add 1 beaten egg, 1 tablespoon more oil and season with salt and pepper to taste.

Place this well-mixed eggplant back into the shell and bake at 350° for 1/2 hour. Remove and cover with the crab meat which has been sprinkled with lemon juice and cooked in butter in skillet. Cook for 15 minutes more.

Serves: 2

Wine: Dry champagne or
Pouilly-Fuissé (French
white wine)

Caribbean Room
Pontchartrain Hotel
New Orleans, Louisiana

OYSTERS À LA HARLEQUIN

- 2 shallots, chopped
- 4 artichokes
- 2 ounces butter
- 1 cooking spoon flour
- 1 cup water (added to oysters)
- 2 dozen oysters
- 1 bay leaf
- 2 whole allspice

Bring artichokes to boil; let simmer and skim water surface. Sauté shallots in butter until curled. Add 1 spoon of flour, blend well. Add oysters and liquid, stir to a smooth sauce. Take outer leaves of artichokes and scrape, combine with diced bottoms, add to sauce. Place each heart in casserole and put oysters around. Sprinkle with bread crumbs, brown and serve.

Serves: 4

Wine: Imported or American
dry white Chablis

Masson's Restaurant Français
New Orleans, Louisiana
Chef: Robert Finley

CANAPÉ MASSON

- 1/4 pound butter
- 1/2 cup chopped green onions
- 1 clove garlic, chopped
- 1 pound cooked crab meat
- 1 cup heavy white sauce (see below)
- 6 slices toast (trim crusts)
- 3/4 cup grated Cheddar cheese

Sauté onions and garlic in butter until soft. Add crab meat, cook 5 minutes. Add white sauce and continue cooking slowly 3-4 minutes more. Cool until fairly firm. Spread on toast slices and cover with cheese. Bake at 350° for 8-10 minutes or until cheese melts.

White Sauce
- 1/2 pound butter
- 1 cup flour
- 2 cups heated milk
  Salt and pepper to taste

Melt butter in copper or any heavy-bottomed pot. Add flour. Simmer over low heat stirring constantly for 3-4 minutes. Add hot milk. Keep stirring and cook slowly 8-10 minutes until it becomes thickened.

Serves: 6

Wine: Chablis

Gallatin's
Monterey, California

MUSHROOMS À LA CRÈME GEORGE

- 1/2 pound small mushrooms
- 1 tablespoon butter
- 1 tablespoon dry sherry
- 1/2 cup sour cream
- 1/4 teaspoon monosodium glutamate
- 1 teaspoon Worcestershire sauce
  Dash of Tabasco
  Salt
  Pepper

Sauté mushrooms and their chopped stems in butter for 2 minutes. Add dry sherry and cook for another minute. Next, add sour cream, monosodium glutamate, Worcestershire sauce, Tabasco, and salt and pepper to taste. Cook until sauce is good and thick; serve on toast points.

Serves: 2

Wine: Any Moselle wine would
be excellent with this
dish.

Emily Shaw's Inn
Pound Ridge, New York
Prop: John Shaw
Chef: Robert Walser

JOHN SHAW APPETIZER

8   slices white bread
1   cup mayonnaise
1   teaspoon curry powder
1   cup grated Cheddar cheese
    Salt and pepper
1   (14-ounce) can pasteurized lump crab meat

With cookie cutter or rim of drinking glass, shape white bread into rounds. Then toast on one side only under broiler.

Combine mayonnaise and curry powder; blend together thoroughly. Spread the mayonnaise and curry combination on the untoasted side of bread, place fresh crab meat on top of each round. Add salt and pepper to taste. Sprinkle grated Cheddar cheese over all and toast under broiler until cheese melts.

Serves: 8

Wine: Chablis

Coach Inn
Fort Washington, Pennsylvania
Chef: Uwe Hastner

CRAB MEAT À LA MAISON

12 ounces butter
3   ounces Virginia ham, chopped fine
36 ounces Alaska King Crab, 1/2-inch pieces
6   slices fresh white bread, remove crusts and grind into bread crumbs
6   ounces imported Swiss cheese, grated

Heat butter in sauté pan. Add ham and fry until slightly crisp. Add crab meat, sauté until meat is hot—do not brown. Divide into individual casseroles or, if you wish, into one large shallow casserole. Mix fresh bread crumbs and Swiss cheese and top casserole with mixture. Place under broiler until cheese melts and color is a golden brown. Serve piping hot!

Serves: 6

Wine: White wine

The Lemon Tree
Lancaster, Pennsylvania
Chef: Larry Copenheover

PÂTÉ CONTINENTAL

16 ounces liver pâté (canned)
1   tablespoon mushroom base or 3/4 cup finely chopped mushrooms
3   tablespoons butter
2   tablespoons each of chopped parsley and chives
1   tablespoon brandy
1   tablespoon Kirchwasser
1/4 teaspoon Worcestershire sauce
    Salt and black pepper to taste

If using fresh mushrooms, sauté in butter. If not, just add butter and all other ingredients to pâté. Mix very carefully. Mold into shape. Refrigerate for at least 5 hours before using. Can be used as an appetizer or on top of steak after it has been cooked, by spreading on top of steak just before you are ready to remove from the broiler.

Serves: 6

Wine: Tavel rosé

Carriage House Restaurant
Pittsburgh, Pennsylvania
Chef: John Marzina

BAKED ROCKAWAY OYSTERS À LA
CARRIAGE HOUSE

      1 large green pepper, chopped
      3 pimentos, chopped
   1/4 pound butter
      1 pound lump crab meat
      1 teaspoon Worcestershire sauce
         Salt and pepper to taste
    24 oysters
   1/2 cup cracker crumbs

Use half of butter to cook peppers and pimentos until tender. Mix all ingredients, except oysters, thoroughly. Open oysters, leaving meat in deep shell. Spread a portion of the mixture on each oyster, sprinkle with crumbs and use the rest of the butter on top of the oysters. Bake at 450° for 10 to 15 minutes.

Serves: 4

Wine: Rhine

L'Orangerie
New York, New York

DELICES DE GRUYÈRE

      3 tablespoons butter
      4 tablespoons flour
  1 1/2 cups milk
      1 teaspoon salt
         Dash white pepper and nutmeg
      4 egg yolks
   1/2 pound (2 1/2 cups) grated
         Swiss cheese
      2 tablespoons flour
      1 egg, well-beaten
      1 cup fine dry bread crumbs

Melt butter in saucepan and stir in flour until smooth; cook 1-2 minutes. Stir in

milk and cook, stirring constantly, until thick and smooth. Continue cooking over low heat 5 minutes. Stir in salt, pepper, nutmeg, egg yolks and grated cheese. Heat thoroughly and remove from heat. Pour into a flat platter and refrigerate 2-3 hours.

After cheese mixture has been refrigerated, mold into balls size of large walnuts. Coat with flour, dip into beaten egg, roll in crumbs. Fry in deep fat (375°) 3-4 minutes or until golden brown. Drain on paper toweling. Serve with or without hot tomato sauce as hors d'oeuvre.

Serves: 4

Joseph's
Boston, Massachusetts

BAKED CLAMS CASINO À LA JOSEPH'S

      8 littleneck clams
      1 cup finely rubbed fresh bread
         crumbs
      1 teaspoon paprika
      1 tablespoon olive oil
   1/2 clove garlic, chopped fine
      2 strips bacon
         Lemon wedges

Place clams in heat-proof baking dish. Mix bread crumbs, paprika and garlic. Place a generous pinch of bread crumb mixture on each clam. Cut each strip of bacon into 4 equal parts. Place a piece of bacon in each clam. Put in 350° oven and bake until the bacon is crisp. Transfer clams to serving dish. Serve with lemon wedges.

Serves: 2

Stanley Demos Coach House
Lexington, Kentucky
Prop: Stanley Demos

CRABE DEMOS

1 1/2 cups mayonnaise
6 tablespoons prepared mustard
4 tablespoons curry powder
2 tablespoons lemon juice
12 ounces hot lump crab meat
1 1/2 cups hot cooked wild rice
Parmesan cheese

Mix mayonnaise, mustard, curry powder, lemon juice together. Divide the hot wild rice into four sea shells. Cover with crab meat and cover the crab meat with the curry mixture. Sprinkle with Parmesan cheese and place under the broiler until the curry mixture becomes bubbly.

Serves: 2

La Mediterranee
Pontchatrain Hotel
Detroit, Michigan

CLAMS LARRY

5 cherrystone clams
1/2 cup chopped shallots
1/2 cup white wine
1 cup crab meat
4 tablespoons Mornay (or similar) sauce (see index)

Open 5 fresh cherrystone clams and preserve the juice. Chop the clams medium coarse. Add finely chopped shallots which have been sautéed and reduced in white wine. Place the clam mixture in the shells and top with fresh crab meat, chopped medium, which has been mixed with 4 tablespoons of Mornay sauce. Bake in hot oven for 6 minutes. Serve immediately.

Serves: 1

Georges Rey Restaurant
Français
New York, New York
Chef: André Ledoux

MOULES RAVIGOTE FACON "LA POTINIERE"

1/2 gallon mussels
1 tablespoon French mustard
1 cup mayonnaise
1 tablespoon chives
1 tablespoon vinegar

Poach mussels and, when they start to open, take them out of the shell. Mix the mustard with the vinegar, add the mayonnaise and then the mussels. Now add the chives. Add salt and pepper if necessary.

Serves: 6

Putsch's 210 Restaurant
Kansas City, Missouri
Chef: Herman Sanchez

ESCARGOT À LA HERMAN

24 snails with shells (canned)
4 ounces butter at room temperature
1/2 teaspoon salt
1/8 teaspoon white pepper
1/4 teaspoon garlic powder
1 tablespoon shallots, chopped finely
1 tablespoon parsley, chopped
Pinch of nutmeg
2 tablespoons dry white wine (Chablis)
Dash of Accent
Dash of Worcestershire sauce

Drain liquid from snails and set aside. Combine all other ingredients in a glass bowl, mix thoroughly. Place small amount of mixture in each snail shell. Place snail in shell and also a small dab of butter. Place stuffed shells on pie plate or oven-proof platter and place in pre-heated 350° oven for 15 minutes. Serve with thinly sliced toast points.

Serves: 4

Wine: Bouchard Pouilly-Fuissé

Court of Two Sisters
New Orleans, Louisiana

SHRIMP À LA FEIN

2 strips bacon
1 tablespoon butter
10 peeled raw shrimp
2 green onions, chopped fine
Salt, pepper, paprika
Juice of 1/2 lemon
Tabasco sauce
Worcestershire sauce

Dice bacon and sauté in skillet until half cooked. Pour off excess fat. Lower flame. Add butter, peeled raw shrimp, green onions, and season to taste with salt, pepper and paprika. When shrimp are turning pink, add lemon juice and two dashes each of Tabasco and Worcestershire sauce. Serve on toast.

Serves: 4

Cy Bloom's Place in the Alley
Chefs: Vincent Magnani and
Hans Ruppenthal

CLAMS CASINO À LA HANS

5 cloves garlic
1/2 bundle parsley
1/4 pound butter
Worcestershire sauce
Salt
12 medium-sized clams
1/4 cup cracker crumbs
2 slices Smithfield ham

Mince garlic and parsley very finely. Mix with the butter, add a few dashes of

Worcestershire sauce and pinch of salt. Reshape butter into a stick and chill.

Open the clams and place on a metal tray. Sprinkle a small amount of cracker crumbs on each clam. Add a piece of ham the size of the clam and top with a slice of the prepared butter.

Bake in a 450° oven for approximately 10 minutes. Serve with drawn butter.

Drawn Butter
Melt butter over low heat, remove and allow to stand until milk solids settle. Skim butter fat from top.

Serves: 3

Chateau Fleur de Lis
Atlanta, Georgia
Chef: Mario Massari

TOURNEDOS CORDON ROUGE

8 3-inch patty shells
1 cup Béarnaise sauce (see index)
1 cup sautéed mushrooms
1/2 cup ham in julienne strips
8 tournedos (3/4 ounce each from tenderloin of beef)
8 mushroom caps
1 cup Madeira sauce (see index)

Mix Béarnaise sauce with mushrooms and ham julienne, and fill patty shells with the mixture. Bake in 400° oven until puffed up and soufflé-like. Season and sauté pieces of tenderloin to desired point. Sauté mushroom caps. Top filled patty shells with tournedos and pin mushroom caps on. Pour Madeira sauce over all.

Serves: 4

Charles French Restaurant
New York, New York

ESCARGOTS BOURGUIGNONNE

1 1/2 cups Burgundy or dry white wine
1 teaspoon finely chopped shallot
1/4 cup finely chopped parsley
1/2 cup softened butter
1/2 teaspoon minced garlic
Salt and ground black pepper to taste
3 dozen canned snails and shells

Boil the wine with shallot until the wine is reduced by one half. Strain. Blend butter with parsley, garlic, salt and pepper. Pour 1/2 teaspoon wine in each snail shell, insert a snail, and top with a little of the herbed butter. Bake in a pre-heated hot oven (450°) for 10 minutes. Serve very hot.

Serves: 6

Blue Pine
Athens, Greece
Chef: Antoine Karahalios

BLUE PINE CHEESE STICK

8 ounces Swiss cheese
1 cup flour
1 cup grated Parmesan cheese
2 cups fresh bread crumbs
4 beaten eggs
Cooking oil

Cut Swiss cheese into small stick-shaped pieces. Mix flour and water into thin paste. Roll the cheese sticks in enough thin paste to cover. Dip the sticks in beaten eggs and then in grated Parmesan cheese and bread crumbs. Dip them once more in beaten eggs and then fry them in hot oil until golden brown (3 minutes).

Serves: 4

Maine Maid Inn
Jericho, New York
Chef: Herbert Guonzburger

BAKED CLAMS À LA MAINE MAID

2 dozen well-washed fresh cherrystone clams
1 (16-ounce) bottle clam juice
2 medium size white onions and several stalks celery, finely chopped
5 cloves garlic, chopped very fine
2 teaspoons salt
2 teaspoons pepper
3 teaspoons Worcestershire sauce
4 teaspoons sherry wine
1 teaspoon Accent
2 teaspoons oregano
2 teaspoons olive oil
3 cups bread crumbs
Grated Parmesan cheese
Dash of paprika

Pre-heat oven to 400°. Place 2 cups of water and 16 ounces of clam juice in large saucepan, bring to boil. Place clams into saucepan until they are open. At the same time sauté celery, onions and garlic in the olive oil until cooked soft, then add spices. Continue to heat for 2-3 minutes.

Remove clams from shell and chop fairly fine. Put chopped clams into sauteed mixture in saucepan and boil for 3 minutes. Add the bread crumbs and stir; boil for 3 minutes more. Fill the clean shells with about 2 teaspoons of mixture per shell. Sprinkle with Parmesan cheese and paprika. Place on a cookie sheet and bake in 400° oven for 15 minutes or until brown.

Serves: 6

Wine: Chablis or Pouilly-Fuissé

GALANTINE DE NOLAILLE À LA GELEE
(Pâté of Chicken Breast with Pistachios,
Natural Jelly)

1	(4-pound) ready-to-cook roasting chicken
1	calve's foot
2	pounds veal shank
1/2	pound boneless lean pork
1/2	pound boneless lean veal
1/2	pound salt pork, cubed
3	tablespoons cognac
1/4	teaspoon ground mace
1 1/2	teaspoons salt
1	teaspoon ground thyme
1/2	cup heavy cream
1/4	pound fatback
1/4	pound cooked tongue
1	truffle, chopped
1/3	cup pistachio nuts
1	stalk parsley
1	carrot
1/2	cup sliced onions
1/2	cup sliced celery

Have the butcher bone the chicken (or bone it yourself). Make a rich stock from the chicken bones, veal shank and the calve's foot. Reserve.

Split the boned chicken down the whole length of the back and open it out flat, skin side up. Starting at the back, with a sharp knife, carefully cut the skin away from the meat, removing the skin in one piece. Be careful not to pierce the skin. Trim skin at the legs and wings, leaving enough to cover the openings. Cut the meat of the breast and the tenderloin under the breast and that of the drumsticks into thin slices and set aside. Put the remaining chicken meat and the lean pork and veal through a food chopper twice, using the finest blade. Add the next five ingredients and mix well.

Place the chicken skin, outer side down, on a buttered cloth, and spread it with the meat mixture. Cut fatback and tongue into strips and arrange them in alternate layers over the meat mixture. Sprinkle chopped truffle and pistachio nuts between the slices. Cover with slices of chicken.

By lifting the edge of the cloth and pulling gently, carefully shape the arrangement into a firm roll, drawing the edges of the skin together to form a sausage roll. Sew the skin together along the length of the roll and at the ends. Wrap the roll tightly in the cloth, making sure it is smooth and even. Tie it in the middle and at the ends with string.

Following the preceding directions, place the roll with the parsley, carrot, onions and celery in a large kettle.

Pour in stock to cover. Cover the kettle, bring to boiling point then reduce heat and simmer 2 1/4 hours. Make a clear aspic from the stock in which the Galantine was cooked.

Cool the pâté of chicken breast. Remove the cloth and the string with which the skin was sewn. Glaze the roll with the aspic. Chill until firm and cut in thin slices.

Basic Stock
Add 3 quarts water (to chicken and/or meat) bring to boil and then simmer for 2 1/2 to 3 hours or until reduced by half. Strain stock and chill uncovered.

Aspic
Add 2 tablespoons gelatin to 1/2 cup cold water and dissolve in 1/2 cup boiling stock. Pour into wet mold and chill until firm.

Serves: 8

Commander's Palace
New Orleans, Louisiana

OYSTERS BIENVILLE

    4 dozen oysters
    2 slices bacon
  1/3 cup sliced mushrooms
    2 cloves garlic, chopped
  1/4 cup chopped shallots
    3 tablespoons butter
  2/3 cup flour
    1 quart hot milk
       Dash egg color
  1/3 pound shrimp
  2/3 cup oyster juice
  1/3 cup lemon juice
  1/3 cup sherry
  1/4 cup chopped parsley

Broil 4 dozen oysters in the half shell for a few minutes until done. Then cover each oyster with Bienville sauce and bake in hot oven for a few minutes until the top is brown and crisp.

Bienville Sauce
Cut bacon into small pieces, fry until brown. Add mushrooms, garlic and shallots and cook until done (about 3 minutes). Add butter to pan, stir until melted. Then blend in flour. Cook slowly for 5 minutes, then add hot milk and stir until thick and smooth. Add egg coloring, shrimp, oyster juice, lemon juice, sherry and chopped parsley. Cook over low heat for 15 minutes.

Serves: 8

Wine: Cordon D'alsace

The Camelot
Minneapolis, Minnesota
Proprietor: Hans Skalle
Chef: Jage Eriksen

COQUILLES SAINT JACQUES

      2 cups Duchesse potatoes (see index)
      1 medium-size onion, diced
      3 tablespoons butter
    1/2 cup sliced fresh mushrooms
      6 cups scallops (Boston Bay preferred*)
         Domestic Chablis wine (to cover scallops)
  1 1/2 cups Béchamel sauce (see index)
         Salt and ground black pepper at the table

Pipe Duchesse potatoes around 6 sea shells—set aside. Cook onion in the butter with mushrooms, leaving onions transparent. Do not brown (use medium heat). Put into saucepan. Cover scallops with Chablis wine. Add onions and mushrooms and bring to boil very carefully (this is of the utmost importance). Then simmer slowly. Remove scallops and mushrooms after they are done (not overdone). Reduce liquid to 1/4. Strain and add to Béchamel sauce. Add scallops and mushrooms to sauce. Put into shells and heat in moderate oven—350°. Before serving sprinkle with Parmesan cheese and brown under broiler.

Serves: 2

*If Boston Bay Scallops unattainable, cut sea scallops into half or one-third, dependent on size.

Soups

Charles French Restaurant
New York, New York

CREAM OF PEA SOUP

2 cups shelled green peas
1/2 teaspoon salt
 Boiling water
4 tablespoons rice flour
1 cup chicken stock
1 cup milk
1 tablespoon bacon drippings
 Pepper
1 tablespoon butter
1/2 cup heavy cream

Cook peas with salt in inch of boiling water until they are soft. Drain off the water and blend the peas in a blender. Mix rice flour with 1/2 cup of stock until the mixture is smooth, then add the remaining stock along with the milk. Stir and cook for 10 minutes.

Stir in pea puree, salt, pepper, bacon drippings and butter. Bring to boiling point. Stir in cream.

Serves: 6

Bacchanal
Caesar's Palace Hotel
Las Vegas, Nevada

POTAGE GEMINI

4 ounces sorrell (sour grass)
1 quart chicken consommé
4 yolks of eggs
1 cup heavy cream
1 tablespoon butter
 Salt and pepper to taste

Melt butter in pot on range. Add sorrell—simmer. Then add chicken consommé. Bring to boil. Combine and whip egg yolks and cream together. Take pot off range then blend quickly with yolk and cream mixture. Season to taste. (Optional: add 1 ounce dry sherry to eggs and cream)

Serves: 6

Delmonico's
Mexico, D.F. 6
Chef: Joaquin Morales

SHRIMP SOUP "BARRA DE NAUTLA"

12 ounces shrimp
1 1/2 ounces olive oil
1 ounce chopped onions
2 ounces chopped celery
1 pound tomato cubes
1 1/4 ounces dry sherry
26 ounces hot fish stock (see index)
1 cup rice
1/4 ounce Pernod
1/2 ounce chopped parsley

Sauté the shrimp with olive oil, onions and celery until the onions are transparent and tender. Then add the tomato cubes and allow 4 minutes. Put the mixture into the hot fish stock, then pour the sherry and Pernod into it. Before serving, sprinkle the parsley over the soup.

Serves: 6

Wine: Dry sherry

Milord
Luang 1, Bangkok

POT MILORD
(La Soupe de Poissons Milord)

        1   pound fish heads
        1   bouquet garni (thyme, bay leaf,
                parsley)
        1   onion, minced
        1   stalk of celery, minced
        2   tablespoons flour, a knob of
                butter
        1   teaspoon mustard
            Salt and pepper
      1/2   pint dry white wine
        2   cups mixed, chopped seafood:
                crab, mussels, whitefish,
                prawns, lobster
        1   cup fresh cream
        4   crumbled crackers
            Grated Parmesan and Gruyère
                cheese

Put the fish heads in a cooking pot containing 3 pints cold water, salt and the bouquet garni. (If fish heads are not available use a pound of unboned fish.) Bring to a boil and simmer for 2 hours, or as long as time permits, adding the minced onion and celery. After cooking, this should be strained through a fine cloth.

Meanwhile, slightly brown the flour in the knob of butter, adding the mustard and salt and pepper and then the white wine, slowly, until the roux becomes a smooth sauce. Mix with the fish stock, add the chopped seafood and finally the cream. Pour into attractive stone soup pots, top with broken crackers and sprinkle with the cheese. Bake in the oven until brown or grill. Serve immediately in "lily fold" napkins.

Serves: 4 to 6

Wine: A nice dry sherry—Tio Pepe, etc.

Charles French Restaurant
New York, New York

BOULA BOULA SOUP

        3   cups (1 can) turtle soup
        3   cups cream of pea soup
        3   tablespoons dry sherry
        1   cups heavy cream, whipped
            Dash of salt

Combine turtle soup and pea soup, bring to boiling point. Stir in sherry. Pour into serving bowls and top with unsweetened whipped cream (add dash of salt while whipping). Place bowls under pre-heated broiler until cream is lightly glazed.

Serves: 6

Restaurant Laurent
New York, New York

GAZPACHO ANDALUZ

        1   clove garlic, mashed
        1   medium onion, peeled and
                chopped
        5   very ripe tomatoes, peeled and
                chopped
      1/4   cup parsley, chopped fine
        2   tablespoons vinegar
        3   tablespoons olive oil
      1/4   teaspoon paprika
        1   cup beef stock or consommé
            Chopped cucumber; tomatoes;
                green pepper; onion; stale
                white bread, cut into cubes

Put garlic and onion into a blender and liquify. Add next 6 ingredients and run blender for 2 or 3 minutes. Season to taste with salt and pepper. Place in soup tureen and chill in refrigerator.

Serve soup in chilled plates. Pass, separately, chopped cucumber, tomatoes, green pepper, onion and bread cubes to be added to soup at the table.

Serves: 4

L'Orangerie
New York, New York

SOUPE DE POISSON PROVENÇALE
(Hearty Fish Soup)

    1/4 cup olive oil
      4 shallots, peeled and chopped
      4 ribs celery, sliced
      1 cup mushroom stems, chopped
         Few sprigs parsley
      2 leeks (bulbs only), sliced
      4 cloves garlic, crushed
      2 bay leaves
     12 peppercorns, crushed
         Pinch saffron, crushed
         Pinch cayenne pepper
      2 tablespoons tomato paste
      3 to 4 pounds fish heads, bones
         and trimmings
      4 medium tomatoes, coarsely
         chopped
      1 cup dry white wine
      2 quarts water
      2 tablespoons salt
      2 tablespoons butter
    1/4 cup flour
      2 tablespoons Pernod or cognac
         Pepper
         Chopped parsley
         Garlic-flavored croutons

Heat oil in 4-quart kettle. Add shallots, celery, mushrooms, parsley sprigs, leeks, garlic, bay leaves, peppercorns, saffron, cayenne and tomato paste; sauté over high heat 10 to 15 minutes or until lightly browned. Stir in fish, tomatoes, wine and water. Bring to boil, cover tightly, then simmer for 40 to 50 minutes. Strain and reserve.

Melt butter in large saucepan, gradually stir in flour and cook, stirring constantly, until flour begins to brown. Gradually blend in reserved fish stock. Cook and stir until soup is smooth and slightly thick-

ened. Reduce heat and simmer 20 minutes; strain through fine sieve. Adjust seasoning with salt and pepper if desired. Just before serving stir in Pernod or cognac. Garnish with chopped parsley and croutons.

Serves: 6

Plaza III
Kansas City, Missouri

PLAZA III STEAK SOUP

    1/4 pound margarine
      1 cup flour
    1/2 gallon water
      2 cups ground beef
      1 cup chopped onion, partially
         cooked
      1 cup chopped carrots, partially
         cooked
      1 cup chopped celery, partially
         cooked
      2 cups frozen mixed vegetables
      1 small can tomatoes
      1 tablespoon monosodium
         glutamate
      2 tablespoons beef base
      1 teaspoon pepper

Melt 1 stick margarine and whip in one cup flour to make smooth paste. Stir in 1/2 gallon water. Sauté 2 cups ground beef, drain off grease and add to soup. Add 1 cup each, onion, carrots, celery (which have been partially boiled). Add 2 cups frozen mixed vegetables, 1 can tomatoes, 1 tablespoon monosodium glutamate, 2 tablespoons beef base, 1 teaspoon pepper. Bring to a boil, reduce to simmer and cook until vegetables are done. Do not add salt.

Serves: 6

Alta Vista
Manila, Philippines

CORN SOUP, PHILIPPINE STYLE

2 cups fresh corn or canned cream-style corn
1 tablespoon cooking oil
2 cloves garlic, chopped
2 tablespoons sugar
1 teaspoon salt
Dash pepper
3 cups chicken stock or water
40 pieces tender pepper leaves

Sauté chopped garlic in oil until brown. Discard garlic and, to the oil, add the corn. Simmer for 5 minutes. Add stock or water, and the rest of the ingredients. Simmer for another 15 minutes or until fresh corn is cooked. Add pepper leaves and serve hot.

Serves: 6

Old Club Restaurant
Alexandria, Virginia

PEANUT BUTTER SOUP

1 quart rich chicken stock
3 ounces minced onions
3 ounces minced celery
8 ounces peanut butter
3 ounces butter
1 tablespoon flour
1 cup half and half
1 teaspoon salt
1/4 teaspoon pepper

Bring to boil and then simmer first three ingredients for 45-60 minutes. Strain out onion and celery and discard. Stir in peanut butter until dissolved. Mix flour with remaining ingredients and simmer together 15 minutes. If too thick, thin to proper consistency with milk. Garnish with 1/2 teaspoon bacon crumbs or minced country ham.

Serves: 6

The Inn of the
Eight Immortals
Falls Church, Virginia
Chef: William Mon

LETTUCE WITH MASHED CHICKEN SOUP

1/2 pound chicken white meat, boned
2 peeled water chestnuts
1 teaspoon salt
1 teaspoon pepper
1/4 cup cold water
1 1/2 pints chicken broth
1 teaspoon monosodium glutamate
1/2 head Iceberg lettuce, cored, washed and shredded (1/8-inch wide)
4 drops sesame oil
2 ounces cooked ham (Smithfield), chopped fine

Chop chicken and water chestnuts together very fine, season with 1 teaspoon of salt and white pepper; then smash the mixture with the back of knife. Put mashed chicken mixture in a bowl and thin it into a batter with 1/4 cup of cold water.

In a 2-quart deep pot heat the broth to boil then stir in the chicken batter mixture to eliminate lumps. Season the soup to taste with salt and monosodium glutamate. Add lettuce, bring to boil again. Remove from heat immediately. Drop in sesame oil and sprinkle chopped ham on top.

Serves: 4

Salamandre
Pontchatrain Hotel
Detroit, Michigan

ONION SOUP—LES HALLES

      4 onions
      1 cup butter
      1 tablespoon flour
1 1/2 quarts beef consommé
         Bread croutons
      6 ounces Parmesan cheese
      6 ounces Gruyère cheese

Peel and slice four onions. Cut the onions very fine. Sauté in melted butter to a golden brown. Sprinkle with flour, stirring constantly with wooden spoon. Add beef consommé. Cook on low fire covering the pot and letting simmer gently for 20 minutes.

Season to your taste.

Place the soup in an oven-proof casserole and cover with a large bread crouton topped with Parmesan and Gruyère cheese.

Place in the oven and bake until top of the cheese is golden brown and sizzling ready to serve.

Serves: 2

Russian Tea Room
New York, New York
Chef: George Lohen

ROSZOLNICK SOUP

      2 quarts beef stock
      1 large onion
      2 carrots
      2 white parsley roots
      2 stalks celery
      2 large potatoes
      1 quart milk
   1/2 pint sour cream
      2 tablespoons flour
      2 dill pickles with 1 glass pickle
         juice
         Chicken giblets—as much as
         desired

Cut up vegetables and partially boil. Set aside. Make white sauce of milk, sour cream and flour. (Be careful not to curdle it.) Put into pot with vegetables and then put in cut dill pickles and juice to flavor along with giblets. Bring to a boil and then simmer for 20 minutes.

White Sauce
Stir flour slowly into milk and sour cream. Simmer and stir until thickened.

Serves: 4 to 6

Wine: Pouilly-Fumé or Chablis

SECTION TWO

Fish Entrées

Poultry Entrées   *Oriental Entrées*

Meat Entrées   *Vegetables*

Salads, Dressings, Eggs and Sauces

Fish Entrées

Casa Del Sol
Holiday Inn
Atlantic City, New Jersey

BAKED STRIPED BASS PROVINCIAL

    1   cup olive oil
    2   slices onion
    2   slices green pepper
    2   cloves garlic, chopped
    1   pint claret wine
    1   dozen fresh mushrooms, sliced
    6   tomatoes, peeled and sliced
  1/2   can pimentos, sliced
    6   pounds striped bass
        Salt and pepper and paprika
    8   slices bread
        Chopped parsley

In a wide fish pan place olive oil, onion and green pepper and fry. When done, add garlic and let it set in hot oil for a second. Then add claret, mushrooms, pimento and tomatoes. Bring to a boil and add bass cut in 2-inch thick slices. Season with salt, pepper and paprika. Cover and simmer for 30 minutes.

Cut slices of bread the same thickness as for eating, fry them in hot oil. Rub the fried bread with a piece of garlic. Lay on a deep platter and place fish on top of fried bread. Place the sauce over the fish and sprinkle with chopped parsley.

Serves: 6

Wine: White wine

Maison Rouge Restaurant
Tampa, Florida
Chef: Elmer Dobbins

OLD ORLEANS LOBSTER FRA DIAVOLO

  1/4   cup olive oil
1 1/2   cups diced cooked clams
  1/4   cup chopped Spanish onions
    1   teaspoon finely chopped garlic
  1/2   cup chopped green sweet
        peppers
    2   cups tomato puree
    1   teaspoon chopped parsley
    1   teaspoon oregano leaves
  1/4   teaspoon sweet basil
  1/2   teaspoon salt
  1/4   teaspoon freshly ground black
        pepper
    1   cup dry white wine
    2   (2-pound) Florida lobsters,
        cooked and cleaned

Remove lobster meat carefully from shells. Try not to break them. Save the shells. Cut meat into bite-size pieces. Gently stir into sauce. Remove from heat and put mixture into the lobster shells. Bake in a 325° oven for 10 minutes. Serve piping hot. Garnish with lemon stars.

Sauce
In a heavy saucepan sauté the onions, garlic and peppers in oil until tender, do not brown. Add tomato puree, mix well. Add the spices, simmer slowly for 30 minutes. Then add wine and stir in well.

Serves: 4

Wine: Dry white wine

Pier 1 Restaurant
Hampton, Virginia

MR. MCNAMARA'S SEAFOOD FRA DIAVOLO

      4 lobster tails, 10 to 12 ounces
         each
      8 cherrystone clams in the shell
      8 medium peeled shrimp
      8 oysters
      1 quart prepared pizza sauce
      1 cup California sauterne wine
      2 ounces anchovies, diced
      3 ounces grated Parmesan cheese
      1 pound spaghetti
    1/4 cup olive oil
      1 teaspoon granulated garlic
      1 tablespoon oregano
         Salt and pepper
      1 teaspoon monosodium
         glutamate
         Chopped parsley

Split lobster tails, remove meat from the shell and place on back of the shell. Broil with butter until completely cooked.

Put 1/4 cup olive oil in frying pan, add cherrystone clams (do not open or remove from the shell), peeled shrimp, oysters (removed from shell), add pizza sauce, wine, diced anchovies, garlic, oregano, Parmesan cheese and salt and pepper to taste and simmer until clam shells open.

Cook spaghetti, adding 1 teaspoon monosodium glutamate. Add lobster tails to sauce and simmer for 5 minutes. Serve over spaghetti, garnished with chopped parsley and Parmesan cheese. Serve with garlic bread.

Serves: 4

The Plaza Hotel
Miami Beach, Florida
Executive Chef: Stephen
Spaneas

FRUTTI DEL MARE ALLA VERNA

      2 1 1/2 pound lobsters
      1 dozen cherrystone clams
      1 dozen mussels
    1/2 pound squid, sliced
      1 dozen shrimp, peeled and
         deveined
    1/4 cup olive oil
    1/2 cup onions julienne
      2 cloves garlic, minced
      4 tomatoes, peeled, seeded and
         cubed
    1/2 cup parsley, chopped
      1 bay leaf
    1/2 teaspoon thyme, crushed
  1 1/4 quarts clam broth or fish stock
      8 ounces dry white wine
         Salt and fresh ground black
         pepper to taste

Clean and scrub shellfish. Cut lobster into 8 pieces and clean squid. Pour oil into brazier and add onions, garlic, tomatoes and seasonings. Arrange lobster and shellfish over vegetables, cover and simmer for 8 to 10 minutes until the juices have been extracted. Add clam broth and white wine; cover and bring to a boil then lower heat and simmer gently for 20 minutes. Serve with linguine al dente.

Serves: 4 to 6

Wine: Dry white wine

Coach Inn
Fort Washington, Pennsylvania
Chef: Arne Hestner

CRAB MEAT À LA MAISON

- 12 ounces butter
- 3 ounces Virginia ham, chopped finely
- 36 ounces Alaska King Crab—1/2 inch pieces
- 6 slices fresh white bread—crusts removed and ground into bread crumbs
- 6 ounces imported Swiss cheese—grated

Heat butter in sauté pan. Add ham and fry until slightly crisp. Add crab meat. Sauté until crab meat is *hot*—do not brown. Divide into individual casseroles or, if you wish, into one large shallow casserole. Mix fresh bread crumbs and Swiss cheese and top casserole with this mixture. Place under broiler until cheese melts and color is a golden brown. Serve piping hot.

Serves: 6

Wine: Chilled white wine

Disneyland Hotel Restaurant
Anaheim, California
Chef: Jack Sullivan

FRUIT OF THE BAYOU

- 1/4 pound scallops
- 1/4 pound raw shrimp, fanned
- 1/4 pound lobster meat, diced in 1-inch squares
- 12 tablespoons (6 ounces) butter
- 1/4 pound mushrooms, sliced
- 1 tablespoon shallots, chopped
- 1 ounce flour
- 3 ounces sauterne
- 1/2 quart half and half cream
  Salt and pepper to taste
- 1 teaspoon rosemary
- 1 tablespoon Accent

Sauté scallops, shrimp and lobster meat in melted 8 tablespoons of butter for 7 minutes. Sauté mushrooms and shallots in 4 tablespoons of butter. Lightly brown and add to shellfish. Sprinkle flour over all and blend in. Add sauterne and hot half and half cream. Blend everything gently and simmer for 3 minutes. Add seasoning and rosemary. Remove from fire, add crab meat and sprinkle Accent over the top, stirring when ready to serve.

Serve above with rice in casserole or patty shells.

Serves: 4

Wine: White or rosé

Cabaret La Boheme
Pontchatrain Hotel
Detroit, Michigan

LOBSTERS À L'AMERICAIN

6 chicken lobsters
Salt and pepper to taste
6 tablespoons olive oil
4 shallots, chopped fine
3 cloves garlic, crushed
1 glass fine cognac
3 glassfuls dry white wine
8 fresh tomatoes, pressed and
chopped
2 tablespoons parsley, chopped
Dash of tarragon
Dash of cayenne
4 tablespoons butter

Sever claws from lobsters and split tail sections in 4. Remove and discard the sac. Season the lobster with salt and pepper and fry in the olive oil in a sauté pan over hot fire until the meat is stiffened. Pour out oil from pan and sprinkle lobster with shallots, garlic, cognac, and simmer for 5 minutes. Add the dry white wine, tomatoes, parsley, tarragon and cayenne, cover and cook for 20 minutes in medium oven. Place lobster in separate dish and reduce liquid in pan to 1/3. Add butter and season to taste. Pour over lobster, then sprinkle with hot cognac and flambé to serve.

Serves: 6

Wine: Dry white wine

Casa Del Sol
Atlantic City, New Jersey

BAKED STUFFED SHRIMP

1/2 pound crab meat
2 small shallots
2 tablespoons chopped green
pepper
4 tablespoons butter
1 cup thick cream sauce (see
index)
2 tablespoons sherry
3 egg yolks
1/2 cup bread crumbs
1 teaspoon English mustard
1/4 teaspoon chopped chives
1/2 teaspoon Worcestershire sauce
12 large shrimp

Simmer crab meat, finely chopped shallots and green pepper in butter. Add cream sauce and sherry. Bring to a boil. Bind with egg yolks and bread crumbs. Add chives, Worcestershire sauce and English mustard. Put in a flat pan and cool.

Split bottom sides of 12 large shrimp. Roll crab meat mixture into 1 1/4-inch oval balls. Put in bottom of shrimp. Pull tail over top. Place in pan. Bake in preheated 450° oven for 15 minutes.

Serves: 3

Wine: White wine

Highland Pheasant "Gordon"

GOODWOOD PARK HOTEL

SINGAPORE

Chef : J. S. Rouffiat

Gordon Highland Pheasant

TIBERIO RESTAURANT
LONDON, ENGLAND
Prop : Mario and Franco
Chef : Carlo Avogadri
Astaco Alla Diavola

RESTAURANT
DEL LAGO
MEXICO CITY, MEXICO
Prop : Dalmu Costa
Filet of Pompano Chapultepec

The Flagship
Washington, D.C.
Chef: Alfred Williams

OYSTERS ROCKEFELLER

    4   cups boiled leaf spinach
    1   ounce Pernod
    1   ounce sherry
    2   garlic cloves
    1   medium size onion
    5   strips bacon
        Salt and pepper to taste
   24   fresh shucked oysters
        Rock salt
        Parmesan cheese

Drain well 4 cups boiled leaf spinach, add Pernod, sherry, garlic, onion, bacon, and salt and pepper to taste. Place in food chopper, grind finely.

Have ready 24 fresh shucked oysters, with same remaining on the half shell. Then, using aluminum sizzling platter, fill with rock salt and place oyster shells directly on salt. Completely cover oysters with spinach mix and top with Parmesan cheese. Place in oven at 350° for 20 minutes. Remove and place under broiler for 1 minute, long enough to brown. This delicacy is served from the sizzling platter.

Serves: 3 to 4

Wine: Chablis

Cafe Ambassador
Sheraton 4 Ambassadors Hotel
Miami, Florida
Chef: Sigmund P. Steher

LE FILLET DE POMPANO EN PAPILLOTE

    1   tablespoon chopped shallots
    8   ounces butter
   10   fresh mushrooms, sliced
   20   fresh oysters
   12   fresh shrimp, peeled and
          deveined
    2   whole pompano
    1   teaspoon salt
  1/4   teaspoon pepper
    1   lemon
   10   ounces dry white wine
    1   pint whipping cream
    1   tablespoon parsley

Sauté shallots and mushrooms in butter. Add oysters, shrimps and pompano. Sprinkle with salt, pepper and lemon juice. Pour wine over and cook until almost all the liquid has evaporated. Take out pompano, add cream and reduce the liquid by half. Prepare two sheets of oiled parchment paper cut in the shape of a heart. Place pompano on one half of the heart, cover it with the sauce, sprinkle parsley over it and close the papillote, folding over the edges like a hem. Place the two papillotes on a tray and put them in the oven at 450°, long enough to puff up the paper and color it a little.

Serves: 4

Wine: Dry Moselle

Eugene's Juneau
Milwaukee, Wisconsin
Chef: J. Reinstein

LOBSTER FRA DIABLO

4	tablespoons butter
1/8	cup minced celery
1/4	cup minced Spanish onion
1/4	cup minced green pepper
1	(#2) can Italian tomatoes
1	teaspoon salt
	Cayenne pepper to taste
	Sweet basil to taste
	Oregano to taste
2	tablespoons tomato paste
4	whole lobsters, boiled until three-quarters done

Sauté celery, Spanish onion and green pepper in butter until celery is clear. Add Italian tomatoes, salt, cayenne pepper, sweet basil and oregano and cook over slow fire until sauce is reduced to half. Then add tomato paste. Pour sauce over the lobsters—finish off in oven. Just before serving, place under broiler until sauce bubbles.

Serves: 4

Wine: White

Commander's Palace
New Orleans, Louisiana
Chef: Mike Roussel

CRAB MEAT IMPERIAL

1	green pepper, diced fine
2	pimentos, diced fine
1	tablespoon English mustard
1	teaspoon salt
1/2	teaspoon white pepper
2	whole eggs
1	cup mayonnaise
3	pounds lump crab meat
	Paprika

Mix green pepper and pimentos, add mustard, salt, white pepper, eggs and mayonnaise and mix well. Add crab meat. Combine mixture with fingers so crab meat lumps are not broken. Divide mixture into 8 crab shells or casseroles, heaping it in lightly. Top with a little coating of mayonnaise, and sprinkle with a little paprika. Bake at 350° for 15 minutes. Serve hot or cold.

Serves: 8

Wine: Meursault

The North Star
Minneapolis, Minnesota

NORTH STAR LOBSTER THERMIDOR

4	live lobsters
2	teaspoons salt
4	tablespoons oil
1	cup white wine
2	cups fish fumet (fish stock and 1/2 cup wine)
8	tablespoons meat gravy
8	tablespoons grated Parmesan cheese
1/4	teaspoon chervil
4	teaspoons tarragon
8	tablespoons chopped shallots
2	cups Béchamel sauce (see index)
2	teaspoons dry English mustard
4	tablespoons butter

Split live lobster in two, lengthwise. Crack shell of claws and pick out the meat. Season both halves of the lobster with salt. Pour oil over them and roast at 425° for 15 to 20 minutes. Dice all of the lobster meat coarsely. Make a stock of white wine, fish fumet and meat gravy and flavor it with chervil, tarragon and chopped shallots. Boil it down to a concentrate and add it to Béchamel sauce and mustard. Boil the sauce for a few seconds and then whisk in the fresh butter. Line the lobster carcasses with this sauce, fill them with the boiled flesh of the lobster and cover with remaining sauce. Sprinkle with Parmesan cheese and melted butter and brown quickly in oven.

Serves: 4

Wine: Fuilley-Puissé

Stone Ends Restaurant
Albany, New York
Chef: Emilio Muniz

SHRIMP À LA STONE ENDS

2 pounds raw jumbo shrimp
6 tablespoons melted butter
Salt and pepper
1 medium shallot or onion, finely diced
2 cloves garlic, finely diced
1 teaspoon chopped chives
1 1/2 teaspoons Worcestershire sauce
1/2 cup white wine
2 cups cooked wild rice

Remove shells from shrimp, but do not cook. Split down back of shrimp by cutting deep, but do not cut all the way through. Remove sand vein. Put shrimp in shallow pan. Pour butter over them. Sprinkle with salt and pepper. Place in pre-heated broiler, 3 inches from heat, and broil 5 minutes.

Pour off butter into saucepan. Add shallot, garlic, chives, and Worcestershire sauce. Simmer for 5 minutes. Just before serving add wine. Put hot cooked wild rice and shrimp in 4 casserolettes, cover with sauce.

Serves: 4

Wine: White dry

Jimmy's Harbor Side
Boston, Massachusetts
Prop: Jimmy Doulos

JIMMY'S BAKED STUFFED FILLET OF SOLE WITH LOBSTER NEWBURG SAUCE

2 slices plain bread, trimmed and chopped fine
1 tablespoon cracker crumbs
1/4 pound butter
2 ounces sherry
1 teaspoon grated cheese
Pinch of salt
1/2 pound lobster meat, cut in small pieces
2 tablespoons flour
3/4 cup warm milk
3/4 cup warm cream
Paprika
Salt to taste
1/4 cup milk

To make stuffing, mix chopped bread with cracker crumbs, 4 tablespoons melted butter, 1 ounce of sherry, grated cheese, a pinch of salt and then one-quarter of lobster meat.

To make Newburg sauce: sauté 2 tablespoons flour in 4 tablespoons melted butter. Add warm milk and warm cream. Simmer until it thickens, then add salt to taste and paprika. Sauté remainder of lobster meat with very little butter and add 1 ounce of sherry, then mix with Newburg sauce.

Place stuffing on each fillet, then roll up. Place stuffed fillets in pan with a little butter in the bottom and add 1/4 cup milk and salt lightly. Bake at 400° for 20 minutes. Just before serving, pour Newburg sauce over fillets.

Serves: 4

Wine: Pouilly-Fuissé

The Matador Restaurant
West Los Angeles, California
Proprietor: William D. Fremont

PAELLA À LA VALENCIA

1 broiler chicken, cut up
2 large white onions, chopped
3 green onions, chopped
1 shallot, chopped finely
2 rock lobster tails, cut up or in thick slices
1/2 pound large shrimp
1 bay leaf
1 tablespoon salt
1/4 teaspoon black pepper
6 ounces olive oil
2 cups rice (large grain)
1/4 pound green peas
1/4 pound string beans
1 large Chorizo (Spanish sausage), sliced
1 thick slice of ham, cut up in squares
2 ripe tomatoes, peeled and sliced
1 pinch saffron
1 (7-ounce) can red pimentos
  Black and green olives
1 dozen well scrubbed or canned clams

Sauté chicken with onions and shallot in large paella pan (or any large pan will do) until golden brown. At the same time, in a smaller saucepan, combine lobster, shrimp, bay leaf, salt and pepper, and sauté in olive oil for 20 minutes. Pour the seafood into the large pan, which contains the chicken, and add: 2 cups of rice, the peas, beans, Chorizo, ham and tomato. Add salt, pepper and saffron. Cover pan with stock and let cook over medium fire until rice is almost done, but still very moist. Decorate with pimentos, black and green olives and clams. Place the paella for 9 minutes in a pre-heated 350° oven.

Serves: 6 to 8

Wine: Sangria or Maravez de Riscal tinto or any Spanish claret

---

Don the Beachcomber
Las Vegas, Nevada
Chef: Ben Owen

LOBSTER CHUNGKING

4 ounces cooking oil
1 teaspoon salt
2 pounds lobster meat
4 ounces cooking sherry
4 cups chicken broth
6 stalks green onions
1/4 teaspoon garlic powder
1 teaspoon Accent (optional)
6 drops sesame oil

Heat cooking pan, pour in oil, add lobster meat, cooking sherry, chicken broth, chopped onions, salt and garlic powder. Cook for 5 minutes over moderate heat then add Accent (optional) and sesame oil. If desired, the juice may be thickened with corn starch—a teaspoon or so.

Serves: 4

Wine: White wine

L'Epuisette
Chicago, Illinois
Chef: Alvin Tomryana

BROOK TROUT STUFFED WITH CRAB MEAT

2 teaspoons shallots, chopped fine
1 ounce butter
1 pound Maryland crab meat
1/3 cup dry white wine
1 ounce mushrooms, chopped fine
1 quart fish velouté (see below)
2 egg yolks
2 teaspoons parsley, chopped fine
1 teaspoon salt
1/8 teaspoon white pepper

Smother shallots with butter in sauté pan over moderate heat. Add crab meat, wine, mushrooms and blend well. Sauté until all moisture is evaporated. Add fish velouté, blend in, and bring to a boil. Add egg yolks while stirring, do not let boil more than 30 seconds. Blend in parsley, salt, pepper.

Fish Velouté
2 cups clam juice
1 cup cream
2 ounces butter
1/2 cup flour

Blend clam juice and cream and heat to warm. Melt butter in a pan. Add flour and stir, then add warm clam juice and cream, let boil, stirring together until smooth and thick.

Serves: 6

Wine: Chablis Vaillon

The Three Thieves
Washington, D.C.
Chef: Alfiero

BOUNTY OF THE SEA À LA BOUILLABAISSE, MAISON

1 large snapper skeleton
   Celery stalks and leaves
   Whole onions
   Parsley leaves and stems
8 tomatoes, skinned and quartered
16 small onions (about 1 inch across)
2 cups hearts of celery, 1 inch square, parboiled
2 cups carrots, 1 inch sections, parboiled
8 clams in shell, cleaned
2 large lobster tails cut into 1 1/2 inch sections
8 large scallops
8 large shrimp without shells
1 pound fillet of sole cut in 2-ounce portions
1 pound red snapper cut in 2-ounce portions
1 ounce chopped parsley
1 teaspoon chopped garlic
1 teaspoon oregano
2 bay leaves
6 ounces dry white wine (Chablis)

Prepare 2 quarts of fish stock by combining first 4 ingredients and simmering for 3 hours. Then combine all ingredients (except wine) in a large pot and simmer for 45 minutes. Add wine 5 minutes before serving. Serve in individual bowls over garlic toast.

Serves: 4

Wine: Piesdorrer Michelsberg

Golden Fox Steak House
Albany, New York
Executive Chef: Vincent
Figliomeni

BOUILLABAISSE MARSEILLAISE

1/2	pound red snapper
1/2	pound perch
1/2	pound tail of cod
1 3/4	pounds striped bass
2	lobsters, cleaned and halved
1 1/4	pounds Spanish mackerel
1	pound skate
1/2	pound shrimp
1/2	pound sea scallops
1/2	dozen clams
1/2	dozen mussels
1	pound eel
3	large leeks, juilienne
1/2	pound fresh tomato, peeled, seeded and chopped
1	medium size onion, julienne
1	large carrot, peeled and juilienne
1	clove garlic
1	bay leaf
2	tablespoons crushed parsley
	Pinch thyme
1	teaspoon saffron
	Pinch fresh fennel
1/2	cup olive oil
1/2	teaspoon dried orange rind
1	tablespoon salt and pepper
	Sliced French bread, 1/4 inch thick

Cut into slices, 1 inch thick, the red snapper, perch, tail of cod, bass, skate, mackerel, eel. Cut lobsters in half, leave in shell. In a large kettle put leeks, onion, carrots, tomatoes, garlic, parsley, saffron, bay leaf, thyme, fennel, orange rind, salt and pepper. Spread the cut-up lobster on top of the vegetables and add all fish except perch, cod, shrimp and sea scallops. Add enough olive oil and enough water to cover the mixture well. Bring to a boil as quickly as possible and boil hard for 8 minutes. Add the remainder of the fish and cook for another 8 minutes. To serve, remove fish and lobster to a large serving dish. Place the sliced French bread in the bottom of a large soup tureen and put the bouillon and vegetables over it. Serve the fish separately.

Serves: 6 to 8

Wine: Champagne, dry white or sparkling rosé

La Bourgogne
San Francisco, California
Chef: Marcel Perrin

DOVER SOLE CHAMBERTIN

4	(16 ounces) Dover soles
1	fifth good red wine (Chambertin)
8	chopped shallots
4	teaspoons demi-glacé (white sauce)
16	ounces butter
1	tablespoon flour

Poach the Dover sole in well seasoned Chambertin (or any other good red wine) with the chopped shallots. Strain and reduce the liquid to half and boil up with the demi-glacé. Thicken with a lump of butter kneaded with the flour. Boil, remove from flame and stir in the rest of the butter. Arrange the Dover sole on a long silver dish, cover with the sauce, glaze quickly with strong top heat.

Serves: 4

Wine: Good Burgundy

T. Pittari's
New Orleans, Louisiana

MAINE LOBSTER À LA PITTARI

       4   tablespoons olive oil
     1/2   cup green onion, scallions or
           shallots, chopped fine
     1/2   cup celery, chopped fine
       2   cloves garlic, chopped fine
     1/4   cup parsley, chopped fine
     1/2   cup cooked shrimp, chopped in
           cubes
     1/2   cup fresh lump crab meat (back
           fin)
       2   cups bread crumbs
           Salt and pepper to taste
       2   (2 1/2 pound) lobsters, split in
           half lengthwise
           Paprika
           Melted butter (enough to brush
           over lobsters)

Heat 4 tablespoons olive oil in a skillet and add onions, celery and garlic. Marinate over very low heat until soft, but do not brown. Add chopped shrimp and let simmer until cooked, stirring regularly to keep it from sticking. Add lump crab meat, sprinkle with bread crumbs and continue stirring frequently. Salt and pepper to taste and let simmer for 20 minutes. Parboil lobster for 2 minutes to the pound. Clean cavity in head, fill it with dressing and sprinkle lightly with paprika. Brush the entire lobster with melted butter and place in broiler for about 20 minutes.

Serves: 4

Wine: Dry white wine, Chablis or sauterne

Frenchy's Restaurant
Milwaukee, Wisconsin
Chef: Mr. Paul LaPointe

SHRIMP DENISE

      12   large shrimp
           Shrimp Denise Butter
      12   5-inch strips of bacon
   1 1/2   cups wild rice, cooked and
           drained
     1/4   pound butter
       2   cloves garlic, crushed finely
       2   teaspoons Worcestershire sauce
       2   teaspoons A-1 sauce
     1/2   teaspoon monosodium gluta-
           mate (optional)
     1/2   teaspoon all-purpose seasoning

Split shrimps down the back halfway through. Stuff the slit with Shrimp Denise butter and wrap with a bacon strip, fastening it with a toothpick. Put the wild rice, cooked and drained, in a long casserole. Broil the shrimps separately for 2 minutes and then arrange them in rows over the rice. Place the entire dish in the oven for 10 minutes. Garnish with fresh parsley and serve. Serve what remains of the butter separately on hot rice.

Shrimp Denise Butter
Soften butter to room temperature and knead in crushed garlic, Worcestershire sauce, A-1 sauce, monosodium glutamate and all-purpose seasoning. Mold the butter into a loaf and wrap it in wax paper. Keep butter very cold in refrigerator until ready to use.

Serves: 4

Wine: Liebfraumilch

Alba Patio de Makati
Makati, Rizal, Philippines
Chef: Juanito Acuna

PAELLA VALENCIANA

1	cup olive oil
4	cloves garlic, chopped
1	cup onion, chopped
2	whole fresh tomatoes, chopped
2	ounces leg of pork, cut in 1-inch squares
2	ounces chicken, cut in 1-inch squares
2	ounces chorizo cantimplos, sliced crosswise
2	ounces smoked ham, sliced square
2	ounces squid, cleaned and cut in 1-inch squares
2	ounces jumbo shrimp, cleaned
	Salt
	Pepper
1	teaspoon paprika
1/2	cup tomato sauce
8	cups chicken broth or consommé
4	cups rice
1	teaspoon paprika
1/2	cup tomato sauce
8	cups chicken broth or consommé
4	cups rice
2	ounces clams, boiled and cleaned
2	ounces string beans, cut in 2-inch pieces
2	ounces green pepper, cut in squares
1	small can pimentos, cut in strips
1/4	package frozen peas
1	teaspoon saffron

Put a cup of olive oil in a large frying pan and add chopped garlic, onions, tomatoes and sauté until golden brown. Then add pork, chicken, chorizo, ham, squid, and shrimp and sauté until medium cooked or half done. Season mixture with salt and pepper and add paprika and tomato sauce. Pour in the chicken broth or consommé and bring to a boil. While boiling, very gently add rice and saffron and stir constantly with wooden spoon until rice is cooked. Add the clams, string beans, green pepper, pimentos and frozen peas and stir for another 5 minutes. Remove the frying pan from the flames and cover. Bake it in preheated oven at 500° for 20 to 25 minutes or until rice is tender. Garnish with hard-boiled eggs, asparagus tips or sliced lemon and chopped fresh parsley before serving.

Serves: 4 to 6

Wine: Red or white Burgundy

O'Donnell's Sea Grill
Washington, D.C.

IMPERIAL CRAB

2	pounds fresh lump crab meat
	Juice of 1/2 lemon
1/2	teaspoon salt
1/8	teaspoon freshly ground pepper
1	teaspoon prepared mustard
2	tablespoons capers
1/2	cup mayonnaise
5	sterilized crab shells
1/2	pound melted butter
	Spanish paprika

Combine the crab meat, lemon juice, salt, pepper, prepared mustard, capers, and mayonnaise in large bowl. Mix carefully in order not to break up crab meat lumps. Pack crab meat mixture into the 5 sterilized crab shells. Brush with melted butter and sprinkle with paprika. Preheat oven to 450°. Place the crabs on baking sheet and bake for 15 minutes, or until they are a golden brown.

Serves: 4

Wine: Chablis

The Two Vikings
Bangkok, Thailand
Chef: Mogens Bay Esdensen

TRUIT VAL DU CHOUES

4 tablespoons butter
4 trout
8 cups cream
  Salt
  Pepper
2 teaspoons fresh chopped dill
2 teaspoons chives, chopped
2 teaspoons parsley
  Pinch of tarragon
3 egg yolks, beaten
1/2 cup cream

Butter pan well, place trout on it and add two cups of cream, salt, pepper. Cover and let cook slowly for 10 minutes, turning once. Remove from pan, skin trout and place on serving dish. Throw herbs into the cream and cook gently to reduce. Add egg yolks to cream mixture to thicken and pour sauce over trout before serving.

Serves: 4

Wine: Chassagne-Montrachet,
white Burgundy

Windjammer
Detroit, Michigan
Chef: Hans Struckmeyer

ALASKA KING CRAB MEAT IN WHITE WINE SAUCE

1 ounce shallots, chopped fine
4 ounces mushrooms, sliced
20 ounces Alaska King Crab meat, boneless and cut in 1/2-inch chunks
4 ounces dry white wine
  Fish sauce (see below)
1/4 teaspoon monosodium glutamate (optional)
1/4 teaspoon salt
1/4 teaspoon white pepper
4 ounces light cream
4 tablespoons butter
1/4 cup onions, chopped
1 tablespoon flour
1 pint fish stock
2 ounces white wine
1/2 cup light cream or half and half
1/4 teaspoon monosodium glutamate (optional)
  Pinch cayenne pepper
1/4 teaspoon dry mustard

Sauté the shallots and mushrooms in light oil. Add all ingredients except cream and heat for 15-20 minutes. Add cream and heat, mixing thoroughly. Serve in patty shells or forked toast and cover with fish sauce before serving.

Fish Sauce
Sauté onions in butter and add flour to make a roux. Add fish stock, white wine and cream and bring mixture to a boil and cook over low heat for 1 hour. Add spices to taste. Strain and keep in refrigerator.

Serves: 4

Wine: Puligny-Montrachet

Jack's Oyster House, Inc.
Albany, New York
Chef: Carlo Lirichild

FISHERMAN'S DELIGHT

    3 ounces olive oil
    1 bay leaf
       Pinch of basil
       Pinch of oregano
    4 (6—8 ounce) lobster tails
    4 King Crab legs, in shell
   12 butterfly shrimp, in shell
   12 cherrystone clams in unopened
         shells
 1 1/2 cups finely chopped scallions
       Dash of vinegar
    6 ounces imported sauterne wine
       Pinch of saffron
  1/2 #10 can imported Italian plum
         tomatoes
    8 ounces tomato juice
       Pinch salt
       Dash of Worcestershire sauce

Brown bay leaf, basil, and oregano in
olive oil until sizzling. Reduce heat and
add seafood and simmer for 5 minutes.
Sprinkle with vinegar, then add wine,
saffron, tomatoes, scallions, tomato juice,
salt and Worcestershire sauce. Cover pan
and cook slowly for 25 minutes over low
heat. Serve over yellow saffron rice mixed
with green peas on a sizzling metal
platter.

Serves: 4

Wine: Imported sauterne

The Jockey Club
New York, New York
General Manager: Sid Edwards

CRAB MEAT À LA JOCKEY CLUB

    8 tablespoons butter
    4 tablespoons flour
    4 cups milk
       Pinch salt
       Pinch pepper
    2 pounds jumbo lump Florida crab
         meat
    4 tablespoons grated imported
         Parmesan cheese

Blend together the butter, flour, milk, salt
and pepper to make a cream sauce. Pour
over the crab meat and sprinkle the top
with Parmesan cheese. Put in salamander
or under broiler for 3 minutes. Then bake
in a moderate oven for 10 minutes until
nicely browned.

Serves: 4

Wine: Chablis or sauterne

Justine's
Memphis, Tennessee
Chef: Justine

SEAFOOD CASSEROLE

    1 cup fresh lump crab meat
    1 cup chopped boiled Maine lob-
         ster in large pieces
    1 cup coarsely chopped shrimp
    1 cup sliced fresh mushrooms
    1 cup chopped green onions or
         shallots
    1 cup grated Cheddar cheese
    3 cups cream sauce (see index)

Combine all the ingredients in a large mixing bowl and mix thoroughly. Put mixture into 4 individual casseroles and cover with grated cheese. Dot with butter. Bake in 350° oven for 20 minutes.

Serves: 4

Wine: Dry sauterne or white Burgundy

Eddie Webster's
Bloomington, Minnesota
Chef: Donald Johnson

BAKED CRAB MEAT CASSEROLE

1	pound drained crab meat
1	teaspoon salt
1/2	teaspoon white pepper
2	teaspoons Worcestershire sauce
1	teaspoon sugar
1	tablespoon dry mustard
1/2	cup white sauce (see index)
1/2	cup shredded Cheddar cheese

Drain and chop crab meat. Add salt and pepper, Worcestershire sauce, sugar and mustard and mix lightly. Add white sauce and mix well. Bake in small, individual casserole dishes, or in coquille shells and top with Cheddar cheese. Bake for 15 minutes at 400°.

Serves: 6

Wine: Sherry

Chateau Henry IV
New York, New York
Chef: Henri Deltievre

LOBSTER THERMIDOR

6	tablespoons butter
4	tablespoons flour
24	ounces light cream of milk
1/2	pound diced mushrooms
1/2	pound cooked lobster meat, diced
2	teaspoons shallots or onions, chopped
2	teaspoons paprika
4	ounces white wine
2	tablespoons mustard
2	teaspoons tarragon and parsley, chopped
	Few dashes Lea and Perrins sauce or Worcestershire sauce
2	egg yolks
	Grated cheese

Melt 3 tablespoons of butter and add the flour. Mix and cook over low flame. Boil the cream of milk and add slowly to the roux. Stir and allow to simmer slowly. Sauté the diced mushrooms in the remaining butter. Add lobster meat, cut in large pieces. Add shallots, paprika, and white wine. Simmer a few minutes and add two-thirds of cream sauce. Then add mustard, tarragon, parsley, Worcestershire and bring to a boil. Remove from heat and add egg yolk. Fill lobster shells with stuffing. Cover with the sauce. Sprinkle with cheese and place under the broiler. Serve with thin fried potatoes and garnish with parsley.

Serves: 2

Wine: White wine

The Four Seasons
New York, New York
Chef: Maurice Chantreau

CRISPED SHRIMP WITH MUSTARD FRUIT

1	tablespoon salt
16	(1 pound) large raw shrimp, shelled and deveined
2	tablespoons butter
2	tablespoons flour
1 1/2	teaspoons prepared mustard
1/2	teaspoon salt
	Dash of pepper
1 1/4	cups milk
1	8-ounce jar mustard fruit, drained, chopped fine to 1/2 cup
	All-purpose flour
1 1/2	cups unsifted all-purpose flour
1 1/2	teaspoons baking powder
1 1/4	cups milk
	Salad oil for deep frying

In a large saucepan combine 1 quart water and 1 tablespoon of salt and bring to a boil. Add the shrimp and simmer for 3 to 5 minutes, or just until tender, then drain well.

In a small saucepan melt butter. Remove from heat. Stir in flour, mustard, 1/2 teaspoon salt and pepper and stir until smooth. Then gradually add the milk and bring to a boil, stirring constantly. Reduce heat and simmer for 3 minutes. Remove from heat and stir in half the mustard fruit. Keep warm.

Split the shrimp down the back and stuff with the remaining mustard fruit. Then roll the stuffed shrimp in the flour. To make the batter, sift flour, baking powder and salt in a medium-size bowl. Add milk and stir until smooth. Meanwhile, in an electric skillet or heavy saucepan, heat the salad oil, 1 1/2-2 inches deep, to 380° on a deep frying thermometer. Dip the shrimp in the batter and fry a few of them at a time for from 3 to 5 minutes. Drain and keep warm while frying the remainder. To serve, arrange shrimp on a platter and cover with mustard fruit sauce.

Serves: 4

Wine: Dry white wine

Vizcaya
Nashville, Tennessee
Chef: Ensebio Herrera

LOBSTER BORDALESA VIZCAYA

2	cloves fresh garlic
2	tablespoons fine minced onions
2	tablespoons olive oil
1/2	pound lobster meat in chunks
2	ounces dry sherry (Manzanilla)
1	tablespoon flour
1/4	cup tomato sauce
1	cup red Bordeaux
1	drop Tabasco
	Salt to taste

Sauté minced onions and garlic very slowly in oil then add chunks of lobster and dry sherry after it is cooked. Add the flour when lobster is cooked, and stir until completely dissolved. Add the tomato sauce, the Bordeaux, Tabasco sauce and salt. Simmer until the sauce turns a rich reddish brown cream. Garnish with fine chopped parsley and serve with steamed rice.

Serves: 1

Wine: Red Spanish table wine, Marqués de Riscal

Joe's Stone Crab Restaurant
Miami Beach, Florida
Chefs: Benson Gardner
Horatio Johnson

SHRIMP CREOLE

1/2	cup chopped celery
1/2	cup chopped onion
1/4	cup chopped salt pork
2 1/2	(# 1) cans tomatoes
6	ounces chili sauce
2	ounces tomato paste
1/2	teaspoon thyme
1	teaspoon Maggi seasoning
2	cloves garlic, finely chopped
2	pounds cooked, cleaned shrimp
	Salt
	Pepper

Simmer celery, onions and salt pork. When cooked, add all ingredients but shrimp. Cook over a low flame for half an hour. Then add previously boiled shrimp to sauce and heat. Spoon over white rice and serve.

Serves: 4 to 6

Wine: Any white wine

The Three Farthings
New York, New York
Prop: Ernest Short

BAKED STUFFED SHRIMP PANAMA

1	pound (large—10-12 to the pound) fresh shrimp, peeled and deveined
1/4	pound King Crab meat
1/4	pound butter, softened
3	cups bread crumbs
1/2	cup dry sherry
	Dash of garlic powder
	Salt
	Pepper

Cut the shrimp open in a butterfly split. Combine remaining ingredients in a mixing bowl, making sure to have butter soft but not melted. Lay the shrimp on their backs on an oiled baking sheet, and stuff them with the mixture. Bake for 10 minutes in 375° oven. Serve with parsley rice and a cup of drawn butter.

Serves: 2 to 4

Commander's Palace
New Orleans, Louisiana
Chef: Mike Roussel

SHRIMP À L'IMPERATRICE

1	pound shrimp, cooked and peeled
1	pint mayonnaise
1	(5-ounce) sweet bell pepper
3	pimentos, chopped
1/2	ounce dry mustard
1	teaspoon salt
6	avocado halves, peeled
	Paprika
1	quart Duchesse potatoes (mashed potatoes with egg yolk mixed in)

Mix shrimp and mayonnaise with all ingredients. Make a border of Duchesse potatoes around small casserole. Place halved avocados in center of casserole and fill with shrimp mixture. Sprinkle with paprika. Bake for about 10 minutes in a medium oven, 400°.

Serves: 6

Wine: Piesporter Riesling

Charles French Restaurant
New York, New York

TURBOT DE LA MANCHE POCHE AVEC
SAUCE MOUSSELINE

2	pounds fish bones
1	large onion, quartered
6	mushrooms, sliced
2	tablespoons chopped parsley
	Juice of 1 lemon
1	teaspoon thyme
1 1/2	quarts cold water
1	cup dry white wine
6	slices, 7 ounces each, imported turbot
1	whole onion
1	whole clove
1	bay leaf
3/4	cup soft butter
3	large egg yolks, well beaten
4	teaspoons lemon juice
1/3	cup heavy cream, whipped
	Dash of salt and cayenne pepper
	Parsley sprigs
	Lemon wedges
	Broiled tomato halves

To prepare fish stock, in a deep pot combine fish bones, quartered onion, sliced mushrooms, chopped parsley, lemon juice, thyme, cold water and white wine. Bring to a boil, then simmer for 20 minutes. Strain through a cheesecloth into fish cooker.

To poach turbot, place slices along with whole onion, clove and bay leaf in fish stock and simmer for 20 minutes or until turbot flakes with a fork. Carefully remove turbot to heated platter and keep warm.

To prepare Mousseline sauce, place 1/3 cup of butter in top of double boiler. Beat in egg yolks and 4 teaspoons lemon juice and place over hot water and beat constantly until butter is melted. Beat in remaining butter, a bit at a time, and continue beating and cooking until mixture thickens. Remove from heat and fold in whipped cream and seasonings.

To serve, garnish turbot with parsley sprigs, lemon wedges and broiled tomato halves. Pass Mousseline sauce in sauceboat separately.

Serves: 6

Wine: Dry white wine

Four Flames
Memphis, Tennessee

OYSTERS HARLON

	Salt and pepper to taste
24	oysters
	Flour for coating oysters
1/8	cup or 2 tablespoons fresh lemon juice
1	cup A-1 Steak sauce
2	tablespoons Worcestershire sauce
2	jiggers sherry or Madeira
2	tablespoons flour
3	tablespoons water

Salt and pepper 24 oysters. Dredge in flour and grill on lightly buttered grill on top of stove until browned on both sides. If grill is not available then use heavy skillet.

Heat in a saucepan on low fire, never allowing to boil: lemon juice, A-1 sauce, Worcestershire sauce, sherry. Blend flour into 3 tablespoons water and stir into sauce to thicken it after it has heated.

Place freshly grilled oysters on a hot serving platter and dress with sauce. Insert frilled toothpicks to serve.

Serves: 2 to 4

Wine: White wine

Charles French Restaurant
New York, New York

SUPREME DE SOLE MARGUERY

12	small fillets of sole, plus bones from sole
1	bay leaf
1	small onion, sliced
1	carrot, sliced
4	stalks celery, sliced
1/2	cup butter
3	tablespoons flour
2	tablespoons shallots, chopped
1/2	teaspoon salt
	Dash of pepper
12	large mushrooms, sliced
12	large cooked shrimp
12	oysters
	Juice of 2 lemons
1	cup dry white wine
2	egg yolks
1/2	cup heavy cream, whipped

Combine fish bones, bay leaf, onion, carrot and celery in 1 quart of water in a saucepan. Cover and cook over moderate heat for 20 minutes. Strain. Reserve liquid.

Melt butter in a saucepan. Stir in flour, smoothly, and cook a minute or two. Add 2 cups of the fish stock and cook, stirring constantly, until sauce bubbles. Reduce heat and simmer slowly for about 15 minutes longer. Set aside.

Butter a shallow pan generously. In the bottom sprinkle the shallots, salt and pepper. Fold each fillet of sole in half and place them side by side on top of the shallots. Pile mushrooms, shrimp and oysters on the fillets. Add lemon juice, white wine, and remaining fish stock and a little more salt and pepper to taste. Put a sheet of waxed paper over the ingredients and cover with a lid. Cook over a low heat for 10 to 12 minutes. Transfer fillets, mushrooms, shrimp and oysters to a large platter and keep warm.

Cook liquid, in which the fish poached, over a high heat until reduced to one third, then stir it into the thickened fish sauce. Stir in the egg yolks and whipped cream and pour over the fish. Place in a preheated broiler, about 4 inches from broiling unit, for several minutes or until surface is a delicate golden brown.

Serves: 6

Wine: Dry white wine

Grenadier
New York, New York

SHRIMP PANAMA

1	pound shrimp
2	ounces butter
1/4	pound onions, finely chopped
1	pound crab meat
2	ounces cracker meal
1	cup sweet cream

Open and clean shrimp. Season to taste. Put aside.

Sauté onions in butter, add crab meat, cracker meal and cream. Simmer for 15 minutes.

Cut partially through back of shrimp to form pocket for stuffing and stuff with mixture.

Bake for 10 minutes.

Serves: 4

Wine: Pouilly-Fuissé

The Inn at Ridgefield
Ridgefield, Connecticut
Chef: Harold Anche

SPANISH SHRIMP À LA CHANTAL

       12 to 16 large red Spanish shrimp
        2 teaspoons finely chopped
             shallots
        1 teaspoon finely chopped garlic
        1 teaspoon thyme
        2 cups old sherry wine
      3/4 cup beef stock
        6 tablespoons flour
        2 teaspoons butter
        2 cups heavy cream
        2 teaspoons finely chopped
             parsley
           Salt, pepper and Maggi to taste

Place shrimp in a small shallow casserole. Add shallots, garlic, thyme, sherry and beef stock and poach the shrimp slightly for 10 to 15 minutes. Drain the broth of the shrimp into a skillet and thicken by adding flour (add 1 teaspoon at a time and blend well to prevent lumping), or blend all of flour with butter and then add to broth. Add the heavy cream, parsley, salt and pepper and a dash of Maggi to the sauce and blend thoroughly. Bring the sauce to a boil and remove from the flame. Serve the shrimp on Rice pilaff and pour the sauce over.

Serves: 4

Wine: A white wine, Chablis Grand Cru

Matteo's
Los Angeles, California
Chef: Alex Lucidine

PESCHI À LA SUNTA

        6 medium-size fillets of Lake
             Superior whitefish
       12 large fresh shrimp
       12 cherrystone clams
        1 can (#2 1/2) Italian plum
             tomatoes (with basil)
        3 tablespoons olive oil
      1/2 teaspoon chopped parsley
           Pinch oregano
           Salt and pepper to taste

Clean fish. Devein and clean shrimp. Scrub clams to remove sand. Crush plum tomatoes, by hand or in a blender, until pulpy; salt lightly to taste. Add olive oil to baking dish and arrange the fish, shrimp and clams on top of the oil in order mentioned (fish on bottom, covered with shrimp and clams). Pour plum tomatoes over fish, sprinkle with parsley, oregano, salt and pepper. Bake in a moderate oven (350°).

Serves: 6

Wine: Pouilly-Fuissé

Harvey House
Baltimore, Maryland

HARVEY DELIGHT

       12   ounces lump crab meat
        4   tablespoons mayonnaise
        2   egg yolks, whipped
            Salt and pepper to taste
            Dash of Worcestershire sauce
        4   tablespoons dry cracker meal
            Dash of dry mustard
        4   portions of boneless Chesapeake
            Bay Rockfish, 10 ounces each
      1/4   pound butter
        1   lemon

For stuffing combine crab meat, mayonnaise, whipped egg yolks, salt and pepper, Worcestershire sauce, dry cracker meal and mustard and blend thoroughly. Bone the fish and stuff cavity of each one with equal portions of the stuffing. Bake in a moderate oven (400°) for 15 to 20 minutes. Place fish on 12-inch oak plank and garnish border with whipped potatoes and fresh vegetables. Baste with butter and lemon juice and place on broiler rack for 5 minutes. Garnish with fresh slices of tomato and lemon wedges and serve.

Serves: 4

Wine: Dry white wine

Miller Brothers
The Hilton Inn
Baltimore, Maryland

BROCHETTE NANTUA

       24   fresh clams
       24   fresh oysters
        2   cups white wine
        4   tablespoons parsley, chopped
        4   tablespoons shallots, chopped
      1/2   teaspoon thyme
        1   bay leaf
            Salt and pepper to taste
       48   1-inch squares of bacon
        1   cup flour
        2   eggs, beaten
        1   cup fine bread crumbs

Scrub the clams and oysters and wash them several times. Put them in a kettle of water with the white wine, parsley, shallots, thyme, bay leaf, salt and pepper. Cover the kettle and steam the clams and oysters until they open. Remove them from their shells and skewer them alternately with squares of bacon in between. Roll the skewered clams and oysters in flour, dip them into the beaten eggs, and then roll them in fine bread crumbs. Fry them in hot deep oil at 375° until they are golden brown and drain them on absorbent paper. Serve with Béarnaise sauce and fried potatoes.

Serves: 4

Wine: White wine

Sovereign Restaurant
Cincinnati, Ohio
Chef: Gustaf Nye

DOVER SOLE VERONIQUE

4 (1/4 pound) Dover sole
4 cups milk
2 cups flour
1/2 cup oil
1/2 cup butter
1 bay leaf
8 slices fresh carrot
4 thin slices onion
8 small pieces celery
8 teaspoons flour
4 cups cream
2 cups sauterne
Salt and pepper to taste
1 bunch seedless grapes

Skin both sides of sole and remove the head and tail. Marinate the fish in the milk for 10 minutes, remove and dust with flour. Pre-heat sauté pan with oil and butter and sauté fish until golden brown on both sides (about 6 minutes). Remove the fish and, to the pan drippings, add the bay leaf, carrot, onion and celery. Simmer for 10 minutes or so. Then add the 8 teaspoons of flour and stir into a smooth paste. Add the cream and cook into a smooth sauce, stirring constantly. Remove mixture from heat and add sauterne. Strain through a fine strainer. Add salt and pepper to taste and pour over fish to serve. Garnish with seedless grapes.

Serves: 4

Wine: Puligny-Montrachet

Brennan's French Restaurant
New Orleans, Louisiana
Chef: Paul Blanger

CRAB MEAT MARINIÈRE

1/2 cup butter
1 cup shallots, chopped fine
3 tablespoons flour
2 cups milk
1/2 teaspoon salt
1/4 teaspoon cayenne
1/3 cup white wine
1 1/2 cups crab meat
1 egg yolk, beaten
Paprika

In a nine inch skillet melt the butter and sauté the shallots until tender. Blend in the flour and cook slowly for 3 to 5 minutes, stirring constantly. Stir in milk until smooth. Add salt, pepper and wine. Cook about 10 minutes more. Add crab meat and heat thoroughly. Remove from heat and quickly beat in the egg yolk. Spoon into 8-ounce casseroles. Sprinkle with paprika. Heat under broiler flame and serve piping hot.

Serves: 3 to 4

Wine: Liebfraumilch

La Mediterranee
Pontchartrain Hotel
Detroit, Michigan

STUFFED BOSTON SOLE

- 3 shallots, chopped fine
- 4 ounces butter
- 3 tablespoons flour
- 6 ounces cream
- 12 ounces King Crab meat
- 6 fillets of sole, cleaned and boned
    Salt
    Pepper
    Sherry wine

Sauté shallots in butter in saucepan until they are golden brown. Add the flour and keep whipping until cooked to a light brown color. Add cream and cook for 2 minutes. Add the crab meat and keep steaming until well mixed. Season to taste.

For the stuffing, make a pocket in the top part of the sole and stuff with 2 ounces of the mixture. Place in a pan with butter and paprika added lightly over the top. Add salt and pepper and broil for 7 minutes. Baste with sherry wine and cook until golden brown.

Serves: 6

Wine: White

La Scala
Beverly Hills, California
Chef: Emilio Nunez

LINGUINI GENOVESE

- 1 1/2 pounds imported linguine
- 1/2 cup olive oil
- 1 (1 1/4 pound) live Maine lobster cut into small pieces
- 8 imported red shrimp, shelled and deveined
- 3 cloves garlic, chopped fine
- 2 shallots, chopped fine
- 1 teaspoon salt
- 1/2 teaspoon white pepper
- 1/2 teaspoon whole oregano
    Pinch saffron
- 1 cup dry white wine
- 2 tomatoes, peeled and chopped
- 1 tablespoon chopped chives
- 12 littleneck clams, washed and cleaned
- 1/2 cup clam juice
- 2 ounces cognac

Cook the linguine pasta in plenty of salted water for about 6 minutes, or until firm. Drain water and arrange pasta on platter. To prepare sauce, take a large heavy saucepan and warm olive oil in it. Sauté the lobster and shrimp with garlic and shallots in the oil. Do not let it burn. Add salt, pepper, oregano, saffron and wine. Reduce it to a half and then add tomatoes, chives, clams and clam juice. Keeping on a high heat, cover and cook for about 10 minutes or until the clams open. Put shellfish and sauce over pasta. Sprinkle with cognac and serve at once.

Serves: 4 to 6

Wine: Caruso Ravello bianco

Cheshire Inn
St. Louis, Missouri
Prop: Stephen J. Apted

CHAMPIGNONS PARISIENNE

Crab meat Stuffing

1	tablespoon chopped onion
4	tablespoons butter
6	tablespoons flour
1 1/2	cups hot milk
1/3	cup cream
1 1/2	pounds crab meat, flaked
1	egg, beaten
1	teaspoon Worcestershire
1/16	teaspoon cayenne pepper
1 1/2	teaspoons salt
2	tablespoons parsley, chopped
1/2	teaspoon sugar
1	tablespoon lemon juice
1	cup stale bread crumbs
	Large mushrooms, 5 or 6 to person—depending on size

Sauté onions in butter until clear but not brown. Add flour to make a roux. Add hot milk and cream and cook over low heat until thickened. Add remaining ingredients and mix until well combined. Refrigerate until ready to assemble. Remove mushroom caps and reserve stems for Savory Rice. Simmer mushroom caps in butter, deep enough to cover them, for about 3 minutes. Drain them in a strainer and set aside.

Savory Rice

1	small onion, chopped
1	small green pepper, chopped
3	tablespoons salad oil
1 1/2	cups uncooked rice
	Chopped mushroom stems
3	to 4 cups strong chicken stock
	Salt and pepper to taste
2	tablespoons pimento, chopped

Sauté onions and pepper in oil until clear but not brown. Add rice, mushroom stems, and sauté until coated with oil. Add chicken stock, cover, and simmer until rice is done. Do not overcook. If rice is too dry, add more stock. Salt and pepper to taste and add the pimento last for color.

Sherry Cheese sauce

1/2	cup butter
1/4	cup flour
1/4	pound grated Cheddar cheese
1	cup milk
1	tablespoon Worcestershire
1/2	teaspoon paprika
3/4	cup sherry wine

Melt butter then add flour to make a roux. Add cheese, stirring until cheese is completely melted. Add milk gradually, mixing until smooth. Add seasoning. Add wine last after removing other ingredients from the heat.

Preparing the casserole

Stuff mushroom caps with crab meat mixture. Place a bed of Savory Rice in a shallow casserole or in individual serving dishes. Top with mushroom caps, stuffed side down, and press into rice. Spoon Sherry Cheese Sauce over each mushroom cap. Sprinkle lightly with paprika and place under broiler to heat and until lightly browned.

Serves: 8

Wine: Red or white wine

Hugo's
Cohasset Harbour,
Massachusetts
Chef: Francis Trecariche

LOBSTER NEWBURG À LA HUGO

    2   (2 pound) live lobsters
        Juice of 1/4 lemon
  1/2   cup butter, melted
    1   teaspoon paprika
  1/2   cup sherry
    3   tablespoons flour
    4   egg yolks, beaten
    3   cups light cream
        Salt to taste

Boil the live lobsters in sea water or salted fresh water. Remove 15 minutes after they have come to a boil and cool. Remove the meat and cut into medium-size chunks. Squeeze the lemon juice over the lobster meat and let it be absorbed. Pour the melted butter into a saucepan, add lobster meat and sprinkle with the paprika. Sauté for 2 or 3 minutes being careful not to burn the paprika. Add the sherry and sprinkle the flour evenly over the meat. Thicken by cooking over a low fire for a minute or so, stirring constantly. Beat the egg yolks together with the light cream and add to lobster mixture, fold it over until smooth and bubbling. Salt to taste. Just before serving add another dash of sherry and spoon over toast forks.

Serves: 4 to 6

Wine: White

Chez Nous
Watermill, Long Island
New York
Chef: Helga Alden Gould

PAELLA MOULIN À L'EAU

  1/2   pound fresh shrimp
1 1/2   pounds lobster meat
    8   small hard-shelled Long Island
        clams, washed
    2   hot Italian sausage
    1   tablespoon olive oil
    2   cups white long-grained rice
  1/4   teaspoon saffron
  1/2   bottle dry white wine
    2   cups clam juice
        Salt and pepper to taste
    8   mussels, washed

Boil shrimp until red; when cooked, shell and clean. Boil lobster until red. Remove all meat from shell and cut into small pieces. Set shrimp and lobster aside. Boil sausage for 5 minutes. Then place in skillet and brown on all sides for 10 minutes. When cooked, cut into pieces.

Pour olive oil in casserole and heat over low flame. Add rice and stir for 3 minutes, adding saffron. Pour in wine and clam juice in small amounts allowing rice time to absorb liquid. Cook for 15 minutes.

Preheat oven to 400°, mix sausage, shrimp and lobster into rice. Salt and pepper to taste. Arrange clams and mussels on top. Leave casserole open and place in oven and bake for 15 minutes. Paella is done when clams and mussels open. Serve at once.

Serves: 4 to 6

Wine: Rosé or Sangria

La Hacienda De Los Mora
Mexico City, Mexico
Chef: Lorenzo Ponti

DICES OF COOKED LOBSTER

Newburg Sauce

1	pound boiled lobster
1/2	cup finely chopped onions
1/2	cup finely chopped carrots
1/4	cup finely chopped celery
1	glass brandy
1	spoon tomato puree
	Dash of paprika
1	teaspoon flour
1/2	pint heavy cream
	Butter

Remove the lobster meat from the shell. Dice and set aside. Grind shell and add the chopped onions, carrots and celery. Pour on the brandy and flambé. Then add the tomato puree, paprika and flour. Add the cream and boil the mixture for 15 minutes. Strain, add the butter and finally the diced boiled lobster.

Soufflé

1 1/2	cups fine butter
2	cups flour
1/2	pint hot milk
6	egg yolks
2	cups boiled lobster puree
6	egg whites, beaten stiff

Melt butter in a casserole. Add flour, stirring constantly. Add hot milk and continue to cook for 5 minutes while stirring to prevent ingredients from sticking to pan. Remove from heat and mix egg yolks in thoroughly. Let cool. Add lobster puree, stiffened egg whites and stir gently.

Butter another casserole and dust with flour. Place the above in this casserole and cook for 25 minutes or until the soufflé is puffed. Serve hot—immediately—with Newburg sauce on the side.

Serves: 6

Chiapparelli's Restaurant
Baltimore, Maryland

SHRIMP LIMONE

24	jumbo shrimp
8	tablespoons olive oil
4	cloves garlic
4	tablespoons chopped onions
4	teaspoons chopped parsley
4	slices lemon
4	thin slices ham
4	tablespoons butter
6	ounces dry white wine

Devein and clean raw shrimp and sauté in olive oil for 5 minutes or until the shrimp curl and turn white. Add the garlic, onions, parsley, lemon, ham and butter. Simmer for 5 minutes more. Then add the dry white wine and let simmer for 2 additional minutes. Garnish with parsley.

Serves: 4

Wine: Dry white wine

Brennan's French Restaurant
New Orleans, Louisiana
Chef: Paul Blanger

TROUT AMANDINEII

    6   fillets of trout, 1/2 pound each
        Salt and pepper
    1   cup flour
    2   eggs
  1/2   pint milk
    2   cups vegetable oil
    1   pound almonds, shelled and
          crushed
    1   cup butter
    1   lemon
    1   teaspoon Worcestershire sauce
    1   tablespoon parsley, chopped

Season trout fillets with salt and pepper and roll in flour. Dip in milk and then into the beaten eggs. Fry slowly in deep fat until golden brown. Remove fish from fat and cover with crushed almonds. Sauté butter until golden brown, remove from heat and squeeze in the lemon, add Worcestershire sauce and parsley. Pour over fish and serve.

Serves: 6

Wine: Chablis

Italian Village
Chicago, Illinois

SPAGHETTI ALLE VONGOLE

    3   tablespoons olive oil
    1   clove garlic, minced
    2   teaspoons minced parsley
    2   cups Italian tomatoes (1 16-
          ounce can) or fresh peeled
          and chopped tomatoes
        Strained juices from clams
    2   dozen small steamed clams

Heat olive oil in a saucepan. Add garlic, parsley and tomatoes. Add the strained juices from clams. Simmer the sauce until it has a good consistency and then remove clams from shells and add clams to sauce. Serve over spaghetti noodles. Cheese is *not* served with this sauce.

Serves: 2

Cafe Europa
New York, New York
Chef: Peter Colthop

SHRIMP AND MUSHROOM POLONAISE

    1   bunch scallions, chopped
    1   tablespoon butter
    1   ounce Madeira
    2   tablespoons flour
    1   pound shrimp
    1   pound mushrooms, halved
    1   pint sour cream
    2   tablespoons chopped parsley
        Salt and pepper to taste

Sauté the scallions in butter for 3 minutes. Add Madeira and stir in the flour mixing thoroughly. Add the shrimp, mushrooms, sour cream and parsley. Cook slowly for about 5 to 10 minutes, or until the shrimp are pink. Add salt and pepper to taste, and serve on hot toast.

Serves: 4

Wine: A dry white wine

Orsini's
New York, New York
Chef: Rinaldo Morandi

RISOTTO À L'AMMIRAGLIA

12   medium shrimp
18   littleneck clams
18   mussels
2   tablespoons chopped Italian parsley
4   tablespoons butter
2   tablespoons olive oil
1   finely chopped medium onion
1   clove garlic
1   stalk celery, diced
2   cups rice
1   cup dry white wine
1   ounce brandy
1/2   teaspoon saffron

Thaw the shrimp, if frozen, shell and devein, then cut into small pieces. Steam the clams and mussels in 2 cups of water with some parsley. Remove from the shells and cut into small pieces. Strain the juice and set aside for later. Over low heat, sauté 2 tablespoons of butter, oil, onion, garlic and celery. When garlic is golden, remove it. Add mussels, clams and shrimps. Cook for 2 minutes. Add rice and cook for 2 more minutes, stirring constantly.

Mix the wine and brandy and dissolve the saffron in it, then add to rice and fish mixture. Keeping the heat low, stir in 1 cup of fish stock that was set aside earlier. When this liquid is absorbed, add more fish stock. Repeat this procedure until all fish stock is used. The rice must cook until fluffy. (If there is not enough fish stock to cook the rice then use chicken broth. Depending on the quality of the rice used, it may take more stock to cook it.) Remove from heat, mix in remaining butter and parsley, and serve immediately on a platter.

Serves: 6

Wine: White wine

Mario's Villa d'Este
New York, New York
Chef: Alfredo Zambrana

SCAMPI ON RICE

30   jumbo shrimp
1/4   pound soft butter
8   cloves garlic, chopped
4   tablespoons parsley, chopped
3   teaspoons Worcestershire sauce
    Salt, pepper and paprika to taste
1   8-ounce glass of dry sherry

Remove shells from raw shrimp and split shrimp evenly without cutting through completely. Clean and devein shrimp and place in a heavy pan. Blend in all the ingredients except the sherry. Pour mixture over the shrimp and broil for about 10 minutes. Serve over rice and sprinkle with sherry.

Serves: 6

Wine: White wine

Hugo's
Cohasset Harbour,
Massachusetts
Chef: Francis Trecariche

BAKED OYSTERS HUGO

24 oysters or cherrystone clams
1 pound loaf of stale bread
1/2 cup fresh parsley, chopped
Juice of 1 lemon
2 drops Tabasco sauce
1 teaspoon Worcestershire sauce
Parmesan cheese
1/2 cup melted butter
Dash of garlic powder
6 strips of bacon, cut into fourths

Wash shells thoroughly and open carefully so as not to lose natural juices. Trim edges of bread and chop into fine crumbs. Mix chopped parsley with lemon juice, Tabasco, and Worcestershire, then mix well with crumbs. Add 2 tablespoons of Parmesan cheese and melted butter. Mix so that all ingredients are evenly distributed. Add a dash of garlic power if desired. Pack crumbs down on oysters or clams and sprinkle with cheese. Place piece of bacon on top and bake at 400° for 15 minutes.

Serves: 6

Wine: White wine

Restaurant Del Lago
Mexico City, Mexico
Prop: Dalmu Costa

FILLET OF POMPANO CHAPULTEPEC

2 pompano fillets, 2 pounds each
3 ounces butter
2 ounces shallots, chopped
7 ounces mushrooms
3 ounces raw morels
1/2 pint thick cream
2 ounces cognac
1 quart velouté with fish fumet (fish stock, see index)
3 ounces cooked lobster
3 ounces cooked shrimp
Salt, pepper and cayenne to taste

Cut the fillets into halves and pound them as thin as possible without tearing. Brown in butter until golden brown, then add shallots, mushrooms, morels, cream, cognac and one-quarter of the velouté. Let simmer slowly. Add lobster and shrimp and season with salt, pepper and cayenne to taste. Cook until consistency thickens.

Take fillets of pompano and season them with salt and pepper. Place in center of each 2 tablespoons of sauce and fold in a little package shape. Place in appropriate pan with butter and chopped raw shallots on bottom and cover with equal parts of white wine and fish fumet. Cover with aluminum foil and place in 200° oven for 20 minutes.

Reduce sauce to half and add the rest of velouté. Mix in egg yolks, pre-whipped in a double boiler. Cover the fillets with this sauce and glaze in salamander. Serve with whole mushrooms.

Serves: 8

Wine: Vina Oncala white

Brennan's French Restaurant
New Orleans, Louisiana
Chef: Paul Blanger

OYSTERS ROFFIGNAC

	Rock salt
3/4	cup butter
1/3	cup mushrooms, cooked and chopped fine
1/3	cup finely chopped shallots
1/2	cup onion, chopped fine
1/2	cup boiled shrimp, chopped fine
2	tablespoons garlic, minced
2	tablespoons flour
1/2	teaspoon salt
1/8	teaspoon pepper
	Dash cayenne
1	cup oyster water
1/2	cup red wine
2	dozen oysters

Fill 4 pie pans with rock salt and place in hot oven to preheat salt.

While salt is warming make sauce. In a 9-inch skillet melt butter and lightly sauté mushrooms, shallots, onion, shrimp and garlic. When onion is golden brown, add flour, salt, pepper and cayenne. Brown well, about 7 to 10 minutes. Blend in the oyster water and wine and simmer over low heat for 15 to 20 minutes.

Place 6 half shells on each pie pan and place an oyster in each. Put stuffing in pastry bag and cover each oyster. Bake in preheated moderate oven (400°), for 10 to 12 minutes or until the edges of the oysters begin to curl.

Serves: 4

Wine: Meursault

The Starlight Roof,
Doral Hotel On-The-Ocean
Miami Beach, Florida
Chef: Claus-Dieter Erstlez

PETIT ALASKA KING CRAB CLAWS "EL CASINO"

40	Alaska King Crab claws
1 1/2	pounds fresh white bread crumbs
1	pound butter
	Juice of 1 lemon
2	ounces parsley
8	cloves garlic, crushed to a mousse with 1/4 teaspoon salt
1	dash Worcestershire sauce
5	fillets of anchovy, chopped
4	stuffed green olives, chopped

Combine lemon juice, parsley, garlic, Worcestershire sauce, anchovies and olives in the melted butter, then add bread crumbs and blend thoroughly. Dip the crab claws in the butter sauce and then in the bread crumbs and broil until golden brown. Bake them in a 350° oven for 5 minutes. Serve with remaining El Casino butter sauce.

Serves: 6

Wine: Château d'Yquem, 1964

Cafe Renaissance
New York, New York
Chef: Ildefonso Valesquez

PESCADO EN PAPILLOT

4	portions of pompano fillets, red snapper or striped bass
1/2	teaspoon chopped parsley
1	clove garlic, chopped fine
4	jumbo shrimp, diced
2	large mushrooms, chopped
1/2	onion, chopped fine
1/4	pound butter
	Flour
1	cup consommé or stock

Sauté all the ingredients in butter for 10 minutes. Add the flour and a cup of consommé or stock and cook gently for 5 minutes. Cut 4 pieces of heavy brown wrapping paper 8 inches x 10 inches, and brush with melted butter on the inside. Use one-quarter of the sauce for each portion in the following manner: ladle spoonful of sauce onto the paper, place fillet in sauce, pour remaining sauce over fillet. Fold paper securely and bake in the oven for 15 minutes at 350°.

Serves: 4

Wine: Any white wine

Voisin
New York, New York
Chef: Gabriel Barragan

CREVETTES MARSEILLAISE

25	pieces fresh shrimp
1/2	pound butter
1/2	teaspoon shallots
1	pinch garlic
2	ounces sherry
1	pinch saffron
1	cup fish stock (see index)
1	cup lobster sauce
	Salt and pepper to taste
1/2	ounce brandy

Sauté the shrimp in butter, adding shallots and garlic, and let mixture steam for 5 to 10 minutes. Add the sherry to the mixture. Flambé the wine for 2 minutes. Add the saffron, fish stock and lobster sauce and let it boil very slowly. Add salt and pepper to taste. If sauce is too thin add 1/2 teaspoon or less of cornstarch or butter and flour. Just before serving add brandy and serve.

Lobster Sauce
Grind shell from small lobster. Melt 1/4 cup butter in double boiler, add 1 tablespoon water and ground shells. Strain hot butter into bowl of ice water. Skim off butter when it hardens.

Serves: 4 to 5

Wine: Dry white wine

Rotisserie of Manila Hilton
Manila, Philippines
Chef: Wilhelm Dilger

KING LAPU-LAPU ROLLS "PACIFICA"

4 pounds escalop of Lapu-Lapu (whitefish or pompano)
Salt and white pepper
1 freshly squeezed lemon
1 tablespoon saffron, cooked in rice for 10 minutes
1/4 pound truffles, chopped
Salt
1 tablespoon parsley, chopped
2 pounds baby prawns
Grated orange and lemon peel
Cognac
White wine, Chablis
2 tablespoons stock of saffron rice

Filling
1/2 pound Lapu-Lapu
1/2 cup marrow fat
1/4 pound pâté au choux (round small pastry shells)
1/2 pound avoset cream (or white sauce)
1 egg white

Grind together first 2 ingredients, add pâté au choux, avoset cream and egg white.

Marinate a thin escalop of Lapu-Lapu with salt, white pepper and freshly squeezed lemon juice. Spread 2 tablespoons of filling on every escalop. Mix saffron rice with chopped truffles, parsley and a dash of salt. Sprinkle mixture on fish with filling. Marinate the cleaned prawns with grated lemon and orange peel, lemon juice, cognac and white wine. Place a marinated prawn in each of the stuffed fish escalops and roll up and wrap in individually buttered aluminum foil. Arrange wrapped rolls in a container and pour 1/2 pint of stock of saffron rice with 1/2 pint of white wine. Cover the container and heat to a boil. Transfer container with rolls to the oven and poach at 350° for 10 minutes.

Unwrap Lapu-Lapu rolls and slice them. Top with Hollandaise sauce and garnish with pastry shell cones stuffed with mashed potatoes and parsley.

Hollandaise Sauce
3 egg yolks
1/2 pound butter
1 teaspoon lemon juice
3 tablespoons cold water

Melt butter. Place egg yolks and water in a thick shallow saucepan over double boiler. Using whisk, beat the sauce rapidly until it is thick and foamy. Remove from heat and beat in melted butter a little at a time. Add lemon juice and season with salt, white pepper and cayenne, strain and keep lukewarm to serve with the fish.

Serves: 4

Wine: Zeltinger Riesling, 1966
Deinhard, Kablenz Am Rhein

Cherry Creek Inn
Denver, Colorado
Chef: Roger Hough

LOBSTER THERMIDOR

    1/2 onion, minced
      1 pound lobster meat, diced in
         1/2 inch cubes
      6 ounces mushroom stems and
         pieces
      1 teaspoon paprika
    1/2 teaspoon mustard powder
    1/4 cup cherry wine
    1/2 cup half and half (cream)
      6 egg yolks, whipped
      1 cup whipping cream
         Salt and pepper to taste

Put onion, lobster meat, mushrooms, paprika, mustard and wine in a saucepan and cook until lobster meat is cooked thoroughly. Stir with *wooden* spoon so as not to break the chunks of meat. Add half and half and bring to a simmer. Add whipped egg yolks and stir until sauce thickens—stir slowly but *constantly*. DO NOT BRING TO A BOIL. Add whipping cream and bring to a simmer again, stirring constantly. Salt and pepper to taste. Serve over patty shells or toast points.

Serves: 4

Wine: Dry white wine, Chablis or sauterne

Maritim Restaurant,
Strand Hotel
Stockholm, Sweden
Chef: Karl Kratzert

PAUPIETTES DE SOLE À LA MARITIM

      3 sole fillets, approximately 12
         ounces each
    1/2 yellow onion
      1 sprig parsley
    1/2 cup white wine
      6 white peppercorns
      1 small boiled lobster, diced
      1 teaspoon salt
      1 small shallot, chopped
      8 oysters
      2 cups thick cream
      2 egg yolks
      1 cup whiskey
    1/2 lemon
    1/2 teaspoon cayenne pepper
      1 cup water

Clean and fillet the soles. Prepare a bouillon from the fish bones, onion, parsley, white wine, water and peppercorns. Cook for 20 minutes. Fill the sole fillets with diced lobster and roll. Salt the rolls and put into covered pan with the chopped shallot. Cook for 5 minutes, making sure the lid is on tightly.

Shell the oysters. Place cleaned shell halves on oval serving dish. Put rolls of sole in them.

Strain the bouillon, and mix with 3/4 of the heavy cream and cook over low flame, stirring into a thick sauce. Mix the egg yolks with the remainder of the cream and stir into the sauce. Season with whiskey, lemon juice, salt, cayenne pepper and pour over fish rolls.

Decorate 4 of the rolls with lobster heated in whiskey, and the remainder with oysters fried in butter and parsley. Serve with rice.

Serves: 4

Sulo Restaurant
Makati, Rizal, Philippines
Chef: Lamberto Credo

ADOBONG SUGPO

- 2 pounds fresh prawns
- 3 cloves garlic, chopped
- 1 cup wine vinegar
- 1 cup water
- 1/2 teaspoon freshly ground black pepper
- Salt to taste
- 1 bay leaf
- 1 cup shortening
- 1/4 cup flour

Shell prawns and set aside. Mix together garlic, vinegar, water, black pepper, salt and bay leaf. Pour over the shelled prawns in an earthenware casserole, cover tightly, bring to boiling point and let simmer for 5 minutes. Remove prawns and strain remaining liquid from the casserole. Set aside the liquid and strained-out pieces.

Put 1/2 cup of shortening in a saucepan over low fire and add strained-out pieces. Add flour and stir constantly until mixture is golden brown. Pour in strained liquid, gradually, beating constantly with a wire whisk until sauce is smooth. Put the remaining 1/2 cup of shortening in a skillet, begin to heat, then add prawns, turning twice as it fries. Remove from skillet, arrange on platter and cover with sauce. Serve over steamed rice.

Serves: 4 to 6

Wine: Chablis

The Vieux Carré
New Orleans, Louisiana

SHRIMP CREOLE

- 1/2 pound butter
- 1 heart of celery, chopped
- 2 medium onions, chopped
- 3 shallots, chopped
- 4 garlic cloves, diced
- 4 cups whole tomatoes
- 1 tablespoon Worcestershire sauce
- 1/2 teaspoon Kitchen Bouquet
- 3 bay leaves
- 2 cans consommé
- 2 pounds raw shrimp, cleaned and deveined
- 1 package frozen okra
- 2 teaspoons filé powder

In a large saucepan melt butter. Add celery, onions, shallots and garlic and sauté until tender. Add tomatoes, Worcestershire sauce, Kitchen Bouquet, bay leaves, consommé and shrimp. Mix ingredients thoroughly and cook over medium heat for 45 minutes. Add okra and filé powder. Cook an additional 5 minutes and serve hot over fluffy, steamed rice.

Serves: 6

Wine: White wine

Columbia Restaurant
Tampa, Florida
Prop: Cesar Gonzmart

RED SNAPPER ALICANTE

1	pound red snapper steak
1	onion
1/4	cup olive oil
1/2	teaspoon salt
	Pinch white pepper
1/2	cup brown gravy
1/2	cup white wine
12	almonds, grated
3	green peppers
3	shrimp supreme
4	rings of breaded eggplant
	Parsley

Place the red snapper steaks on top of three slices of onion, spread over the bottom of a clay casserole. Over the fish add olive oil, salt, white pepper, brown gravy, white wine, grated almonds and green pepper rings. Bake at 350° for 25 minutes. Garnish with breaded eggplant rings and the shrimp supreme.

Serves: 2

Wine: Bodega or any white wine

Klein's Restaurant
Pittsburgh, Pennsylvania
Chef: Jules Leve

SHRIMP À LA ROMANO

1	cup rice
36	green shrimp
8	large ripe tomatoes
1	cup vegetable oil
1	tablespoon salt
1/2	tablespoon (black) pepper
1	teaspoon oregano
1	pinch cayenne pepper
2	tablespoons minced parsley
2	stalks chopped celery
3	cloves of finely chopped garlic
5	teaspoons grated Romano cheese
	Grated Parmesan cheese

Cook rice in normal way and set aside. Partly cook unshelled shrimp in water—when water comes to boil, remove from water, shell and clean shrimp. (Shrimp should be undercooked.) Take a large casserole, make a bed of the rice and place cleaned shrimp on rice bed.

Take tomatoes, scald with boiling water, remove skins and cut into large pieces. Add oil to tomatoes and blend in a simmering saucepan. Add other ingredients and spices until completely mixed and blended. Ladle over shrimp. Sprinkle generously with grated cheese and bake in a preheated oven at 350° for 15-20 minutes. Serve hot.

Serves: 6

Salum Sanctorum
New York, New York
Chef: Jean Pierre Germain

BASS CHAMBORD

2 fresh tomatoes
1 large onion
4 stalks celery
4 carrots
1 clove garlic
Fresh parsley
Thyme
Bay leaves
6 pounds of striped bass
Salt and pepper
1 cup olive oil
1 cup water
10 cups red wine
Lettuce leaves, poached in hot water
1/4 cup white vinegar
1/4 pound mushrooms, sliced
Butter

Chop all vegetables, including garlic and parsley, thyme and bay leaves, into large pieces, place on bottom of pan as a layer. Salt and pepper inside of bass. Place it on the bed of vegetables. Spread over it the olive oil and 1 cup of water and 6 cups of red wine. Cover with foil and bake in the oven for about 45 minutes at 350°. Remove pan from oven, if cooked to satisfaction. Skin bass and place on long platter. Cover with lettuce leaves (poached in hot water to prevent drying while sauce is being prepared).

Place pan containing vegetables on open fire and add 1/4 cup white vinegar and simmer for 10 minutes. Strain essence from vegetables and put in small pan and reduce with an additional 4 cups of red wine.

Sauté the mushrooms lightly in butter, then blend with essence. Remove lettuce leaves from bass and place sauce over the fish. Leave remaining sauce on side.

Serves: 4

Wine: White Burgundy,
Chassagne-Montrachet,
Abbay de Morgeot

Charles French Restaurant
New York, New York

FROGS' LEGS SAUTÉ PROVENÇALE

3 shallots, chopped fine
1 clove garlic, crushed
1/3 cup olive oil
12 small tomatoes, peeled and diced
1/3 cup finely chopped parsley
Salt and pepper to taste
18 frogs' legs
1/2 pound butter

Sauté shallots and garlic in olive oil until soft. Stir in tomatoes, parsley, salt and pepper and simmer for 20 to 30 minutes or until sauce is thickened. Sauté frogs' legs in hot butter until golden brown on all sides. Add prepared sauce and simmer 10 minutes. Serve on heated platter with sprinkling of additional chopped parsley.

Serves: 6

Wine: Dry white wine

PAUL YOUNG'S
RESTAURANT
WASHINGTON, D.C.
Prop: Paul Young
Chef: Nino Longo
Tournedo Jetée Promenade

SULO RESTAURANT
MAKATI, RIZAL, PHILIPPINES
Chef: Lamberto Credo
Adobong Sugpo

STARLIGHT ROOF, DORAL HOTEL ON-THE-OCEAN

MIAMI BEACH, FLORIDA

Chef: Klaus-Dieter Erstlez

Petit Alaskan King Crab Claws "El Casino"

Commander's Palace
New Orleans, Louisiana
Chef: Mike Roussel

TROUT ALEXANDRA

1	(3-pound) speckled trout
1/2	pint milk
3	bay leaves
	Salt and pepper to taste
6	ounces mushrooms
4	ounces butter
1 1/2	pounds boiled shrimp
1/2	Florida lobster
1	clove garlic
4	green onions
2	tablespoons flour
1/2	pint cream
1/4	pint fish broth
2	ounces sherry
4	sprigs parsley

Tenderloin and poach trout in milk and a little water with salt and bay leaf. Sauté mushrooms in butter until nearly brown. Add shrimp and lobster. Let sauté for 5 minutes. Add garlic, green onions, and salt and pepper to taste. Cook until done. Blend in flour, add cream, milk and fish broth and cook slowly for 10 minutes. Add sherry and parsley and serve piping hot.

Serves: 4

Wine: Chablis

Restaurant Drouant
Paris, France
Prop: Jean Drouant
Chef: Georges Laffon

PÂTÉ DE BROCHET NEWBURG

1	(3-pound) pike
1	cup shallots, minced
1/2	cup tarragon
1	glass white wine
1	jigger cognac
4	eggs, separated
1	pound butter, softened
1	pint fresh cream
1	tablespoon anchovy sauce
	Salt and pepper

Clean and fillet the pike. Butter an oven dish, put in shallots, tarragon, fish fillets and white wine. Place in hot oven for a moment only, then remove the fish and transfer the juices to a saucepan. Add cognac and simmer until volume is reduced by at least 1/3.

Work the eggs and the softened butter into the fish fillets by kneading them in a cool saucepan. Season with salt and pepper, add the fresh cream and then the cognac sauce as prepared above, and lastly the anchovy sauce.

Butter a pâté dish and place layers of fish, covered with foil to avoid browning. Cook for 1 1/2 hours.

Serves: 8

Wine: White Burgundy

Jimmy's Kitchen
Hong Kong
Chef: Harry Cheng

SPICED GAROUPA JIMMY'S
(Spiced Fillet of Fish Jimmy's)

    2 pounds 4 ounces filleted fish
       (preferably garoupa or mahi
       mahi or mainland equivalent.
       Pompano will also do)
    1 egg
    1 cup flour
    1 cup bread crumbs
    1 cup peanut or vegetable oil
    1 cup equal parts garlic, ginger
       and red chili, finely chopped
  1/4 pound butter
    2 large onions, finely chopped
    1 cup sesame oil

Cut filleted fish into approximately 16 equal parts (4 per serving). Beat the egg, then roll the fish in the egg, then flour, then bread crumbs, then deep fry in oil until golden brown.

Sauce
Chop up, finely, the equal parts of garlic, ginger and red chili and make a paste of same. Sauté this in a small amount of butter and add finely chopped onions. Let boil, then add a small amount of sesame oil and boil again. Pour this over the fish fillets. Serve with noodles or boiled potatoes.

Serves: 4

Wine: Chateau Mayne Leveque
Grave 1967 (dry)

L'Orangerie
New York, New York

MOULES MARINARA

    6 to 8 quarts mussels
1 1/2 cups dry white wine
    6 shallots, chopped fine
  1/3 cup finely chopped parsley
  1/3 cup sweet butter
       Cayenne pepper and salt to taste
       Lemon juice
       Additional chopped parsley

Put mussels in large colander, rinse under running water. Scrub shells with stiff brush to remove all traces of sand and rinse again. Place mussels, wine, shallots and parsley in large cooking utensil. Cover and steam over low heat, 8 to 10 minutes, or until all shells open. Transfer mussels to soup plates.

Strain stock, bring to a boil. Remove from heat and stir in butter piece by piece. Season to taste with cayenne pepper, salt and lemon juice and pour over mussels. Sprinkle with additional chopped parsley and serve piping hot.

Serves: 6

Wine: White wine

Mario's
Nashville, Tennessee
Chef: Vito Vianello

SCAMPI MARIO

 1 onion, chopped
 Garlic as desired
 1 1/2 tablespoons mustard
 5 ounces vinegar
 1 cup consommé
 1 cup tomato sauce
 24 shrimp
 Olive oil
 Seasoned bread crumbs

To chopped onion and a little garlic, add mustard, vinegar, and consommé. Boil 5 minutes. Add 1 cup tomato sauce, cook for 10 minutes. Split and roll shrimp in olive oil and in seasoned bread crumbs. Broil until brown and serve with sauce on the side.

Serves: 4

Wine: Verdicchio (white)

Miller Brothers
The Hilton Inn
Baltimore, Maryland

MARYLAND EEL MILLER BROTHERS

 1 pound smoked eel
 1 quart beer
 1/2 pound butter
 1 cup chives
 8 eggs

Boil smoked eel in beer approximately 4 minutes. Sauté quickly in butter. Serve with scrambled eggs and cut chives.

Serves: 4

Brennan's
Houston, Texas
Chef: Paul Paulyc

TROUT BLANGE

 1/2 cup butter
 1 tablespoon minced garlic
 3/4 cup raw shrimp, peeled
 3/4 cup raw oysters
 1/2 cup sliced cooked mushrooms
 1/2 teaspoon Spanish saffron
 2 cups whole canned tomatoes
 1 cup fish stock (see index)
 1/4 teaspoon cayenne
 1 teaspoon salt
 2 tablespoons cornstarch
 1/4 cup water
 2 trout (2 pounds each) cleaned, boned. (Save heads, skin, bones for making stock)
 2 cups seasoned mashed potatoes

In a 10-inch skillet melt butter and sauté garlic, shrimp, oysters, mushrooms and saffron. Add tomatoes, fish stock, cayenne and salt. Simmer 15 to 20 minutes. Combine cornstarch and water, add to sauce to thicken. When desired consistency is obtained, remove pan from heat and add parsley. Keep warm.

Grill or broil trout to a golden brown and remove to warm serving platter. Place mashed potatoes in a pastry bag and flute a wall around extreme edge of fish platter. Cover fish with warm sauce. Garnish with whole mushrooms and shrimp. Sprinkle potatoes with paprika. Place under flame until potatoes are lightly browned.

Serves: 4

Wine: Chablis

Brione's Italian Restaurant
Brooklyn, New York
Chef: Romano Bernoy

LOBSTER TAILS À LA BRIONE

16 baby lobster tails
3 ounces olive oil and 2 ounces butter
1 cup finely chopped onions
1 ounce chopped Italian ham (prosciutto)
2 cups consommé (chicken or beef)
2 cups dry champagne (or chablis)
1 tablespoon chopped Italian parsley
Salt and black pepper to taste

Cut open the top of the lobster, lenghwise. Loosen the meat of the tails, individually, so as not to break shells.

Add olive oil and butter to a large frying pan with onions and sauté until pale brown in color. Add lobster tails and stir until onions are a golden brown. Add ham, simmer for 2 minutes. Pour in consommé and simmer for 10 more minutes. Pour in the champagne, or wine, with parsley and black pepper and salt, if needed. Simmer for additional 10 minutes; with a cover on pan.

Serves: 6

Wine: Bolla Soave

Maxim's de Paris
Tokyo, Japan
Chef: M. Pierre Cassier

SOLE ALBERT

1 sole fillet (16 ounces)
1 cup bread crumbs with melted butter
1 cup vermouth (French)
3 shallots
Salt
Pepper
1/4 cup chopped parsley
2 tablespoons tarragon
Butter
1/2 lemon

Bread sole with bread crumbs and melted butter. Place in pan. Pour enough vermouth to half submerge the fish without soaking the bread crumbs. Add shallots, salt, pepper and tarragon. Place in a hot oven (425°) and brown for 30 minutes. Reduce juice and finish with butter and lemon juice. Garnish with parsley before serving.

Serves: 6

Wine: White Burgundy

Old Original Bookbinders
Philadelphia, Pennsylvania
Chef: Nathan

SHRIMP DU JOUR

3	pounds uncooked shrimp, shelled
1/4	pound butter
2	teaspoons Worcestershire sauce
1	clove garlic, chopped
1/4	cup chives, chopped
1/4	cup parsley, chopped
	Salt and pepper
	Grated cheese
	Bread crumbs
	Drawn butter

Sauté shrimp in butter with Worcestershire sauce, garlic, chives, parsley, salt and pepper for 5 minutes. Drain butter sauce and place in a large casserole. Sprinkle with grated cheese and bread crumbs. Pour butter, in which shrimp were cooked, over all. Bake in a hot (400°) oven for about 8 to 10 minutes, or until golden brown. Serve with drawn butter.

Serves: 6

Hotel Malaysia
Singapore
Chefs: Gunther Nuhel and
Monty Derksen

COLD LOBSTER SANUR BARI

2	medium-size fresh lobsters
1	teaspoon lime juice
1/2	cup carrots
1/2	cup celery
1/2	cup onions
	Salt, pepper and Worcestershire sauce to taste
1/4	teaspoon curry powder
3 1/2	ounces fresh pineapple, in chunks
3 1/2	ounces mango fruit, in chunks
3	tablespoons mayonnaise
	Lettuce

Boil the fresh lobsters in water with the lime juice, carrots, celery and onions for 10-15 minutes, depending on the size of the lobsters. Let the lobsters cool. Cut into dices, being careful not to break the shell.

Mix the pepper, Worcestershire sauce, curry powder and salt together in a bowl. Add pineapple, mango and mayonnaise, then add lobster.

Place the lobster shells on a tray with a bed of sliced lettuce in each shell. Place the lobster mixture inside the shells and garnish with parsley, pimentos and olives.

Serves: 2

Wine: Gewürz-traminer

The Ledges
Coral Gables, Florida
Chef: Vincent McNulty

DOLPHIN FLORENTINE À LA VINCENT

1 (16-ounce) dolphin (or yellow-
　　tail), filleted
　Paprika
8 ounces creamed spinach (fresh,
　　frozen or canned)
2 hard-cooked eggs, chopped
1/2 cup condensed milk

Sprinkle fish fillet with paprika and bake at 350° for 15 minutes.

Combine and heat together spinach, chopped hard-cooked eggs and condensed milk. Place hot mixture on the bottom of a flat casserole. Place baked fish atop this mixture and cover with Hollandaise sauce. Put under broiler until lightly browned (about 3 minutes). Garnish with a ring of lemon, parsley and olives.

Hollandaise sauce
1 egg yolk
1 tablespoon water
1 tablespoon butter
　Dash of salt, pepper, Worcester-
　　shire sauce and lemon juice to
　　taste

Cook all ingredients in double boiler, slowly, stirring constantly, until custard thickens.

Serves: 2

Wine: Chablis

Topinka's on the Boulevard
Detroit, Michigan
Prop: Kenneth Nicholson

CRAB MEAT IMPERIAL

1/2 cup butter
2 cups flour
3/4 gallons milk
1/2 cup light sherry
1 green pepper, diced
1/2 cup red pepper, diced
2 tablespoons dry mustard
3 drops Worcestershire sauce
　Salt and pepper to taste
3 pounds King Crab meat, cooked
　　and cut into pieces

Melt butter and blend in flour. Add the milk that has been heated, gradually, stirring constantly. Reduce heat and cook three minutes longer and add sherry, gradually, while stirring. Add remaining ingredients with the exception of the crab meat. Blend well and then add crab meat. Bring to serving temperature and serve in casserole with toast points or patty shells.

Serves: 12

Wine: Chablis

Port St. Louis
St. Louis, Missouri

OYSTERS BIENVILLE PORT ST. LOUIS

    Ice cream salt
1 dozen oysters on the half shell
4 green onion tops, chopped fine
2 tablespoons butter
3 tablespoons flour
1/3 cup dry white wine
2/3 cup milk
1/2 cup chopped shrimp
1/2 cup chopped mushrooms
    Parmesan cheese

Place ice cream salt in a pie plate, arrange oysters in shells atop the salt.

Fry onions in butter until lightly browned, add the flour slowly, stir well and place over low heat. Add milk and wine, stirring constantly. Add shrimp and mushrooms. Cook for about 10 minutes over low heat, stirring constantly as mixture thickens. Season to taste. Spoon a little sauce over each oyster, sprinkle bread crumbs and grated cheese (Parmesan) fairly thickly atop each oyster. Place under broiler until just lightly browned.

Serves: 2

Wine: Any good dry white

Duke Zeibert's
Washington, D.C.
Chef: Joseph Kerriod

FLOUNDER STUFFED WITH CRAB MEAT

4 (1-pound) whole flounders
    Salt and pepper
1 pound lump crab meat
8 ounces butter
    Cracker meal
    Oil

Split the back of the flounder, removing meat on both sides. Place flounder with dark side down, spread open top, season with salt and pepper. Spread crab meat on fish and top with butter. Fold top side of fish over crab meat, brush with oil and sprinkle with cracker meal. Brown stuffed fish in broiler, then bake at 350° for 15 minutes.

Serves: 4

Wine: White wine

Sea Fare of the Aegean
New York, New York

STRIPED BASS CRETE ISLAND

2	to 3 heads of striped bass
1	gallon water
1/2	cup diced carrots
1	cup diced celery
1/2	cup diced onions
1	mixed cup of Italian parsley and dill (weed or powder)
1/2	teaspoon chopped garlic
1	tablespoon olive oil
1	tablespoon melted butter
1	tablespoon fresh lemon juice
1/4	cup sherry
4	portions fillet of striped bass, 3/4 pound each
	Salt and pepper to taste

Boil the heads of striped bass in one gallon of water until a quart of stock remains in order to be a strong broth. Strain the stock and place the above ingredients, with the exception of the bass fillets, into the broth and boil for 8 minutes.

Place the striped bass fillets in individual casseroles and cover with mixture.

Cook for 15 minutes or until done.

Serves: 4

*Wine: Pouilly-Fuissé or
Hymetus (Greek)*

Le Cordon Bleu
Dania, Florida
*Chefs: Rene Palisson and
Louis Chardentier*

LE FILLET DE SOLE GENERAL PATTON

8	fillets of English sole
2	chopped shallots
	Sprig of chopped parsley
2	jiggers of dry white wine
1	small cooked lobster
1	cup butter
2	tablespoons flour
1/2	cup heavy cream

Take fillets of sole, butter a shallow pan nicely and lay the fillets on it. Sprinkle with 2 chopped shallots, chopped parsley and dry white wine. Cover with wax paper and bring to the boiling point. Put it in the oven at 400° for 10 minutes.

On the side, take some cooked lobster, slice the tail into scallops and warm in butter. Take fillets out of the oven, pour the juice into a deep pan. Thicken with butter, flour and heavy cream. Put the lobster scallops on top of fillets, pour the sauce over and place under broiler until brown.

Serves: 4 to 6

*Wine: Dry Alsatian—served
very cold*

Sultans Table, Dunes Hotel
Las Vegas, Nevada

SCALLOPS NANTAISE

    Butter
6   scallops
2   shrimp
2   oysters
1   cup white wine
1   cup heavy cream
1/2 cup Béchamel sauce (roux, see
      index)
    Salt and pepper to taste

Sauté scallops, shrimp and oysters in butter for 5 minutes until scallops are solid to the touch. Add the white wine. Boil and cook for a few minutes, add heavy cream. Boil for 5 minutes, thicken with roux. Season to taste with salt and pepper.

Serve in scallop shells, decorated with a truffle slice and Duchesse potatoes around the edge. Sprinkle bread crumbs on top. Put under salamander browner or under broiler until lightly browned.

Serves: 1

Wine: Pouilly-Fuissé

Steve's Pier and Jimmy's
Backyard
Port Washington, New York
Chef: Steve Karathano

MIXED SEAFOOD À LA STEVE

1/4   pound shrimp
1/4   pound scallops
1/4   pound crab meat
1 1/2 dozen oysters
1   garlic clove
2   pounds salt butter
1   cup flour
1   quart milk
1   quart heavy cream
1   cup dry sherry
1   teaspoon salt
1   teaspoon white pepper
1/4   teaspoon nutmeg
1/4   teaspoon celery salt
1/4   pound sliced smoked ham
1/4   pound diced sharp cheese

Sauté in butter—shrimp, scallops, crab meat and oysters with clove of garlic, in heavy skillet.

Make white sauce by combining and heating together, while stirring, butter, flour, milk and cream with sherry, nutmeg, celery salt, salt and pepper. Mix into white sauce the sautéed ingredients.

Place seafood into casserole dish. Add sliced ham on top of seafood, top with diced sharp cheese. Bake in 250° oven until brown.

Serves: 4

Wine: White wine

Gull Harbor Inn
Kalamazoo, Michigan
Chef: Arthur Merrick

SEAFOOD CASSEROLE—HENRI DUVERNOIS

- 4 peeled and chopped shallots
- 1 teaspoon butter
- 1 cup shrimp
- 1 cup lobster
- 1 cup oysters
- 1 cup blanched scallops
- 1 ounce cognac
- 1 cup sliced, cooked mushrooms
- 1 cup white wine sauce (velouté)
- 1 tablespoon chives
- 1 cup Hollandaise sauce (see index)

Sauté shallots in teaspoon of butter, add shrimp, lobster, oysters and scallops. Sauté for 2 minutes and flame with cognac. Mix in the mushrooms and white wine sauce. Let simmer for 3 minutes. Add chives. Pull pan from fire. Let stand for 5 minutes and then fold in Hollandaise. Serve in casserole with potato bordure or rice.

Serves: 4

Wine: Dry white wine or rosé

King Cole
Indianapolis, Indiana
Chef: Dieter Krug

FILLET OF DOVER SOLE WALEWSKA

- 4 fillets of Dover soles or lemon soles
- 1/2 cup white wine
- 3 cups fish fumet
- 2 cups lobster chunks
- 1 cup Hollandaise sauce (see index)
- 1 cup whipped cream
- 8 thin slices of truffle, or black olives

Poach fillets in 1/2 cup white wine and 3 cups fish fumet. Arrange the poached fillets on a dish and surround with lobster chunks. Blend a delicate lobster sauce of Hollandaise and whipped cream, and cover each fillet. Place under broiler and glaze. Before serving add a thin slice of truffle or black olive on top of each fillet.

Serves: 4

Wine: White

Park Schenley Restaurant
Pittsburgh, Pennsylvania
Chef: Gino Croce

SHRIMP BARSAC

20 shelled shrimp
2 tablespoons butter
1/2 teaspoon chopped garlic
1/2 teaspoon chopped parsley
3 ounces Barsac wine (sauterne)
1/4 teaspoon salt
2 tablespoons bread crumbs
1 tablespoon Parmesan cheese

Sauté 20 shrimp in a skillet with butter until golden brown. Add garlic and parsley and simmer. Pour Barsac wine over and reduce heat for 1 minute. Take off stove and arrange shrimp in casserole. Sprinkle with bread crumbs mixed with Parmesan cheese, salt lightly, and moisten with leftover Barsac wine. Put under broiler for 2 minutes. Serve hot.

Serves: 2

Wine: Puligny-Montrachet,
B & G

The Blue Fox
Cleveland, Ohio
Chef: Frank Ardito

ROLLED STUFFED FLOUNDER

1 small onion, chopped
1 pound fresh mushrooms, sliced
1/2 pound cooked spinach
1/2 pound flounder, chopped
5 egg yolks, beaten
Flour
Paprika
Salt and pepper to taste
Butter
Dash of Worcestershire sauce

Sauté the onion, add the mushrooms and cooked spinach and cook for about 10 minutes over a medium to low flame. Add the chopped flounder and cook until flounder is done. Cook the mixture and add the beaten egg yolks and mix thoroughly. Stuff the flounder fillets with the mixture and roll in flour to which paprika, Worcestershire sauce, salt and pepper have been added. Sauté in butter until all sides are slightly browned, then bake in 400° oven for 10 minutes. Serve with Almondine Sauce.

Almondine Sauce

4 tablespoons butter
Juice of 1/2 lemon
2 tablespoons shaved almonds

Melt the butter until brown. Add lemon juice and almonds just before serving

Serves: 4

Wine: Dry white wine

Tiberio Restaurant
London, England
Prop: Mario and Franco
Chef: Carlo Avogadri

ASTACO ALLA DIAVOLA

2 (1 1/2 pound) live lobsters (or cooked frozen)
1/2 pound butter
4 large cloves garlic, chopped
1 large spoon made-up English mustard
1 bunch fresh tarragon, 6 branches, chopped
1 sherry glass brandy
Salt, cayenne pepper to taste
3 ounces fresh white bread crumbs

Wash, cut lobsters in half, remove the stomach and discard. Remove raw coral.

Place in mixing bowl with butter: half the garlic, half the tarragon, the mustard and the brandy, add the seasoning. Mix cold until emulsified.

Season lobster. Spread mixture evenly in pan with lobsters and sprinkle fresh white bread crumbs over the lobsters. Place in hot oven for 20 minutes at 375°.

Serve with mixed salad and the mayonnaise mixed with the remaining garlic (pounded to a paste), and the remaining tarragon.

Serves: 4

Wine: Verdicchio

Stanley Demos Coach House
Lexington, Kentucky
Prop: Stanley Demos

DOVER SOLE MY WAY

1/2 cup vegetable shortening
6 fillets of Dover sole
1 cup flour
2 tablespoons butter
2 tablespoons shallots, chopped
1 cup drained and chopped canned tomatoes
1 clove garlic, chopped fine
Salt and fresh ground pepper to taste
1 cup Hollandaise sauce (see index)

Melt vegetable shortening in a heavy skillet. Roll fillets in flour and sauté in skillet until tender. Remove and serve.

To prepare the sauce, melt the butter into a saucepan, add shallots and cook until they are transparent. Add tomatoes, garlic, salt, pepper and parsley and simmer for 10 minutes. Top each fillet with the tomato sauce and then with Hollandaise and place under the broiler for a minute until glazed.

Serves: 4

Savoy Philippines Hotel
Manila, Philippines
Chef: Daniel Mallenergne

FILLET OF LAPU-LAPU VERONIQUE

3   pounds black Lapu-Lapu [fillet of sole, red snapper or any other white fish]
3   ounces butter
2   ounces shallots, chopped
4   ounces white wine
    Dash of salt and pepper
3   ounces flour
4   ounces avoset cream (or white sauce)
1   pound white grapes, peeled and seeded

Place fillets of Lapu-Lapu in a pan with a bit of the butter. Add shallots, white wine, salt and pepper, and cook for 5 minutes. Drain stock, set skillet aside. Simmer the stock until it thickens. Add 2 ounces of butter mixed with the flour. Stir gently and boil for two minutes. Add the avoset cream and pour over the fillet. Garnish with grapes.

Serves: 4

Wine: Muscadet of Pouilly-Fuissé

Hotel Russell
Dublin, Ireland
Prop: Hector Fabron
Chef: Pierre Rolland

ST. JACQUES À L'IRLANDAISE

1   cup flour
20 scallops
2   ounces butter
1   pint fresh cream
1   tablespoon chopped parsley
2   minced shallots
    Jigger Irish Mist
    Salt and pepper to taste
4   egg yolks

Flour scallops and sauté them with half the butter, cooking for about 3 minutes. Add cream, shallots and parsley and then the Irish Mist. Season with salt and pepper to taste. Simmer for another 3 minutes. Remove scallops from pan and place them in 4 empty scallop shells. Reduce sauce to half, add rest of butter and the 4 egg yolks. (Once the eggs are in the sauce be careful not to overcook.) Mix and pour over the scallops.

Serves: 4

Wine: Meursault Blagny, 1967 or Corton-Charlemagne, 1963

Mayfair Farms
East Orange, New Jersey
Chef: Dave Moyer

MOUSSE OF SOLE, BONNE FEMME

3 pounds fillet of sole, reserve
    bones
2 ounces shallots
3 egg whites
    Salt and pepper to taste
1 pint heavy cream

First, grind up raw sole, shallots, egg white, salt and pepper very finely and strain through a fine wire-mesh strainer. Add heavy cream, mix with wooden spoon so that it combines well. Form the mixture into quenelles or the size of an ordinary roll. Then place quenelles in pan and poach in a white Chablis wine with no water. Let it cook slowly.

Bonne Femme sauce
1/2 cup flour
1/8 pound butter
  1 pint fish stock (see index)
  1 cup heavy cream
  1 cup Chablis
    Salt and pepper
  8 cooked mushroom heads, sliced
    finely
  3 tablespoons Hollandaise sauce
    (see index)
  1 cup heavy cream, whipped

Make a roux out of a little flour and butter, then add pint of fish stock made from bones of the sole. Add 1 cup of heavy cream and 1 cup of Chablis, a little salt and pepper to taste. Cook very slowly for 4 or 5 minutes making a nice cream sauce. When ready, combine with cooked

mushroom heads, sliced finely. Add 3 tablespoons of Hollandaise sauce, 1 cup of whipped cream. Mix everything very finely with wooden spoon in bowl in folds.

Place quenelles in a pan, cover thoroughly with sauce. Place under broiler until slightly browned.

Serves: 4

Scoma's Restaurant
San Francisco, California
Chef: Sam Patane

CRAB CIOPPINO SCOMA

   Oil and butter (enough to braise
      onion and garlic)
 1 large onion, finely chopped
 4 cloves garlic, finely chopped
   Pinch of oregano
 4 bay leaves
   Pinch of sage
 1 (10-ounce) can tomato paste
 1 cup water
12 prawns
 3 cracked crabs
12 clams
 6 oysters
12 scallops

Combine and heat oil and butter, then add finely chopped onion and garlic and braise. Add oregano, bay leaves, sage, tomatoes, tomato paste and 1 cup water. Season with salt and pepper. Let cook for 1 hour. After sauce is cooked, strain, and add prawns, cracked crabs, clams, oysters and scallops. When clams open, Cioppino is ready.

Serves: 6

Wine: Any white wine

Sea Wolf Restaurant
Oakland, California
Chef: Guy Holt

CRAB LEGS SAUTÉ À LA SEA WOLF

2	ounces olive oil
1	ounce garlic butter
1	cup flour
1	pound fancy crab legs
2	small green onions, chopped fine
4	ounces sauterne
4	ounces consommé
	Salt
	Pepper
	Monosodium glutamate
1/2	cup rice

Into frying pan add olive oil and garlic butter. Heat and add crab legs which have been lightly floured.

Moderate heat for about 3 minutes, or until lightly browned, and add green onions. Sauté for 1 more minute. Add wine and consommé and continue cooking until sauce is reduced by one-half. Add salt, pepper and MSG to taste.

Saffron Rice

1 1/2	ounces butter
1	green onion, chopped fine
1/2	cup rice
3	cups chicken broth
1/8	teaspoon saffron
	Salt, pepper, MSG —to taste

Into a saucepan put butter and onion and place over medium heat until butter is melted. Add rice. When rice turns to a light brown add chicken broth and saffron. Reduce heat and cook until liquid is absorbed by the rice. Add salt, pepper and MSG to taste.

Serves: 4

Wine: Dry white (Chablis or sauterne)

Poultry Entrées

Mirabelle
London, England

SUPREME CURZON

3 each: carrots, onions, celery stalks
6 leaves tarragon, sprig of parsley
Salt, pepper, butter
2 (3-pound) chickens
1 double whiskey
1 glass dry white wine
1/2 pint cream

Chop very fine: carrots, onions, celery, parsley and tarragon. Put in a saucepan with a nut of butter and cook gently for 10 minutes stirring now and then. Take the legs and skin off the chickens, then remove the breasts.

Put half of the cooked vegetables in a saucepan with butter. Lay the breasts of the chicken on top, then the rest of the legs, salt and pepper. Let the chicken simmer gently for about 5 minutes, turn on the other side, put the whiskey, white wine and cream on top and let it cook, boiling gently, for about 12 minutes. Take out the breats. Let the sauce thicken, then pour over the chicken and serve. (The legs can be used in the same way but allow 20 minutes for cooking.)

Serves: 4

Wine: Champagne or white Burgundy

King's Arms Restaurant
Burbank, California
Chef: Charles Crozer

BONED BREAST OF CAPON—KING'S ARMS

8 breasts of capon or chicken
3/4 cup flour
1/2 cup oil
6 ounces butter
1 small onion
3 cups milk
3 teaspoons salt
1/2 teaspoon pepper
4 ounces sherry
1 (4-ounce) can sliced mushrooms, drained

Remove bones from breasts, dredge in flour. Heat oil in large skillet and add chicken and cook covered until tender, pour off oil. Use 2-quart pan, add minced onion and butter, sauté over medium flame until golden brown, add flour and continue to cook for 2 minutes. Add warm milk and stir until it thickens. Add salt, pepper and wine, then strain over chicken and drained mushrooms and simmer 10 minutes.

Serves: 4 to 6

Wine: Grey Riesling

Hotel Singapura Intercontinental
Singapore
Chef: Mr. Hanspeter Graf

SUPREME DE VOLAILLE "SINGAPURA"

1	(6- to 7-ounce) chicken breast
1/4	ounce thinly sliced smoked ham
1/2	ounce slice of Swiss cheese
	Salt
	Pepper
	Grated nutmeg
	Flour
	Egg, beaten
	Butter
1/2	small shallot, finely chopped
1	ounce sliced mushrooms (champignons)
1	ounce chopped peeled tomatoes
1	ounce white wine
1 1/2	ounces fresh cream
1	thin slice of truffle

Slit open the chicken breast and stuff with slices of smoked ham and cheese. Season with salt, pepper and a little grated nutmeg. Sprinkle with flour and coat with beaten egg. Sauté in butter until nearly cooked, add chopped shallots, mushrooms, tomatoes. Sauté for a few seconds longer, sprinkle with wine and add fresh cream. Simmer for 2 more minutes. Place chicken on a dish, pour thickened sauce over and top with a thin slice of truffle.

Serves: 1

Wine: Any good white wine

Diamond Harbor Inn
Cassopolis, Michigan
Chef: Karl Gissat

COQ AU VIN—THE HARBOR INN'S WAY

2	cups boiled rice pilaff
2	tablespoons Parmesan cheese
2	tablespoons diced ham
1/2	cup chicken stock
4	(6-ounce) boned breasts of chicken

Mix rice, cheese, ham, garlic and chicken stock. Cook slowly for about 5 minutes. Season to taste. Flatten out chicken breasts with cleaver. Season with salt and pepper. Place some of the rice, cheese and ham mixture on each. Fold together and set into small sauté pan. Brush with butter and cook in medium oven (400°) for 15 minutes.

Sauce

4	slices bacon
4	shallots, chopped
1	cup pearl onions
1	cup cooked sliced mushrooms
1	cup brown sauce
1	cup red wine

Cut bacon into finger-thick pieces. Sauté in pan until light brown. Add the chopped shallots, mushrooms and onions. Sauté for about 2 minutes, then fill up with red wine and brown sauce, let simmer for about 5 minutes. Set ready chicken breasts in casserole. Top with sauce, let simmer for a few minutes and serve.

Serves: 4

Wine: Dry white wine

The Mandarin
San Francisco, California

BEGGAR'S CHICKEN

- 1 (3-pound) chicken
- 2 teaspoons sesame oil
- 1 teaspoon cornstarch
- 1/4 teaspoon anise seed
- 1/2 teaspoon salt
- 1 tablespoon (additional) sesame oil
- 1/3 cup dried mushrooms
- 1/2 cup boneless pork, sliced thin
- 1/4 cup bamboo shoots, sliced thin
- 1 tablespoon soy sauce
  Ceramic clay for baking

Wash a 3-pound chicken. Mix 2 teaspoons sesame oil, 1 teaspoon cornstarch, 1/4 teaspoon anise seed and 1/2 teaspoon salt. Rub this mixture over chicken, inside and out. Heat 1 tablespoon sesame oil in a skillet and sauté 1/3 cup dried mushrooms, which have been soaked in water for 2 hours, then sliced thin. Stir for 2 minutes before adding 1/2 cup boneless pork and 1/4 cup bamboo shoots, both sliced thin. Blend in 1 tablespoon soy sauce and cook for 2 minutes. Stuff this mixture into chicken. Wrap bird in 2 layers of foil and 1 layer of butcher's paper. Encase wrapped chicken in wet clay about 1/4-inch thick. (Ceramic clay can be found at most art supply shops.) Bake in preheated 400° oven for 50 minutes. Lower heat to 200° and bake another hour. To serve, crack clay with mallet and open paper.

Serves: 4

Wine: Pinot Chardonnay
Wente Brothers

Shelter Island's Bali Hai
San Diego, California
Chef: Li Fun Yip

CHICKEN OF THE GODS

- 1 2 1/2- to 3-pound chicken, boned
- 1 egg, beaten
- 1/4 teaspoon salt
- 3 teaspoons sherry
- 1 teaspoon soy sauce
  Dash of white pepper
- 1/2 pound chestnut flour
  Cooking oil
- 1/2 cup soft butter
- 1/2 cup flour
- 2 tablespoons cornstarch
- 4 cups chicken stock
- 1 cup cream
- 2 teaspoons browned sesame seeds

Marinate chicken in mixture of egg, salt, sherry, soy sauce and white pepper for 15-20 minutes. Coat each piece with chestnut flour. Brown chicken in oil.

Melt butter over medium heat and blend in flour and cornstarch. Bring stock to a boil and stir rapidly while adding butter mixture. Reduce heat and add cream and seasoning.

Cut chicken pieces into slices and arrange on hot platter. Cover with cream sauce. Sprinkle sesame seeds over top.

Serves: 4 to 6

Wine: Blue Nun—
Liebfraumilch

Historic Smithville Inn
Smithville, New Jersey
Chef: Earl Robenson

"CHICKEN PYE" WITH DUMPLINGS

- 1 capon or heavy stewing chicken
- 1 strip celery
- 1 small onion
- 2 small carrots
  Finely chopped parsley

For a full-flavored pot pie use either a capon or heavy stewing chicken. Cook in a large kettle with tight-fitting lid. Place whole chicken in the kettle with the vegetables. Add water to cover, bring to a full rolling boil. Lower heat to simmer and cook until tender. Remove chicken to a tray to cool. When cool, remove skin and bones. Cut meat into serving pieces.

To serve, place in tureen or large serving dish with the dumplings and gravy, sprinkle finely chopped parsley over the top. Serve immediately.

Dumplings
- 2 cups Bisquick
- 2/3 cup milk
- 1/2 teaspoon baking powder

After the chicken is removed to cool, mix above ingredients together and drop by tablespoonful into boiling liquid. Cover tightly. Steam 12 minutes. Remove dumplings to the tureen with chicken, strain the broth and thicken slightly with flour mixed with water, cook until thickened and pour over the dumplings.

Serves: 4 to 6

Michel's
Honolulu, Hawaii
Chef: Gerald Ikeda

BREAST OF CHICKEN, MICHEL'S

- 4 whole boned and skinned chicken breasts
- 1 cup all-purpose flour
  Salt
  Pepper
  Accent
- 1/2 pound drawn butter
- 2 teaspoons shallots, chopped
- 1/4 teaspoon garlic, chopped
- 8 ounces whole petite fresh mushrooms
- 8 ounces artichoke hearts, quartered
- 1/2 cup sherry
- 1/2 cup white wine
  Demi-glacé (brown sauce reduced)
- 1/2 cup Hollandaise sauce (see index)

Season chicken breasts with salt, pepper, Accent and flour. Sauté on medium flame in 1/2 pound of drawn butter until golden brown. Then add shallots, garlic, whole mushrooms and artichoke hearts and sauté for 5 to 8 minutes until mushrooms are tender. Then add 1/2 cup each of sherry and white wine and simmer 10 minutes, or until one-half the liquid is gone. Add demi-glacé made of brown sauce which has been reduced to half by cooking. Simmer for 10 to 15 minutes until done. Check seasoning.

Before serving, fold Hollandaise sauce into sauce, also chopped parsley. Serve with rice pilaff.

Serves: 4

Wine: Graacher Himmelreich Spätlese Prum

Au Trou Normand
Hong Kong
Chef: B. Vigneau

POULET TROU NORMAND

    1   2-pound lobster
        Salt and pepper to taste
  1/3   pint oil
    2   ounces butter
    2   shallots, chopped
  1/3   pint dry white wine
    1   brandy glass cognac
  1/4   teaspoon cayenne pepper
    1   teaspoon paprika
    1   pint fresh cream
    1   3-pound chicken

Take a whole raw lobster, split it, season the pieces of lobster with salt and pepper. Put these pieces into a sauté pan, containing 1/6 pint of oil and 1 ounce of butter, both very hot. Fry them over an open fire until the meat has stiffened well and the carapace is of a fine red color. Then remove all grease by tilting the sauté pan with its lid on; sprinkle the pieces of lobster with 2 chopped shallots; add 1/3 pint white wine, 1 small glassful cognac, cayenne and the paprika. Then add 1 pint of fresh cream, cover the sauté pan, and set to cook in the oven (350°) for 18 to 20 minutes. After, take the tail of the lobster out, remove the shell, cut the meat in slices.

Take off the carcass of a fresh chicken, then you have 2 legs and 2 pieces of breast, put these pieces into a sauté pan containing 1/6 pint of oil and 1 ounce of butter, both hot. Fry them over an open fire until the meat is colored and well cooked (20 minutes). Then put these pieces of chicken into a cocotte dish, put the sliced lobster meat on top and keep warm aside.

Take off all grease from the sauté pan, then strain the ready-made sauce into this sauté pan, cooking for a few minutes until the sauce is thickened. Then coat the chicken with the lobster sauce. Serve with steamed rice or boiled potatoes.

Serves: 2

Auberge le Vieux St. Gabriel
Montreal, Canada
Chef: André Carpenter

POUSSIN AU MIEL
(Honeyed Cornish Game Hen)

    6   Cornish game hens
        Salt
        Pepper
    1   pound maple smoked bacon
    4   ounces honey
    3   ounces butter
        Cognac

Place hens in a casserole. Salt and pepper them. Wrap hens with bacon. Pour melted butter and honey on the hens. Heat oven at 400° and cook for 1 hour. When ready to serve, cognac can be poured over. This dish can be served with rice.

Serves: 6

Wine: Chablis

L'Orangerie
New York, New York

CANETON COTE À L'ORANGE FLAMBÉ
(Crisp Roasted Duckling, Flambéed
with Grand Marnier)

    1   (5- to 6-pound) duck
        Salt and pepper
    2   tablespoons shortening
    1   onion, coarsely chopped
    1   carrot, coarsely chopped
    3   celery leaves, coarsely chopped
    1   bay leaf, crumbled
  1/2   teaspoon dried thyme

Rub duck with salt and pepper; place on rack in roasting pan. Add shortening and roast in preheated oven (450°) 20 minutes, basting frequently and turning twice. Add onion, carrot, celery and herbs. Reduce heat to 350°; continue roasting 1 to 1 1/2 hours or until tender. Remove from pan and keep warm.

Sauce
    4   oranges
  1/2   cup dry white wine
    1   (7 1/2-ounce) can brown
        gravy
    2   tablespoons sugar
    2   tablespoons currant jelly
  1/2   cup Grand Marnier
        Salt

While duck is roasting, carefully coarse-shred peel of oranges. Cut rind into julienne (very thin) strips. Parboil strips in boiling water for a few minutes; drain. Remove all the white membrane from oranges; separate orange sections (do this over a bowl to save juice). Stir wine and brown gravy into duck roasting pan drippings until smooth; simmer about 15 minutes. Strain into saucepan and skim off all fat that rises to surface. Combine sugar with enough water (a few drops) to

moisten and stir over low heat until golden brown. Stir in julienne orange peel, reserved orange juice, currant jelly and Grand Marnier. Cook and stir until jelly has dissolved. Combine with gravy in saucepan, simmer a few minutes. (If sauce appears thin, blend 1 tablespoon cornstarch with 1 tablespoon Grand Marnier until smooth; stir into sauce.) Correct seasoning.

To serve, carve duck and arrange attractively on hot serving platter. Spoon half the sauce over duck and garnish with orange sections. Light to reduce alcohol. Serve remaining sauce in heated sauceboat.

Serves: 4

Little Harry's
Detroit, Michigan
Chef: Clarence Stokes

SPECIAL CHICKEN

    1   (2-1/2 pound) chicken
        Salt
        Pepper
        Flour
        Shortening
    3   ounces cooked crab meat
    2   ounces sliced Swiss cheese
    2   ounces Burgundy wine
    2   ounces mushroom sauce

Bone chicken, season and add to flour. Sauté in 8-inch skillet. When done drain excess shortening. Top with crab meat, mushroom sauce, and Swiss cheese. Add Burgundy wine and place in oven at 450° for 15 minutes or until Swiss cheese is well melted.

Serves: 2

Wine: Pouilly-Fuissé

Caprice
London, England
Chef: Gino Scandolo

CANARD À LA PRESSE

- 1   duck for 2 persons, 2 ducks for 4 persons
- 1   glass red wine (Burgundy preferred)
     Salt, pepper, cayenne, peppercorns, zest of orange
- 1   slice of foie gras
- 2   ounces of butter
- 1   small jigger of brandy
- 1/2 lemon

The ducks should be slightly cooked—roasted—about 8 to 10 minutes. In the first stages of this preparation it requires 2 people for the initial proceedings, which are: remove the legs and place to one side for later use. The duck is then skinned, the breast carved into finely-cut slices and placed around the edge of an oval hot platter. The carcass is pressed in the appropriate appliance to extract the blood, which should be retained for later use.

While this is being done, a chafing pan is heated containing the red wine, peppercorns and zest of orange and reduced to about half.

The foie gras, butter and seasoning are mixed together to a smooth consistency. This is then placed in the middle of the platter on which the carved duck is already prepared. Strain the reduced wine onto the foie gras mixture, add a little gravy residue from the roasting of the duck. The process of binding the sauce must be done on a low flame and must not be allowed to boil. It is important that the chafing dish must be continually rotated while making this sauce, thus allowing the sliced duck to warm gradually.

The blood extracted from the carcass is now added little by little. Taste occasionally to correct seasoning and add a few knobs of butter to cohere the sauce to a smooth consistency. It cannot be too strongly emphasized that this sauce must not boil. At this stage, it is advisable to remove from flame and continue the rotary movement without heat. Add a little brandy, and a few drops of lemon juice at the last moment.

In the old days, when this dish was prepared in front of clients, it was customary, with the clients' permission, to take the bottle of champagne off the table (they usually drank champagne) and add it to the dish in preparation.

May it be pointed out that "Canard à la Presse" is a seasonable dish. May we also add that we think an ideal accompaniment to this dish is an orange salad and crisp pommes soufflés.

In serving this dish, when a client has nearly finished, it is customary to serve the legs of the duck. These, however, must go to the kitchen to be bread crumbed, coated with mustard and grilled, and then served.

Serves: 2 per duck

Le Cygne Restaurant
New York, New York
Chef: Bernard Hermann

QUAILS WITH GENEVER

8	quails
16	thin slices of lard
	Salt
	Pepper
	Butter
12	cracked Genever balls (small box black pepper)
1	onion, sliced
1	carrot
1	ounce Genever Gin (made from above)

Use 8 quails and roll them with lard very thin. Season with salt and pepper. Cook in casserole with butter for 12 minutes, after 6 minutes of cooking add 12 little balls of Genever cracked, and add onion and carrot, and light-cook the remaining 6 minutes. Take the lard and flambé with Genever Gin and a reduction of game, and finish the seasoning of the sauce to your personal taste.

Serves: 4

Wine: Pomerol

Ben Gross Restaurant
Irwin, Pennsylvania
Chef: Robert Lilly

CORNISH HEN WITH GRAPES

4	16-ounce Cornish hens
1/2	lemon
12	pieces bacon
1/2	pound butter
2 1/2	pounds seedless grapes
1/2	teaspoon salt
	Pinch white pepper
1	teaspoon M S G
2	cups Rhine wine
1/2	cup fresh chopped parsley
2	teaspoons thyme
8	whole peppercorns
1/2	teaspoon chopped shallots
	Requires a 4-quart pot with cover

Rinse out insides of hens, rub inside with lemon. Put half the bacon into pot, add butter. Over low heat brown the hens on the bacon, about 8 minutes per side. Remove the hens. Stuff with grapes. Season with salt, pepper and M S G. Put in pot on the cooked bacon, breast up. Cover with remaining bacon. Add wine, parsley, thyme, peppercorns and shallots. Cover the hens with the remaining grapes. Cover tightly and put in preheated oven at 375°. Cook for 1 hour and 15 minutes. DO NOT REMOVE TOP UNTIL IN THE DINING ROOM. When top is removed a most beautiful aroma will fill the room.

Serves: 4

Wine: Rhine or Moselle

Sultans Table, Dunes Hotel
Las Vegas, Nevada
Chef: Emile Hellegouarch

TURKEY SCALLOPINI PRINCESS

4	turkey breasts
1/4	pound butter
1/2	cup mushrooms, julienned
1/4	cup shallots
1/2	cup sherry
1	jigger brandy
1	cup heavy cream
1/2	pound cooked asparagus

Fillet and slice raw turkey breasts into 3-ounce pieces. Break slightly and fry fillets in butter. Sauté mushrooms in butter until slightly colored, add shallots until colored slightly. Déglacer with sherry and jigger of brandy. Add heavy cream and cook until thickened.

To serve—lay cooked asparagus on plate, cover with sauce. Place turkey on top— serve with rice pilaff on the side.

Serves: 4

Wine: Saint-Emilion

Le Mistral
New York, New York
Chef: Max Thomas

LA POULARDE CARMARGUAISE
(Roast Chicken Carmarguaise)

1	3-pound chicken
2	pinches fine herbes
	Salt and pepper
1	pinch thyme
1	pinch oregano
4	ounces vegetable oil
3	ounces white wine

Sew edges of chicken's cavity together with twine, then tie legs and tail close. Season chicken with fine herbes, salt and pepper, thyme and oregano. Roast chicken in pan with vegetable oil, baste it over chicken for 30 minutes while turning chicken on its sides in 400° oven. Remove chicken, pour out most of the cooking oil, add white wine, stir it on hot heat and reduce this sauce. Cook chicken another 5 minutes to make it very crisp, then serve it with sauce on the side.

Serves: 2

Nancine's
Great Neck, New York
Chef: Nancy Perachino

NANCINE'S CHICKEN À LA NANCY

8	breasts of chicken, in strips
1	cup flour
1	cup olive oil
1	lemon rind
3	slices prosciutto
1/4	pound melted butter
1	garlic clove
1/2	cup lemon juice
1/2	cup white wine
1/4	teaspoon salt
	Dash of pepper
1/2	cup chicken stock

Flour chicken strips, sauté in hot oil until golden brown. Discard oil from pan. Add lemon rind and prosciutto, also add chicken stock, melted butter, white wine, garlic, salt and pepper, simmer for 10 minutes. Garnish with parsley and serve.

Serves 6

Wine: White

Raimondo's
Miami, Florida
Chef: Raimondo Laudisio

CHICKEN GLORIA

4	breasts of chicken
	Salt, pepper, nutmeg
1	egg
2	ounces milk
1	cup almonds
1	cup prosciutto, julienne
1/2	cup grated cheese
1/2	cup white bread crumbs
2	ounces drawn butter
2	ounces olive oil
1/4	pound butter
1	tablespoon flour
1	cup dry white wine
1	lime
	Lime wedges
4	cherry tomatoes
4	black olives
	Parsley

Skin chicken (first removing all bones except wing bone) and slice paper thin. Season, then dust lightly with flour. Dip in batter (next 6 ingredients) and bread crumbs. Cover the bottom of a sauté pan with butter and olive oil. Heat until butter melts then slowly sauté chicken until golden brown. Place on warm serving platter and keep warm. Melt 1/4 pound butter, cream in 1 level tablespoon flour. Add 1 cup white wine and juice of one lime. Pour over chicken. Garnish with lime wedges, tomatoes, black olives and parsley.

Serves: 2 to 4

Wine: Soave Bolla

The Ocean Room
The Claridge Hotel
Atlantic City, New Jersey
Chef: Jules Seligmann

BREAST OF CAPON WITH CHABLIS SAUCE

    4   breasts of capon—9 to 10
        ounces when boned
    2   ounces butter
    1   cup Chablis wine

Bone 4 breasts of capon, but leave wing bones on. Take top skin off, and sauté breasts in small skillet in 2 ounces of butter, slowly, 1 minute on each side. Do not brown. Add 1 cup of Chablis, bring to a boil, cover and cook in preheated oven at 350° for about 10 minutes, until done. Remove from oven and put on side; keep warm.

Chablis Sauce
    2   ounces butter
    1/2 small onion, sliced
    1/2 small carrot, sliced
        Small piece of celery, sliced
    1/2 bay leaf
        Pinch of rosemary
    1/2 cup chicken broth
    1   tablespoon cornstarch
    1/2 ounce caramel color
        Egg color

In small saucepan, put butter, add to it onion, carrot, celery, 1/2 bay leaf and pinch of rosemary. Sauté for about 2 minutes, add liquid from capons and chicken broth. Let simmer slowly for about 10 minutes. Dilute a little cornstarch in a little cold water; while stirring, add to Chablis sauce, tighten up gravy slightly. Add a little caramel color and a little egg color for appearance. Strain and keep warm.

Mushroom Topping
    8   fresh medium-size mushrooms
    2   shallots, chopped coarsely
    1   ounce butter
    1/2 cup sherry wine
    1/2 cup light cream
    1/2 ounce cornstarch
    5   ounces fine noodles
1   1/2 ounces butter
        Hollandaise sauce (see index)

Take mushrooms, chop them but not too fine; chop 2 shallots and sauté them in 1 ounce of butter in small saucepan for 1 minute. Add to chopped mushrooms. Add 1/2 cup sherry, let simmer for a few minutes. Add 1/2 cup light cream. Tighten up with a little cornstarch diluted in a little cold water and pour it into mushroom topping. It will stay on top of capons.

Cook fine noodles in salted water. When cooked, strain into a colander or strainer and add a little cold water to take off starch. Put back into cooking pan, add 1 1/2 ounces butter, mix with fork. On bottom of serving dish place fine noodles, put capons on top. Cover capons with mushroom topping, spoon some of the Chablis sauce over it and cover with Hollandaise sauce. Brown under hot broiler or salamander, pour rest of the Chablis sauce around the platter and serve.

Serves: 4

Wine: White

Aperitivo
New York, New York
Chef: Oreste Sabatini

CHICKEN APERITIVO

1 (2 1/2-pound) chicken, cut in
   pieces
5 tablespoons olive oil
1 small onion, minced
2 shallots
2 sprigs chives
4 slices minced prosciutto
3 large mushrooms, sliced very
   thin
2 bay leaves
1 pinch thyme
2 pinches minced parsley
   Salt and pepper to taste
1 cup dry white wine
1 cup consommé
1 cup fresh small green peas

In a frying pan large enough to hold the chicken, heat the olive oil. Sauté the chicken until golden brown on all sides. Remove from heat and set chicken aside. Sauté the minced onion, shallots and chives; add the prosciutto, mushrooms, bay leaves, thyme, parsley and seasoning.

Cook for about 5 minutes. Add the chicken and the wine; cook, uncovered, for 3 more minutes. Add consommé. Simmer covered, until chicken is cooked (25-30 minutes) and the sauce is reduced.

Preboil 1 cup of fresh small green peas and when the chicken is ready to be served, sprinkle on top to garnish.

Serves: 2

Dewey Wong's
New York, New York

ORANGE DUCK À LA DEWEY WONG

1 (6 1/2 to 7 1/2 pound duck)
1 bunch scallions, cut into 3
   pieces
   Several cloves
1 1/2 ounces star anise
1/2 teaspoon hot pepper
1 3/4 cups soy sauce
1 cup flour
1/2 cup water chestnuts, slivered
6 cups peanut oil

Remove any large fatty pieces from duck cavity. Soak duck in boiling water 40 minutes. Braise until golden brown. Halve lengthwise, bone and trim remaining fat. Prepare light paste of plain flour and cold water. Roll pieces in paste, stuff with scallions, cloves, anise, hot pepper and soy sauce; reassemble duck halves. While still damp, roll duck in water chestnuts and flour and deep fry in 6 cups of peanut oil at 215° for 15 minutes.

Orange Sauce
4 cups water, 1 cup white vinegar, 4 tablespoons sugar
2 whole fresh oranges, sliced
2 whole fresh lemons, sliced
1 medium onion, sliced thin
1/2 teaspoon cornstarch

To 4 cups of water add 4 tablespoons of sugar, 1 cup of white vinegar. Add sliced oranges, lemons, onion. Boil 15 minutes or until 2 cups sauce remain. Thicken with 1/2 teaspoon cornstarch.

To serve: Slice duck as desired, cover liberally with sauce, top lightly with Grand Marnier (French liqueur). Garnish with fresh sliced orange and maraschino cherries.

Serves: 4

Wine: Chablis

Goodwood Park Hotel
Singapore
Chef: J. S. Rouffiat

GORDON HIGHLAND PHEASANT

- 1 tender cock pheasant
- 2 tablespoons butter
- 4 tablespoons olive oil
- 2 tablespoons finely chopped carrot
- 2 tablespoons finely chopped onion
- 1 good pinch thyme
- 1 crumbled bay leaf
  Pheasant liver
- 1 tablespoon honey
- 1 glass whiskey
- 1/2 pint thick cream
  Butter
  Button mushrooms
- 2 slices toasted sandwich loaf
  Salt and freshly ground black pepper

Clean and truss pheasant and brown on all sides in butter and olive oil in a flame-proof casserole. Add finely chopped carrots, onions, thyme, bay leaf, honey and liver. Cover casserole and simmer for 30 minutes. Flame with heated three-fourths of the whiskey. Moisten with cream; cover casserole and simmer until pheasant is tender and sauce has reduced a little.

Remove and mash the pheasant liver with a little butter and one-quarter of the whiskey and spread the toasts with this mixture. Remove bird; pass the sauce through a fine sieve and season to taste. Place pheasant on the toast, add button mushrooms sautéed in butter and cover with sauce, which should be quite thick.

Serve with mashed turnips, mashed potatoes, green peas and button mushrooms.

Serves: 4
Wine: Château Haut-Brion—1958

The Blue Horse
St. Paul, Minnesota
Chef: George Wandzel

DUCKLING BIGARADE

- 1 large duckling
- 1/2 cup diced celery
- 1/2 cup diced carrots
- 1/2 cup diced onions
  Parsley
  Thyme
  Bay leaf
- 4 teaspoons sugar
- 1 tablespoon red wine vinegar
- 1 cup brown gravy
- 1 orange
- 1 lemon
  Curaçao or Grand Marnier

Truss a large Long Island duckling. Put it into a braising pan on a foundation of diced celery, carrots and onions. Add a bouquet garni composed of parsley, thyme and bay leaf. Season. Cook with a lid on for about 15 minutes. Then, remove the lid and cook at about 375° for 1 1/2 hours, or until well done and nicely browned on all sides. Remove all grease.

Dilute the thick juices in the roasting pan with a stock that's prepared in the following way: Combine 4 teaspoons of sugar soaked in a tablespoon of red wine vinegar in a pan, and cook to form a pale caramel. When the sugar begins to change color, pour in 1 cup of brown gravy. Pour this mixture into the roasting pan and blend with the juices. Cook this mixture over a strong heat for 5 minutes. At the last moment, add the juice of an orange and a squeeze of lemon juice. Strain through a cloth. Add 2 tablespoons of orange peel cut in a fine julienne (thin strips), blanched, cooled in cold water and drained. Bigarade sauce can be flavored with a small quantity of Curaçao or Grand Marnier added at the very last minute. Pour sauce over duckling. Garnish platter.

Serves: 2

The Vieux Carré
Treasure Island, Florida
Chefs: Joseph and Patricia
Cerquone

POULET EVANGELINE
(Boneless Chicken Breast Topped with a White Wine Mushroom Sauce)

1/2	pound butter or margarine
	Salt and pepper
4	(6-ounce) boneless chicken breasts

In large skillet or frying pan melt butter. Salt and pepper chicken breasts and place in skillet. Sauté to a light golden brown, turning breasts often until they are completely cooked.

Sauce

1/2	pound butter
2	bay leaves
1	bunch green shallots, diced
1	small onion, diced
1	heart of celery, diced
	Salt and pepper
1	cup enriched flour
1	quart half and half cream
2	cups mushrooms, sliced
1/2	cup white wine (Chablis)
4	slices American yellow cheese
4	slices natural Swiss cheese
	Paprika

Place butter in heavy saucepan and melt. Add bay leaves, shallots, onion and celery. Salt and pepper lightly. Sauté ingredients until tender. Add flour, stirring constantly over heat, until mixture becomes a smooth paste. Add cream, mushrooms and wine, again stirring constantly over heat, until mixture becomes silky and smooth. Remove from heat.

Place cooked chicken breasts into individual ramekins. To each breast add 1 slice American cheese, a cover of sauce, 1 slice Swiss cheese, and a final topping of sauce. Sprinkle with paprika, and place in heated oven (375°) for 10 minutes, or until mixture becomes bubbly.

Serves: 2

The Old Mill
Toronto, Canada
Chef: Joseph Internicola

BROME LAKE DUCKLING—ORANGE SAUCE

1	(5 pound) duckling
2	oranges
1	tablespoon red currant jelly
2	tablespoons brown sugar
3	ounces red wine (Medoc)
6	ounces demi-glacé (see index)
1 1/2	ounces Grand Marnier

Roast duckling at 450° for 20 minutes. Reduce oven temperature to 350° and roast for 1 1/2 hours or until tender.

To prepare sauce: Cut peel of oranges in small strips and boil for 5 minutes. Drain. Put the red wine, brown sugar, juice from the 2 oranges and red currant jelly in a saucepan. Simmer for 10 minutes. Add the demi-glacé and simmer for 20 minutes. Strain the sauce and add the Grand Marnier and orange peel.

Serves: 2 to 3

Wine: Red Burgundy

Rosewood Room
Northstar Inn
Minneapolis, Minnesota
Chef: Hans Gilgen

ROASTED DANISH DUCKLING

2   (3-5 pound) ducklings, thawed
     and rinsed in water
2   cups pitted, dried or canned
     prunes
4   apples, peeled, cored and sliced
2   small onions, diced
4   celery stalks, diced
4   cups chicken stock (1 bouillon
     cube)
9   teaspoons flour
     Currant jelly
4   oranges
     Salt and pepper

Preheat oven to 375°. Mix apples and prunes and stuff into duckling. Rub outside with salt. Put onion and celery in a roasting pan with duckling on top. Roast in oven approximately 1 3/4 to 2 hours. (If you prefer your duck to be dark and crisp, pour the prune juice over the duckling after about an hour of cooking time.) While duckling is roasting, sauté the neck and gizzard in small casserole; add the chicken stock, let reduce to approximately 1 1/2 cups.

When duckling is done, remove to serving platter. Drain the fat from the roasting pan and sprinkle with flour to absorb the grease from the vegetables. On a medium heat, on top of the stove, stir in the stock and let thicken. When smooth, strain it back into the casserole, season with 4-5 teaspoons of currant jelly and the orange juice; let simmer 5 minutes before serving. Serve with boiled white potatoes and sweet and sour red cabbage.

Serves: 4

Wine: Charmes-Chambertin
Domaine Amiot 1961

Riviera Restaurant
Costa Mesa, California
Chef: Jean Jacques Bouché

BREAST OF CAPON "NEPTUNE"

4   boneless breasts of capons
       Clarified butter
1/2   cup dry vermouth
8   large mushroom caps, sliced
       thin
8   medium-size shrimp
8   Alaska King Crab legs, 2 inches
       long
2   tablespoons shrimp butter
1/2   cup whipped cream
       Rice
4   large mushroom caps
8   fleurons

Braise dry breasts of capons in clarified butter, 8 minutes on each side, in oven at 375°, add vermouth. Let it reduce to one third. Add mushroom caps. Cut shrimp and crab legs in pieces and mix in the chicken velouté. Bring this to a rapid boil and then add shrimp butter and cream. Remove from heat.

Serve capon breasts in the sauce with rice, 4 large mushroom caps that have been sautéed in butter, and 8 fleurons.

Chicken Velouté (2 1/2 cups)
4   tablespoons butter
6   tablespoons flour
1/4   teaspoon white pepper
2   cups chicken broth

Mix all ingredients thoroughly together. Cook over double boiler for 15 minutes, stirring occasionally.

Shrimp butter
       Shrimp shells
       Shrimp shells' weight in butter

Crush shrimp shells (red scampi from Spain are advisable). Add their weight in butter and strain through a fine sieve. Keep chilled.

Serves: 4

Wine: 1967 Courbois Pouilly-Fumé

Le Poulailler
New York, New York
Chef: Roger Fessaguet

FRICASSEE DE VOLCULLE STANLEY

3 chickens, 3-4 pounds each
2 medium-size onions
1/2 cup oil
2 tablespoons curry powder
2 hands of flour
1/2 quart white wine
3 medium-size tomatoes, diced
2 baking apples
2 bananas
1 pinch of shredded coconut
1 bouquet garni, (parsley stems and herbs)
1/2 gallon chicken or beef stock
1/2 quart heavy cream

Cut the chicken in pieces. Simmer down the onions in oil (don't let them get too brown). Add the chicken—mix together and add the curry power. Simmer down for a few minutes then add the flour, let cook for few minutes (preferably in the oven). Then add white wine, tomatoes, apples, bananas and coconut and bouquet garni. Fill up with the stock, season to taste. Bring to a boil and cook for 25-30 minutes (according to the tenderness of chicken). Remove the chicken. Pass sauce through a sieve. Let cook for 1/2 hour and bring to consistency with the cream. Season to taste. Serve with rice pilaff.

Serves: 6

Atlantis
San Diego, California

BIRD OF PARADISE

6 (15-ounce) Cornish hens
6 ounces wild rice
    Salt and pepper to taste
6 ounces orange sauce

Bone Cornish hens. Cook wild rice per directions on container. Stuff the Cornish hens with the rice, season with salt and pepper to taste. Roll up, tie, and bake them at 375° for 25 minutes.

Split pineapple and scoop out the center, pour in the rest of rice—bake 10 minutes. Place your pineapple on dish, set Cornish hens on top, pour orange sauce on top.

Orange Sauce
4 ounces sugar
4 ounces cider vinegar
1 cup veal stock (see index)
1 cup orange juice
2 teaspoons Grand Marnier

Make a caramel with vinegar and sugar by boiling ingredients over high heat until mixture turns a blond color and begins to thicken. Add orange juice and veal stock. Simmer 5 minutes over medium-low heat and add 2 teaspoons of Grand Marnier. Remove from heat.

Serves: 6

Wine: Chablis

Jacques French Restaurant
Chicago, Illinois
Chef: George Chazand

DUCKLING BIGARADE

1	4-pound cleaned duckling
1 1/2	teaspoons salt
1/4	teaspoon ground black pepper
1	tablespoon butter
1	tablespoon flour
1	cup chicken stock
1/2	cup dry white wine
2	medium-size oranges
2	tablespoons sugar
2	tablespoons water
1 1/2	cups orange juice
2	tablespoons lemon juice

Rub skin and body cavity of duckling with 1 teaspoon salt and pepper. Truss, place on rack in roasting pan and place in preheated (450°) oven. Roast until golden brown, about 20 minutes. Remove duckling to another pan. Pour off and discard all but 1 teaspoon of fat. Add tablespoon of butter to roasting pan and melt. Blend in flour and cook until roux is lightly browned. Add stock, wine and 1/2 teaspoon salt. Stir and cook until sauce slightly thickens. Return duckling to roasting pan, cover and cook in preheated oven (350°) about 1 hour or until duckling is tender.

Cut orange peel in fine strips, place in water to cover and boil 3 minutes. Drain and set aside. Segment orange, discarding white bitter portion, and set aside. Transfer duckling to warmed platter. Skim off and discard fat from sauce in roasting pan. Cook until sauce is reduced to about 1 cup. Cook the sugar and water in a small pan until straw-colored, then add the sauce. Stir in lemon and orange juice. Boil sauce 1 minute. Add orange peel.

Salt to taste. Carve duckling into 4 portions, spooning some sauce over each and serving balance in sauceboat. Garnish with orange slices.

Serves: 4

Chez Cary
Orange, California

SUPREME DE POULARDE À LA CYNTIA
(Breast of Capon in Creamed Champagne Sauce)

3	finely diced shallots
1/2	bottle dry champagne
4	cups chicken consommé
1	tablespoon drawn butter, combined
3	5-pound capons
1	pound rice pilaff
1/2	pint whipping cream
1	cup Hollandaise sauce (see index)
2	ounces Curaçao or Triple Sec
2	avocados, sliced
4	oranges, peeled and wedged
1/2	pound white Muscat grapes, peeled
3	tablespoons flour

Place shallots in skillet with champagne and reduce to 1/2. Add consommé, bring to boil and add butter mixture and flour, finish off sauce. Sauté capon breasts to a golden brown and bake in oven at 350° for 20 minutes. Place capon on rice pilaff. Add whipped cream and Hollandaise to the sauce. Pour Curaçao over capons and cover with sauce. Garnish capons with avocado, orange wedges and grapes. Glacé under broiler until a golden brown.

Serves: 6

Wine: Schloss Johannisberger, Rotlack Rhine wine

THE BLUE HORSE

ST. PAUL, MINNESOTA

Prop : Clifford Warling

Chef : George Wandzel

Roast Fillet of Beef—Périgueux

TRATTORIA GATTI
NEW YORK, NEW YORK
Prop: Fernando
and
Elda Moscini
Chef: Attilio Vosilla
Beef and Chicken A La Gatti

MAINE MAID INN
JERICHO, NEW YORK
Chef: Herbert Guonzburger
Baked Clams A La Maine Maid

Ondine's
Sauselito, California
Chef: Alfred Robun

PHEASANT ONDINE

2 (2 1/2 pound) pheasants
2 ounces of good dry sherry
4 cups water
1 onion, 1 carrot, 1 branch celery,
  1 leek—all finely chopped
1 bay leaf
1 pinch thyme
4 juniper cloves
  Salt and pepper

Disjoint the birds, separating the legs into thighs and drumsticks. Put the thighs aside with the breasts. Cut up the carcasses and drumsticks into small pieces. Place them in a saucepan with the sherry, cover and simmer until the sherry is evaporated. Add the water with the other ingredients and bring to a boil. Cook slowly for 1 1/2 hours.

Velouté

3 ounces butter
3 ounces flour
3 cups stock

Melt the butter in a saucepan, add the flour and stir with a French whip. Add the stock and bring to a boil. Cook for 10 minutes.

Conclusion

4 ounces butter
1 ounce vodka
3/4 cup velouté
8 mushroom heads, sliced
4 shallots, chopped
2 cups sour cream
  Monosodium glutamate
  Salt and pepper to taste

Melt the butter in a large skillet, then add the breasts and thighs. Cover them and cook slowly for 30 minutes, turning them once or twice. The color of the birds must remain pale. Remove them and place them on a warm serving dish. Using the same skillet, sauté the mushrooms quickly. Add the vodka, and when this is almost reduced, add the shallots and cook them quickly so they do not brown. Add the velouté and, stirring with the whip, bring the sauce to a boil. Remove this from the fire and add the sour cream. Put the sauce back on the fire *just long enough to warm the sour cream.* Season to taste, then pour the sauce over the birds and serve.

Serves: 4

Luau
Manila, Philippines
Chef: Mariano Ramos

LUAU'S OWN CHARCO-BROILED CHICKEN

1 broiler chicken
2 tablespoons Calamansi or lime
  juice
2 teaspoons Worcestershire sauce
2 tablespoons pineapple juice
1 tablespoon olive oil
  Salt and pepper to taste
2 tablespoons melted butter
2 pineapple slices
  Buttered rice

Remove chicken entrails and split down the center of the breast bone with a very sharp knife. Remove breast bone. Flatten the chicken to give it a regular shape and even surface. Insert the drumsticks into the skin. Marinate for 2 to 3 hours in lime juice, Worcestershire sauce, pineapple juice, olive oil and salt and pepper. Broil over charcoal until well done. Heat marinade, add melted butter and pour over chicken. Grill pineapple slices, serve on the side with buttered rice.

Serves: 2

Wine: Chablis or Pouilly-Fuissé

Locke-Ober
Boston, Massachusetts

BREAST OF CHICKEN (UNDER GLASS)
RICHMOND

- 1 breast of 3 1/2 pound chicken
  Flour
- 2 large mushroom caps
- 2 tablespoons sweet butter
- 2 ounces Amontillado sherry
- 1 cup basic cream sauce (see index)
- 1 slice Virginia ham, cut very thin, about the size of a slice of bread
- 1 slice fresh toast
- 3 ounces fresh cream
  Chopped parsley
  Paprika

Dredge chicken breast in flour and place with mushroom caps in sauté pan. Sauté in butter on range until the breast is golden brown. Discard excess grease in pan and add 1 ounce of sherry, cream sauce and ham. Place in 350° oven for approximately 25 minutes or until chicken is thoroughly cooked. Place a slice of fresh toast in an au gratin dish. Put the slice of ham on toast and sit breast on ham. Decorate top of breast with mushroom caps.

Add balance of wine and fresh cream to the cream sauce and stir for proper consistency. Strain and pour over chicken. Dust with chopped parsley and paprika. Cover the au gratin dish with glass belle and put in the oven for 5 minutes.

Serves: 1

Petite Marmite
Palm Beach, Florida
Chef: Costanzo (Gus) Pucillo

BREAST OF CHICKEN MAISON

- 6 chicken breasts
- 10 chicken livers
- 1/2 pound butter
  Salt
  Pepper
- 1 cup flour
- 6 eggs, beaten
- 3 cups fresh white bread crumbs

Skin the 6 chicken breasts, halve them, remove the bones including the wing tips, but leave the main wing bones. Put prepared breasts between 2 sheets of waxed paper and pound them thin with the flat side of a cleaver.

Sauté chicken livers in butter and grind in the meat grinder. Place 2 tablespoons of the ground chicken livers on each breast, salt and pepper, fold the chicken breast over the filling to form 6 cutlets of even shape. Dip the cutlets in flour, then in beaten egg, roll them in fresh white fine bread crumbs. In a skillet, in the 1/2 pound butter, sauté the chicken on one side until golden. Turn the cutlets over and bake in a hot oven, 400°, for 15 minutes or until tender.

Serves: 6

Wine: Pouilly-Fuissé

Regency Room, Sands Hotel
Las Vegas, Nevada
Chef: Pierre M. Le Coy

PHARONE À LA CRÊTOISE
(Pharone is the Italian word which
means guinea hen, a domestic bird with
a delicate meat on the dry side.)

    1 (3 pound) guinea hen
    1 jigger brandy
    2 ounces butter
       Salt
       Pepper
       Rosemary
       Clay for baking

Brown the bird in the pan and flame it
with brandy. Stuff the bird with 2 ounces
of butter, add salt, pepper and rosemary.
(One can also stuff the bird with a poultry stuffing.) Wrap the bird tightly in foil.
Then wrap it in clay, completely, thereby
forming head and tail. And pierce a hole
on the back of the bird.

Cook in oven for 40-50 minutes with
maximum heat, then put it on a plate and
break the clay with a hammer in front of
the guests. Then free the bird from its
foil, slice it up and serve with a light
tarragon sauce.

This method can also be used for pheasants or chickens.

Serves: 2

Jena
Mexico City, Mexico
Chef: "El Montanes"

PARTRIDGE À LA JENA

    6 partridges
       Salt and pepper
       Cupful of oil
    5 carrots, chopped
    3 leeks, chopped
    2 celery stalks, chopped
    1 sizeable onion, chopped
    1 cup dry red wine
    1 cup dry white wine
       Red pepper strips

The partridges are cleaned thoroughly
and then are put into a saucepan; they
are seasoned with salt and pepper. Then
they are under-fried in the oil. Then the
chopped vegetables are added together
with the wine as well as enough gravy to
cover the partridges. The partridges are
then put into the oven and allowed to
remain until the meat has softened at
medium heat. Once they are well cooked,
the partridges are put into another saucepan. The gravy is allowed to evaporate
until it becomes a little heavy, after
which it is strained and poured over the
partridges. To serve up these partridges,
small rice timbales are prepared and or-
namented with little strips of red pepper.

Serves: 6

Wine: Red Bordeaux Château
Lafite-Rothschild

L'Odeon Restaurant
San Francisco, California
Chef: Claude Trosha

CHICKEN PLAKA

1/4	pound pitted prunes
2	cups uncooked rice
1/4	cup salad oil
	Salt
	Pepper
1/2	teaspoon rosemary
1/2	teaspoon thyme
1/2	quart hot chicken broth
2	diced apples
1/4	quart seedless grapes, fresh or canned
3	pair chicken livers, sautéed and chopped
1/2	cup pine nuts or slivered almonds (optional)
1	broiler-fryer chicken, cut in quarters as needed
	Salad oil as needed
1	orange (grated rind)
	Salt and pepper as needed
1/2	quart carrot sticks
1/2	quart small whole or halved onions
1/4	cup mushroom caps or pieces, fresh or canned
1/4	cup butter or margarine, melted
2	tablespoons chicken stock base
1/4	cup water

Halve or coarsely chop prunes. Cook and stir rice in the 1/4 cup oil until lightly browned. Add salt, pepper, rosemary and thyme. Gradually add broth until absorbed. Add prunes, apple, grapes, liver and nuts. Divide into 2 greased pans, 20 by 12 by 2 1/2 inches. Rub chicken with cut surface of lemon. Coat with oil, sprinkle with orange rind, salt and pepper. Brown at 475° (hot oven) about 10 minutes. Arrange chicken, skin side up, over rice. Cover with aluminum foil and seal completely. Spread carrots, onions and mushrooms in pan (20 by 12 by 2 1/2 inches). Drizzle with butter; pour on chicken stock base mixed with water; season to taste. Cover with aluminum foil and seal completely. Bake chicken and vegetables at 350° (moderate) about 45 minutes. Serve 1/4 chicken with 1/2 cup each prune dressing and vegetables. Spoon vegetable stock over vegetables and chicken.

Serves: 4

La Cave
Bangkok, Thailand

CHICKEN CURRY

6	cups coconut milk or milk
1/2	cup curry powder
1/2	cup chutney
1	teaspoon paprika
2	chickens cut in appropriate pieces
6	teaspoons soy sauce
2	teaspoons flour

Cook coconut milk at boiling point for a few minutes; put in curry powder, chutney, paprika, cook down. Sauté pieces of chicken in it, cook down. Season with soy sauce and thicken with flour. Serve with rice.

Serves: 4

Wine: Rosé

Le Mont Restaurant
Pittsburgh, Pennsylvania

CHICKEN PARISIENNE

      6 ounces cooked broccoli spears
      2 teaspoons Hollandaise sauce
      6 ounces thin-sliced, boiled breast
         of chicken
      8 tablespoons cream sauce
      1 tablespoon Parmesan cheese

Put broccoli in center of casserole, pour Hollandaise sauce over it, then arrange the sliced chicken and cover it with cream sauce and sprinkle Parmesan cheese lightly over it. Cook in preheated oven (500°) for 15 minutes or until golden brown.

Cream Sauce
      2 ounces butter
      3 ounces flour
      1 pint chicken broth
    1/2 pint milk
    1/2 teaspoon salt

Place ingredients in deep pan, bring to boil and stir for 15 minutes.

Hollandaise Sauce
      1 egg yolk
      1 tablespoon lukewarm water
      4 tablespoons melted clear butter

Put egg yolk in a bowl, add lukewarm water and beat with a wire whisk, constantly, while cooking over hot water (not boiling) until thick and creamy. Away from heat blend in 4 tablespoons of melted clear butter.

Serves: 2

Wine: Tavel-Bellicard E. B.

Madrid
Manila, Philippines
Chef: Mrs. Julia de la Orden
Trullench

SQUABS AU SHERRY
(Pichones al Jerez)

      4 squabs
    1/2 cup butter with 2 cups frying
         oil, enough to fry squabs until
         golden brown
      2 onions, chopped
      2 teaspoons chopped parsley
    1/2 cup chopped celery
         Salt and pepper
      5 teaspoons American, French or
         Spanish sherry
      8 cups chicken broth mixed with
         2 teaspoons beef extract
         (Bovril)
      2 big cans mushrooms (Taiwan
         "555" suggested)
      2 small cans pâté de foie (liver
         paste)
      4 teaspoons brandy

Fry squabs in butter and oil until golden brown. Remove from pan. To remaining butter and oil add onions, parsley, celery, salt and pepper and wine. Allow to boil. Transfer everything to a large pan with the squabs and add enough broth to cover the squabs. Simmer until squabs are half tender. Add mushrooms and pâté de foie. Cover with brandy and continue cooking until done. Try tenderness with a fork.

If after cooking, the dish appears thin or watery it may be thickened by frying 2 ounces butter with 2 tablespoons flour and adding to the liquid, stirring continuously, until it thickens. Pour sauce on squabs and serve hot.

Serves: 4

Wine: Demi-sec white

Lenhardt's
Cincinnati, Ohio
Chef: Anna Lenhardt

VIENNESE CHICKEN PAPRIKASCH AND
NOCKERL

3 medium-size onions, diced
1/2 cup shortening
1 roasting chicken, divided into quarters
3 tablespoons Hungarian sweet paprika
1 cup water or stock
1 tablespoon salt
1/2 teaspoon sugar
1 tablespoon flour
1/2 cup cream

Sauté diced onions to light yellow color in 1/2 cup shortening. Divide chicken into quarters and sauté with onions for 15 minutes, carefully turning occasionally. Remove from heat and add Hungarian sweet paprika, mixing paprika thoroughly into chicken. Replace mixture on the heat, add 1 cup of water or stock. Then add salt and sugar. Continue to cook over slow heat, or in the oven at 350°, until the meat can be pierced easily with the fork. Transfer chicken to a serving platter and to remaining gravy add 1 tablespoon flour combined with 1/2 cup cream. Bring gravy to a quick boil, then strain over chicken. The Viennese Chicken Paprikasch is served with Viennese Nockerl (small dumplings) or rice.

Nockerl (small dumplings)
1 cup flour
5 eggs
Pinch salt

Mix flour and eggs in small bowl until fluffy. Add salt, mix again. Drop mixture by 1/2 teaspoonfuls into lightly salted boiling water. To prevent mixture from sticking to spoon, allow spoon to drop into water each time dough is dropped. When dough rises to top of boiling water, drain and serve.

Serves: 4

Wine: Durnsteiner
Katzensprung

Commander's Palace
New Orleans, Louisiana

CHICKEN GUMBO

1 small stewing hen
2 tablespoons flour
3 tablespoons shortening
2 onions, chopped
1 cup chopped celery
2 cups tomatoes
6 sprigs parsley, chopped
2 cups water or stock
2 bay leaves
1 sprig or 1 pinch of thyme
1 teaspoon celery salt
2 cups okra
Salt and pepper

Cut chicken in serving portions, dredge lightly in flour and sauté in shortening until brown. Add onions and celery, and cook until soft. Add all other ingredients except okra and cook until chicken is done. Add okra and cook 15 minutes. Salt and pepper to taste. Serve with rice.

Serves: 8

Wine: Puligny-Montrachet

Brennan's French Restaurant
New Orleans, Louisiana

CHICKEN FINANCIERE

1	2-pound chicken, disjointed
	Seasoned flour
1/2	cup vegetable oil
1/2	cup chicken livers, coarsely chopped
1/2	green onion, minced
1	teaspoon minced garlic
1	tablespoon flour
1 1/2	cups chicken stock
1/2	cup dry red wine
1/2	cup sliced mushrooms
1/4	cup sliced olives
1/2	teaspoon salt
	Dash cayenne
1	tablespoon Worcestershire

Dredge chicken pieces in seasoned flour. In a large skillet heat vegetable oil and fry chicken to golden brown and tender. Remove chicken to platter and keep warm.

Sauté chicken livers, green onion and garlic. Blend in flour and brown. Stir in chicken stock until smooth. Add remaining ingredients. Simmer 15 minutes. Return chicken to pan and continue to simmer 10 minutes more.

Serves: 2 to 3

Wine: Saint-Emilion

Old Club Restaurant
Alexandria, Virginia

BARBECUED CHICKEN

2	(2 1/2-pound) broilers, each half cut into 3 pieces
8	ounces Chablis wine
6	ounces all-purpose oil
1	teaspoon minced chives
1	tablespoon minced parsley

Marinate the broilers at least 1 hour at room temperature in the above ingredients.

Barbecue sauce

2	tablespoons brown sugar
1/2	cup vinegar
1/4	cup lemon juice
1/4	cup orange juice
1	teaspoon Kitchen Bouquet
1	teaspoon Worcestershire sauce
1/2	small onion, minced
1/4	teaspoon garlic salt
1/2	teaspoon salt
1/8	teaspoon pepper
1	cup chili sauce
1	cup tomato paste
1	cup all-purpose oil

Let ingredients simmer together for at least 1 hour and 15 minutes. Drain marinade from chickens. Add the liquid to barbecue sauce. Broil chickens 5 inches from broiler for 15 minutes each side.

Remove chickens from broiler. Place in pan. Cover with barbecue sauce and cook for 1 1/2 hours in 325° oven.

Serves: 4 to 6

Laffite
Denver, Colorado

CANETON BIGARADE À LA SPERTE

- 1 (5-pound) duckling
- 1 pinch salt
- 1 pinch pepper
- 1 pinch dried thyme
- 1 pinch sage
- 1 cup cut-up celery
- 1 cup cut-up scallions
- 1 cup cut-up carrots
- 1/3 cup brown sugar
- 1/3 cup granulated sugar
- 3 oranges
- 1/2 cup Port wine
- 1/2 cup Triple Sec Liqueur
     Cayenne

Rub the cavity of a clean 4-5 pound duckling with salt, pepper and a little dried thyme and sage. Insert a couple of pieces of celery, scallions and carrot. Put the duck in a shallow roasting pan and roast it, uncovered, in a moderately slow oven—325°—for 2 hours or until the meat on the legs is tender when pressed with the fingers.

In a saucepan combine 1/3 cup each of brown and granulated sugar and cook the mixture, stirring constantly, until it is almost caramelized. Stir in the juice of 3 oranges and 1/2 cup Port and bring the sauce to a boil. Skim off and discard the fat from the pan juices of the roasted duck. Add the remaining duck juices to the orange mixture and cook the sauce for about 5 minutes. To reduce it, add 1 tablespoon finely slivered orange and season the mixture with a little orange-flavored liqueur—Triple Sec—salt and cayenne.

Carve the duck into quarters and arrange them on a heated platter. Pour some of the sauce over the duckling and garnish the platter with peeled orange slices. Serve the remaining sauce separately.

Serves: 4

Cavalier Room, Syracuse Hotel
Syracuse, New York

BREAST OF CHICKEN AND RICE À LA MARSALA

- 1/2 cup bacon fat
- 1/2 cup minced onions
- 1 tablespoon minced chives
- 2 cloves garlic, minced
- 8 chicken breasts
     Flour
- 3 cups Marsala wine
- 2 cups canned tomatoes
- 3 cups beef stock
- 3 cups mushrooms, sliced
- 1/2 cup parsley, chopped
     Salt and pepper to taste

Heat fat, add onions, chives and garlic. Flour chicken breasts—add to onion and chives and brown. Add 3 cups Marsala wine and boil to reduce to 1 cup. Add tomatoes and beef stock. Cook for 30 minutes on a boil—last few minutes add sliced mushrooms and chopped parsley. Season to taste.

Rice ring
- 1/8 pound butter
- 1 onion, diced fine
- 1/4 cup peppers, chopped fine
- 1/4 cup pimentos, chopped fine
- 1 cup rice
     Salt and pepper
- 2 cups chicken stock

Melt butter, add onion and cook until glazed. Add peppers, pimentos and rice and cook a few minutes. Add salt and pepper. Add chicken stock and bring to a boil. Cook 20 minutes.

Serve in a rice ring. Place chicken breasts in center and garnish with watercress.

Serves: 8

Hotel d'Angleterre
Copenhagen, Denmark

FAISON FARCI À L'HUBERTUS

1	pheasant
1/2	teaspoon sage
1/2	cup cognac
1/2	cup Port wine
5	juniper berries
1/2	teaspoon marjoram
1/2	teaspoon rosemary

Bone a big pheasant from the back without damaging the skin. Rub the inside of the pheasant with sage. Place it in a deep dish, pour cognac and Port over it and season it with juniper berries, marjoram and rosemary. Marinate the pheasant for 12 hours.

The Forcemeat

	Pheasant liver, gizzard and heart
1	cup bread crumbs
1	egg
	Cream (enough to soften forcemeat)
	Salt, pepper, sage
1	teaspoon pistachios
2	entire small truffles
	Butter for browning pheasant
1	cup venison bouillon (or chicken)

Make a forcemeat of pheasant liver, gizzard and heart as well as bread crumbs. Mix it with 1 egg and dilute with the pheasant marinade; add some cream until the forcemeat is soft. Season with salt, pepper and sage and add entire pistachios and truffles.

Stuff the pheasant with the forcemeat and sew it up carefully. Brown the pheas-
ant in an iron pot with abundant butter. Pour venison bouillon over it and bring it carefully to the boil. Simmer for 30 minutes.

The Broth

18	leaves of isinglass per cup of broth
2	tablespoons chopped beef
1	tablespoon browned pot herbs
1	twig of thyme
5	juniper berries
2	egg whites

Boil the leaves of isinglass per cup of broth and clear with chopped beef, browned pot herbs, a twig of thyme, juniper berries and approximately 2 whites of egg.

Slice the pheasant and pour aspic over it. Serve with warm rolls and butter.

Serves: 4

Wine: Meursault or Chassagne-Montrachet

Smoke House
Burbank, California

BREAST OF CHICKEN BORDEAUX

4	boneless chicken breasts
1	cup flour
2	tablespoons oil
1	bell pepper, sliced
1	medium onion, sliced
1/4	pound mushrooms, sliced
1	ounce Burgundy wine
	Salt and pepper

Dredge chicken in flour, sauté chicken on both sides approximately 5 minutes in oil. Add vegetables and cook until they are done. Add wine, salt and pepper to taste. Serve over rice.

Serves: 4

Stuft Shirt
Newport Beach, California
Chef: Bob Harris

BREAST OF CHICKEN À LA KIEV

3 whole chicken breasts removed from 3 1/2-pound roasters, cut in half with main wing bones left attached
  Salt, monosodium glutamate, white pepper
1 tablespoon minced shallots
1 tablespoon chopped chives
1/4 pound firm butter
  Flour seasoned with salt and pepper
2 slightly beaten eggs
1 cup bread crumbs
2 cups clarified sweet butter
1 tablespoon oil

Pound chicken breasts with a mallet (dipped in ice water before each pounding) until thin, being careful not to split the flesh. Sprinkle the inside of each 1/2 breast with salt, monosodium glutamate and white pepper. Combine shallots and chives. Cut butter lengthwise into 6 sticks. Place 1 teaspoon of the shallot-chive mixture and 1 stick of butter on the long edge of each 1/2 chicken breast. Starting at the buttered edge, tightly roll each portion, sealing the butter and allowing the wing bone to protrude. Dredge each portion lightly with seasoned flour, dip into beaten eggs and coat with bread crumbs. Heat clarified butter and oil and brown chicken breasts (2 or 3 at a time) quickly on all sides. Transfer browned portions to a shallow, oblong baking dish. Bake in a 350° preheated oven for 15 minutes or until chicken is tender. Drain on absorbent paper. Place a paper frill on each wing bone. Arrange on a heated serving platter and keep warm in a low temperature oven. Serve with Smitane sauce.

Smitane Sauce
1/2 cup sour cream
1 cup whipping cream
1 cup condensed chicken broth
1/2 cup finely chopped onions
1/4 cup sweet butter
3 tablespoons flour
1/2 teaspoon salt
  Dash of cayenne pepper
2 tablespoons dry white wine

Combine sour cream, whipping cream and broth in saucepan and simmer over low heat. DO NOT ALLOW TO BOIL. Stir occasionally. Separately sauté onions in butter until transparent. Blend in flour, salt and cayenne pepper. Add, gradually, hot cream-chicken broth mixture, stirring continuously. Add white wine and pour into heated sauceboat. Serve immediately. Yields 3 1/2 cups.

Serves: 6

Wine: Wente Bros. Pinot Chardonnay

Fourteen 21 Club
Denver, Colorado
Chef: Walter Beuttler

CHICKEN CURRY "MADRAS"

    4 (8-ounce) boneless fresh
         chicken breasts
    2 teaspoons butter
    2 tablespoons flour
    2 teaspoons curry powder
  1/2 pint milk
  1/2 pint heavy cream
    1 teaspoon chicken base
    2 bananas
    3 pineapple rings
    2 ounces Pernod
       Coconut flakes
       Browned almonds
       Chutney

Put chicken in medium hot oven (375°) about 25 minutes. Melt butter in pan, add flour and curry powder. Add milk and heavy cream, stir constantly until it reaches a boil. Add chicken base, 1/2 squashed banana, 1 diced pineapple ring and the Pernod. Pour over chicken breasts. Top with 1/2 broiled banana, 1/2 broiled pineapple ring, coconut flakes, browned almonds and chutney. Serve with rice and water chestnuts wrapped in bacon.

Serves: 4

Pamplona
New York, New York
Prop: M. Gonzalez

POLLO Y LANGOSTA À LA CATALANA

  1/2 pound carrots
  1/4 pound leeks
    2 ounces shallots
    2 ounces fresh garlic
    4 pounds live lobster meat, sliced
    2 ounces brandy
    2 teaspoons Spanish paprika
  1/4 pound flour
       Salt and pepper
    1 pound fresh tomatoes
    1 quart water
    1 (4-pound) chicken
  1/4 pound margarine
    1 tablespoon Pernod

Chop carrots, leeks, shallots and fresh garlic and simmer in a casserole for 15 minutes. Soak lobster in brandy. Next add the paprika and flour and season with salt and pepper. Add tomatoes and mix with wooden spoon. Add a quart of water and keep mixing to prevent mixture from sticking to casserole, then let it cook for 15 minutes. Pass the sauce through a blender.

Cut the chicken in 4 parts and take out the bones. Cover with margarine. Slice the lobster and marinate with salt and pepper. Place chicken and lobster in hot casserole dish, add sauce and Pernod, and place in 400° oven for 25 minutes. The color of the sauce should be old gold. Delicious with rice.

Serves: 4

Trader Vic's
San Francisco, California
Prop: Victor J. Bergeron

EMPRESS CHICKEN

  8 chicken legs
  8 chicken thighs
12 ounces prosciutto ham
1/4 cup sherry
1/4 cup pure soya (Sang Chow)
  1 teaspoon salt
1/4 teaspoon pepper
1/2 teaspoon monosodium
      glutamate
  2 tablespoons oil
     Cornstarch

Wash chicken legs and second joints and bone them carefully, leaving the skin intact. Chop prosciutto ham very fine and fill the cavity of each leg and thigh. Mix sherry, pure soya, seasonings and oil in a bowl and marinate chicken 10 to 15 minutes. Roll pieces in cornstarch, rubbing it in to make a good coating, and fry in deep fat until golden brown. Keep warm in oven while you make the following sauce.

Sauce for Empress Chicken
12 Chinese dried black mushrooms
  2 tablespoons oil
1/4 cup chopped onions
  1 tablespoon minced ginger root
  3 cups chicken stock
1/2 teaspoon salt
  1 ounce sherry
  1 ounce pure soya
  3 tablespoons cornstarch mixed
     with
1/2 cup cold water

Wash and soak mushrooms in warm water for 15 to 20 minutes. When spongy, squeeze out water and cut into strips 1/4 inch wide. Heat pan and add oil; sauté onions and chopped ginger together. Add mushrooms and stir-fry a few seconds, then add chicken stock, salt, sherry and soya and bring to a boil. Thicken with cornstarch mixture, then add fried chicken pieces and let heat through. Serve with steamed rice.

Serves: 6 to 8

Cinelli's Country House
Cherry Hill, New Jersey

CHICKEN À LA OLGA

1/2 spring chicken
     Flour seasoned with salt and
      pepper
  2 tablespoons butter
  2 tablespoons olive oil
  2 artichoke hearts
  4 large mushroom caps
  2 ounces imported Marsala wine
  3 pieces sliced truffles
     Chopped parsley

Cut chicken into 4 pieces and dip in seasoned flour. Sauté in frying pan with butter and olive oil until brown on all sides. Add artichokes and mushroom caps and simmer for approximately 10 minutes in covered pan. Drain off any excess liquid and add wine. Simmer for 2 or 3 minutes. Serve from skillet, garnishing with sliced truffles and parsley according to taste.

Serve: 1

Wine: Imported Marsala

Cafe Johnell
Fort Wayne, Indiana
Prop. and
Chef: John N. Spillson

SUPREME DE VOLAILLE AU CHAMPAGNE

4 whole chicken breasts, skin removed
1/2 cup flour
2 teaspoons salt
1 teaspoon pepper
1/4 cup butter
4 ounces sliced fresh mushrooms
6 ounces half and half
3 ounces champagne

Pound chicken breasts until thin. Roll breasts in flour, salt and pepper. Shake excess flour off. Heat butter in skillet. Cook breasts over low heat until brown on both sides. Add mushrooms, cover and cook 10 minutes. Drain off excess butter. Remove chicken to a warm place. Add half and half to skillet and simmer for 5 minutes. Add champagne, bring to a rapid boil and cook until sauce is reduced to a creamy consistency. If too thick, add a little half and half. Place chicken breasts on hot plate and spoon sauce over them. Garnish.

Serves: 4

Wine: Good dry white

The Empress
London, England
Chef: Gino Scandolo

EMPRESS DUCKLING IN BURGUNDY

1 large duckling
2 large glasses Chambertin
2 shallots, chopped
1/2 bay leaf
1 pinch mignonette pepper
Little grated nutmeg
2 small glasses brandy
1/2 pint veal stock, thickened
2 ounces butter
18 small white mushrooms
1 truffle, diced and cooked

Roast the duckling slightly underdone. Take the meat from both sides of the breast. Detach the thighs, cut off the rump and throw away. Cook the red wine, reducing to two-thirds. Crush the carcass, put it into the casserole in which the wine was reduced and add shallots, bay leaf, pepper, nutmeg, brandy and veal stock. Cook for 30 minutes and press it through a pointed strainer. Re-boil the sauce and reduce until it forms a thick cream. Finish away from the fire with the butter.

Arrange the pieces of duckling in a hollow dish, and add the whole mushrooms and the truffle, sliced and previously cooked. Cover all with the sauce.

Serves: 2

Regency Hyatt House
Atlanta, Georgia

CHEF LUDWIG STRODEL'S COQ AU VIN

3	(4-ounce) chunks of lean bacon
2	quarts water
2	tablespoons butter
2 1/2	to 3 pounds cut-up frying chicken
1/2	teaspoon salt
1/2	teaspoon pepper
1/4	cup cognac
3	cups young, full-bodied red wine such as Burgundy or Chianti
1	to 2 cups brown chicken stock, brown stock or canned beef bouillon
1/2	tablespoon tomato paste
2	cloves mashed garlic
1/4	teaspoon thyme
1	bay leaf
3	tablespoons flour
2	tablespoons softened butter
	Sprigs of fresh parsley

Remove the rind of the bacon and cut into rectangles 1/4 inch across and 1 inch long. Simmer for 10 minutes in 2 quarts of water. Rinse in cold water and dry. In a heavy 10-inch fireproof casserole or an electric skillet (temperature at 260°), sauté the bacon slowly in hot butter until it is very lightly browned. Remove to a side dish.

Dry the cut-up frying chicken thoroughly. Brown it in the hot fat in the casserole (360° for the electric skillet). Season the chicken. Return the bacon to the casserole with the chicken. Cover and cook slowly (300°) for 10 minutes, turning the chicken once. Uncover and pour in the cognac. Averting your face, ignite the cognac with a lighted match. Shake the casserole back and forth for several seconds until the flames subside.

Pour the wine into the casserole. Add just enough stock or bouillon to cover the chicken. Stir in the tomato paste, garlic and herbs. Bring to simmer. Cover and continue to simmer slowly for 25 to 30 minutes or until the chicken is tender and its juices run a clear yellow when the meat is pricked with a fork. Remove the chicken to a side dish.

Simmer the chicken cooking liquid in the casserole for a minute or two, skimming off fat. Then raise heat and boil rapidly, reducing the liquid to about 2 1/4 cups. Correct seasoning. Remove from heat and discard bay leaf.

Blend the butter and flour together into a smooth paste. Beat the paste into the hot liquid with a wire whip. Bring to simmer, while stirring, and let simmer for 2 minutes. The sauce should be thick enough to coat a spoon lightly. Arrange the chicken in the casserole, place the mushrooms and onions around it, and baste with the sauce.

Shortly before serving, bring to simmer, basting the chicken with the sauce. Cover and simmer slowly for 4 to 5 minutes, until the chicken is hot through. Serve from the casserole or arrange on a hot platter. Decorate with sprigs of parsley.

Serves: 4

Swiss Chalet
San Juan, Puerto Rico
Chef: Hans Moosberger

COQ AU VIN À LA GENEVOISE

3 (2 1/2-pound) chickens,
    disjointed
  Salt, pepper, flour
2 cups cooking oil
2 onions, chopped
1 clove garlic, chopped
2 bay leaves
  Rosemary
1 cup tomato puree
3 cups red wine (Chambertin)
3 cups chicken stock (consommé)
1 small can mushrooms, sautéed
1 small can pearl onions

Fry disjointed chicken, which has been prepared with salt, pepper, and flour, in hot oil until brown. Add chopped onions and garlic, bay leaves, rosemary and tomato puree and sprinkle with flour. Add wine and chicken stock, mix well and cook on small fire, covered, for about 20 minutes. Remove chicken, strain sauce when thick enough, add some sautéed mushrooms and pearl onions. Serve very hot in casserole with buttered rice on the side.

Serves: 6

Charles French Restaurant
New York, New York

POT-AU-FEU À LA CHARLES

3 2 1/2-pound chickens
6 carrots
6 celery branches
2 leeks
1 bay leaf
  Salt and pepper
  Water
1/2 pound butter
3 tablespoons flour

Boil the chickens in a pot with water, carrots, celery, leeks, bay leaf, salt and pepper until tender, for 35-40 minutes. Take the chickens and the vegetables out of the broth. Cut each chicken in 4 parts, remove the skin and some bones. Dice vegetables. Put the chickens and the vegetables in the dish you serve the pot-au-feu and keep it hot. Strain the broth. Melt butter, add the flour and stir in the broth and boil for 15 minutes. Pour the sauce over the chicken and vegetables and garnish with matzoh balls.

Matzoh Balls
4 eggs, separated
3/4 cup matzoh meal
1/4 cup dry bread crumbs
1/4 cup water
1/4 cup chicken fat
1/2 teaspoon baking soda
1/2 teaspoon salt
  Pinch of nutmeg

Beat egg yolks hard. Then add all remaining ingredients, except egg whites, and mix until well blended. Beat egg whites until frothy (not stiff) and fold into mixture. Refrigerate 30 minutes. Shape into little balls the size of a walnut, and boil in broth or water for 20 minutes. Yields 2 dozen.

Serves: 6

The Colony
New York, New York
Chef: Claude Millien

CHICKEN GISMONDA

2 whole chicken breasts, boned
   and split to yield 4 sections
1 egg, well-beaten
3 tablespoons cold water
1 teaspoon salt
2/3 cup fine dry bread crumbs
1 package frozen chopped spinach, cooked
1/4 cup butter
   Dash of nutmeg
1/3 pound mushrooms, sliced tops
   only
2 tablespoons sherry
   Oil or other fat for frying

Place chicken sections on cutting board and pound as thin as possible with wooden mallet or base of a heavy saucer. Dip them in egg which has been mixed with cold water. Then dip in bread crumbs mixed with salt. Let stand at room temperature for 10 minutes.

Meanwhile, cook spinach according to package directions, drain, add 2 table-spoons butter and a dash of nutmeg. Keep hot.

Sauté mushroom slices in remaining butter for 5 minutes. Add sherry. Cover and keep hot.

Heat oil in a heavy pan until a one-inch cube of bread browns in 48 seconds. Lower prepared chicken breast halves into it. Cook chicken pieces, 5 or 6 minutes on each side, turning them with a slotted spoon. They will rise to the surface of the fat when they are done. Remove and drain on paper towels.

Arrange 4 servings of spinach on a platter with a cooked chicken breast on each.

Overlap mushroom slices neatly on each chicken breast and spoon some of the mushroom pan liquid over the portions. Serve at once.

Serves: 4

Georges Rey Restaurant
Français
New York, New York
Chef: André Ledoux

CHICKEN SAUTÉ NORMANDIE STYLE

   Small spring chicken
2 tablespoons butter
1 tablespoon finely chopped onion
8 ounces cèpes or mushrooms,
   sautéed
3 to 4 tablespoons calvados
   (apple-jack)
1/2 pint cream
3 tablespoons meat gravy

Cut up the chicken and sauté in butter. When half cooked add the onion and cèpes or mushrooms and continue cooking, taking care that the onion does not become brown. When the chicken is tender, add the calvados and reduce by two thirds. Add the cream and meat gravy and boil for a few minutes.

Put the chicken onto a serving dish and pour the sauce and mushrooms over.

Serves: 2

Cafe Chauveron
New York, New York
Prop: Roger Chauveron

CHICKEN IN CHAMPAGNE SAUCE

- 2 (3-pound) chickens, cut-up
- 1/2 pound butter
  - Salt and pepper
- 1/3 cup white Port wine
- 2 ounces brandy
- 4 ounces dry champagne or dry white wine
  - Shallots
- 1 cup thick cream sauce (see index)
- 3 cups light cream

Sauté chicken in butter. When it is lightly browned, season with salt and pepper and cover. Cook slowly for 25 minutes. Remove the pieces of chicken and pour off the cooked butter. Bring to boil the brandy, Port wine and champagne; simmer for 5 minutes. This will make a sauce. Then add the thick cream sauce and the fresh light cream. Cook over a hot fire for 6 minutes, stirring constantly, but do not boil any more. Put the chicken back in sauce, simmer for 5 minutes. It is now ready to be served. Boiled rice or wild rice can be served with the chicken.

Optional: If you desire to add shallots at the beginning of the sauté, use 1 small head, finely chopped.

Serves: 4

Le Manoir
New York, New York

DUCKLING WITH FIGS

- 1 (4-to 5-pound) duckling, cut into serving pieces
  - Butter, softened
  - Salt and pepper
- 1/4 teaspoon cinnamon
- 1/4 teaspoon cloves
- 1/4 teaspoon nutmeg
- 1/4 teaspoon ginger
- 1 cup dry red wine
  - Butter for basting, melted
- 2 tablespoons Kitchen Bouquet (optional)
- 1 (17-ounce) jar whole figs in heavy syrup
- 1 1/4 cups brown gravy or 1 (10 1/2-ounce) can brown gravy
- 1 tablespoon red wine vinegar
- 1 teaspoon cayenne pepper
- 1 tablespoon cognac

Rub duckling pieces well with butter. Mix salt, pepper and spices together and sprinkle on duckling. Place in shallow oven roaster on rack, skin side up, and roast at 375° for 30 minutes. Turn, roast for an additional 30 minutes, basting every 10 to 15 minutes with red wine and melted butter. For a dark crust, brush with Kitchen Bouquet (about 2 tablespoons) and turn heat to 450° for last 10 minutes of cooking.

In a saucepan, heat figs in syrup, drain figs, place on heat-proof platter with duckling pieces. Drain fat from roasting pan, add 1/2 cup fig syrup and 1 1/4 cups brown gravy (or 10 1/2 ounce can gravy), 1 tablespoon red wine vinegar, 1 teaspoon cayenne pepper and 1 tablespoon cognac. Bring to a boil and simmer for about 5 minutes. Strain over duckling and figs, serve remaining sauce in gravyboat.

Serves: 4

King Cole
Dayton, Ohio
Chef: Dieter W. Krug

CAPON À LA KIEV

2 (3-pound) caponettes
1 ounce finely chopped garlic
1 ounce finely chopped shallots
1 ounce finely chopped parsley
  Dash of salt and white pepper
8 ounces softened butter
  Egg
  White bread crumbs
  Parmesan cheese

Bone caponettes so breasts can be divided into 2 pieces. Completely bone with the exception of the first wing joint which is allowed to remain fastened to breast. Thigh is separated from leg, and bone is removed. You should now have 4 pieces of breast and 4 pieces of thigh (enough to serve 4 persons).

Add garlic, shallots, parsley and dash of salt and white pepper to softened butter and blend together. Using flat side of a heavy knife flatten out breasts and thighs to approximately double their size. Season lightly with salt and pepper. Divide butter mixture into approximately 8 equal parts and place 1 on each breast and thigh. Fold flattened breast or thigh to completely envelope seasoned butter so that butter cannot seap out. Bread each piece in egg wash, white bread crumbs and some Parmesan cheese. Sauté until golden brown and then place in 400° oven for approximately 20 minutes. Serve with supreme sauce (rich chicken sauce) and wild rice.

Supreme Sauce

2 tablespoons butter
2 tablespoons flour
2 cups chicken or veal or fish stock

Stir over low heat until thickened, then cook in double boiler for an hour.

To one and one-half cups of above sauce base made with chicken stock add one cup chicken stock and mushroom cuttings. Bring to boil and strain. Stir in one tablespoon butter and season to taste.

Serves: 4

The Inn of the Eight Immortals
Falls Church, Virginia

PA HSIEN CHICKEN

1 (4-pound) plump roasting chicken, eviscerated, rinsed and drained
1 1/2 teaspoons salt
1/3 cup soy sauce
1 tablespoon hoisin sauce
3 tablespoons dry white wine
1 stalk green onion, cut roots, rinse and smash head lightly
2 slices fresh ginger
2 cups soup stock
2 tablespoons lard
1 clove garlic, peeled, smashed and chopped fine
1 stalk baak-choy or 2 stalks if small, rinse each leaf thoroughly and slit it in half then cut lengthwise
12 slices canned bamboo shoots
12 pieces snow pea pods, with ends pinched out
3 water chestnuts, sliced
6 black mushrooms, soaked, rinsed and sliced
2 tablespoons cornstarch dissolved in water
1/4 cup oyster sauce

Thoroughly rub chicken with marinade of 1 teaspoon salt, soy sauce, hoisin sauce and wine. Stuff chicken with green onion and ginger. Roast the marinated chicken in 375° oven until brown with breast down. In 30 minutes turn the chicken over with breast up. Pour 1 1/2 cups soup stock over chicken and roast 30 minutes more or until done. Remove chicken from pan to cool.

In a hot frying pan melt 2 tablespoons lard, add 1/2 teaspoon salt and garlic, then put in vegetables, bamboo shoots, water chestnuts and mushrooms. Stir-fry 5 minutes, add 1/2 cup soup stock, cover and cook 10 minutes. Thicken the liquid with the cornstarch batter. Stir thoroughly, then scoop into a large serving platter. Split the chicken in half and remove bones with a boning knife. Slice the meat lengthwise into strips about 1/2-inch wide and place on top of vegetables. Strain drippings in roasting pan into saucepan. Add oyster sauce and bring to boil, thickening it with remaining cornstarch batter. Pour oyster gravy over chicken.

Serves: 4

Mandarin Hotel
Hong Kong

LE CANETON POELE "PUERTO PRINCESSA"
(Roast Duckling "Puerto Princessa")

1/2	bottle red wine
4	ounces sugar
8	ounces mango chutney
16	ounces crushed pineapple
2	tablespoons fresh lemon juice
3	tablespoons fresh orange juice
6	ounces tomato catsup
6	ounces chili sauce
1	medium-size red chili
5	pieces cloves
1/4	ounce ginger powder
	Tabasco sauce
	Cornstarch
2	whole roast ducklings

Lightly brown sugar in saucepan and add red wine. Reduce slightly, stir in finely chopped mango chutney, crushed pineapple, orange juice, lemon juice, tomato catsup and chili sauce. Bring to boil. Simmer for about 3 minutes, season with remainder of spices; ginger powder, cloves and Tabasco sauce. Stir the cornstarch with a little cold water and add to sauce. Boil again, stirring all the time, until sauce thickens. Remove from heat and allow to cool. Can be served hot or cold with roast ducklings.

This sauce can be used with various smoked meats: ham, ox tongue, etc.

Serves: 4 to 6

Wine: Nuits-Saint-Georges

Charles French Restaurant
New York, New York

PETITE MARMITE MAISON

  1 chicken breast
  1 pound chicken necks and backs
  2 tablespoons butter
  1 pound plate beef
  1 pound beef ribs
  1 marrow bone
  1 medium-large onion
  1 stalk celery
  2 quarts beef broth
     Salt and pepper to taste
  1 cup diced carrots
  1 cup diced turnips
1/2 cup diced celery
1/2 cup green peas

Lightly brown chicken breast, necks and backs in butter. Drain off the fat and discard. Put chicken in 4-quart saucepan. Add beef, ribs, marrow bone, onion, celery stalk and beef broth. Salt and pepper to taste. Slowly bring to boiling point. Skim. Reduce heat and simmer for 1 1/2 hours. Remove and discard onion and celery.

Remove chicken, beef, ribs and marrow bone from the stock. Cut chicken, meat and plate beef into 1/2-inch squares. Take marrow out of the bone and cut also in small squares. Set aside.

Skim the broth, bring to boiling point, and add carrots, turnips and celery. Cook for 20 minutes or until vegetables are tender. Add peas, chicken, meat and marrow, and cook for 5 minutes or until peas are tender. Serve very hot.

Serves: 6

Inn on the Park
Toronto, Canada
Chef: Georges Chargnet

CAILLES AUX CERISES

    3 (3 ounce) quails—plump with firm white fat
      Butter
1 1/2 ounces cherry brandy
      Juice of half a lemon
    5 ounces game stock or good rich veal stock (see index)
   12 pitted Bing cherries

Truss the quails, then fry quickly in a small amount of butter in a baked enamel roasting dish, until they are lightly colored.

Cover and place in a preheated oven of 425° for about 10 minutes. Remove the quails from the roasting dish. Drain off the fat. Pour the cherry brandy and lemon juice into the roasting dish with the remaining drippings, and reduce by half. Add the stock and replace quails in roasting dish. Bring to a boil on the stove. Return to the oven for 5 minutes (425°).

Sprinkle the pitted cherries over the quails and serve with a diamond-shaped crouton spread with goose liver pâté. The quails may be served in a casserole, pouring the sauce over.

Serves: 2

Oriental Entrées

Sun Luck East
New York, New York
Chef: Jimmy Wong

SAN WOO GAI PAN
(Chicken with Crab Meat Sauce)

2 pieces chicken breast (approximately 1 pound)
2 egg whites
1 tablespoon cornstarch
2 cups vegetable oil
1/4 pound Alaska King Crab meat
2 thin slices Virginia ham
  Handful snow pea pods (approximately 1/4 pound)
1 or 2 ounces canned sliced mushrooms
2 pieces sliced scallions
  Dash soy sauce
  Salt and pepper to taste

Bone the chicken breast and slice into strips. Dip chicken strips into egg white and cornstarch. Fry in hot oil until brown.

Prepare sauce by sautéing the crab meat, ham, mushrooms, scallions and pea pods. Then add soy sauce, salt and pepper. Mix with egg whites and cornstarch mixture. Pour sauce on top of the chicken.

Serves: 6

Aku Aku Restaurant
Las Vegas, Nevada
Chef: Wing Ng

CHEF WING SPECIAL FRIED RICE

1 ounce frying oil
2 cups well-cooked steamed rice, sitting on side
1/4 cup chopped fresh shrimp or canned dwarf shrimp
1/4 cup chopped ham
1/4 cup chopped barbecued pork
1/4 cup chopped green onions
1/4 cup chopped well-done fried eggs
2 ounces clean bean sprouts
2/3 teaspoon salt
1/4 teaspoon Accent
1 ounce Chinese soy sauce
  Few drops sesame oil

Prepare medium-hot pan with 1 ounce of oil. Sauté shrimp, pork and ham about 1 minute. Put rice in to cook together for 2 minutes then add onions, eggs and bean sprouts for another 2 minutes. Add salt, Accent, Chinese soy sauce with a few drops of sesame oil mixed into it.

Serves: 2

Yamato
Century Plaza Hotel
Los Angeles, California
Chef: Taijai Asai

SUKIYAKI
(Braised Meat and Vegetables)
    Suet
2 pounds top sirloin or rib steak, cut bacon thickness
3 bunches green onions, cut about 1 1/2 inches long
2 pounds dry onions, sliced lengthwise
2 bunches spinach
1 cake bean curd (tofu), cut in small squares (optional)
1/2 #2 can bamboo shoots, sliced
1/2 pound bean sprouts
1/2 pound mushrooms, sliced
6 stalks celery
1/2 pound shiratake (or saifun) long rice
    Soy sauce

Place skillet on stove, or electric skillet may be used at the table. Cook suet in frying pan. Add the meat and sear until brown. Add vegetables and 1/2 of the cooking soy sauce and serve while vegetables are still slightly crisp. Meat and vegetables should be attractively arranged on a large plate. Sukiyaki for the above recipe should be made in 2 cookings. Sugar and sauce should be added if necessary.

Sukiyaki sauce
2/3 cup Japanese soy sauce
2/3 cup consommé or beef stock
2 heaping teaspoons sugar (add additional to individual taste)
2 ounces Japanese rice wine (Sake)

Blend and stir until the sugar dissolves. Cooking time approximately 8 to 10 minutes.

Rice
1 1/2 pints rice, washed and well-drained
3 1/4 cups water

Bring rice and water to a boil. Turn heat down and simmer 15 minutes. Turn off heat and let rice stand for approximately 7 minutes. If the rice, the first time you cook it, is either too hard or too mushy, adjust cooking water accordingly.

Serves: 6

Aku Aku Restaurant
Las Vegas, Nevada
Chef: Wing Ng

CHICKEN ALMONDS

    Cooking oil
1/2 cup diced meat of chicken
1/2 teaspoon salt
1/2 teaspoon sugar
1/2 teaspoon Accent
1/2 cup water chestnuts, diced
1/2 cup celery, diced
1/2 cup bamboo shoots, diced
1/2 cup snow peas, diced
1/2 cup mushrooms, diced
1 cup rich stock
    Cornstarch
    Browned slivered almonds

Prepare hot pan with thin oil. Blend chicken in pan about 30 seconds. Then put next 8 ingredients in together for 30 seconds. Add stock, cover. Keep cooking about 10 minutes. Use light cornstarch to mix gravy. Sprinkle with brown slivered almonds and serve.

Serves: 2

Kahiki Supper Club
Columbus, Ohio
Chef: Philip C. W. Chin

KAHIKI HONG KONG STEAK

    1   (16-ounce) prime New York
        strip steak, trimmed of fat and
        tail

Broil steak to degree of doneness desired.
Slice to bite-size, 1/4-inch thick.

    1   tablespoon peanut oil
  1/4   teaspoon salt
    6   pieces celery in 2" x 1/4"
        strips
    6   pieces bok chop
    6   sliced water chestnuts
    6   sliced bamboo shoots
  1/4   yellow onion, sliced
  1/4   cup black mushrooms
  1/4   cup sliced mushrooms
    2   ounces snow peas
  1/2   cup beef stock
    2   tablespoons oyster sauce
        Cornstarch
    2   ounces pineapple
    1   kumquat

In kettle heat peanut oil and salt. Mix
with celery, Bok chop, water chestnuts,
bamboo shoots, onion, black and sliced
mushrooms and snow peas. Add beef
stock, bring to boil, add oyster sauce.
Thicken with cornstarch.

Put mixture over pre-broiled steak, garnish with pineapple and kumquat.

Serves: 2

Bill Chan's Gold Coin
New York, New York

PINEAPPLE GAI KEW WITH WALNUTS

  3/4   cup chicken broth
  1/4   cup pineapple juice
    1   tablespoon soy sauce
    1   tablespoon dry sherry
    3   drops sesame oil
    1   tablespoon cornstarch
  1/2   cup blanched walnuts
    4   sprigs parsley
    2   tablespoons cooking oil
  1/2   teaspoon salt
  1/8   teaspoon pepper
    1   pound boned chicken (bite-size)
  1/4   cup French mushrooms, sliced
  1/4   cup water chestnuts
  1/4   cup bamboo shoots, sliced thin
    1   cup snow peas or string beans

In a 1-cup measure mix chicken broth,
pineapple juice, soy sauce, sherry and 3
drops sesame oil. Set aside. Mix cornstarch with enough water to obtain a
medium consistency. Set aside. Measure
the blanched walnuts and parsley sprigs
and set aside.

Into a hot deep skillet, add cooking oil
and salt and pepper. Now add the
chicken and stir-fry for 2 minutes. Immediately add mushrooms, water chestnuts,
snow peas or bamboo shoots, celery and
string beans. Toss together well, then add
1 cup of the prepared broth, cover and
simmer 2 minutes. If needed, add salt
and pepper to taste. Thicken slightly with
cornstarch and water mixture. Serve
topped with walnuts and decorated with
parsley.

Serves: 4

Christopher Inn
Columbus, Ohio
Chef: Kenneth L. Garver

China Doll Restaurant
Phoenix, Arizona
Chef: Park Tsang

CHINESE PEPPER STEAK CHRISTOPHER INN STYLE

1	tablespoon sesame oil
1 1/4	pounds beef tenderloin tips, sliced
3	medium green peppers, cut in 3/4-inch squares
2	medium onions, cut in 3/4-inch squares
	Salt and pepper
2	cups chicken stock
3	tablespoons soy sauce
1	cup sherry wine
1	cup bamboo shoots
1	cup water chestnuts
1	cup bean sprouts
1	cup sliced mushrooms
	Cornstarch or arrowroot
2	cups uncooked white rice
	Chopped green onions

Put sesame oil in hot sauté skillet, add beef, pepper, onions, salt and pepper. Brown well. Add chicken stock, soy sauce and wine. Bring to boil. Add remaining ingredients, bring to boil, thicken slightly with cornstarch or arrowroot.

Cook rice until fluffy and put in a casserole, packing it in so it will hold together. Spoon in pepper steak around rice and sprinkle chopped green onions on top.

Serves: 6

Wine: Pommard

LITCHI CHICKEN

1	pound boned chicken breasts
1/2	teaspoon salt
1/4	teaspoon pepper
2	eggs
2	tablespoons flour
4	tablespoons cornstarch
8	ounces water
1	pint oil
2	cups water (additional)
1	green pepper, minced
3	tablespoons tomato catsup
4	tablespoons sugar
4	tablespoons salad vinegar
1	(#2 can) litchi fruit

Cut chicken meat to bite-size, sprinkle with salt and pepper, set aside. Make batter by beating eggs, flour, three quarters of the cornstarch and water in a mixing bowl. Heat oil in a saucepan. Coat the chicken meat with the batter and drop them in oil, piece by piece, and fry until well done and crisp outside. Remove from oil and drain. Remove the oil from saucepan and put in 2 cups of water, add catsup, green pepper, sugar, vinegar, litchi and bring to boil. Thicken sauce with the remaining cornstarch (mixed with a little water). Pour over the fried chicken and serve hot.

Serves: 4

Yamato
Century Plaza Hotel
Los Angeles, California
Chef: Taijai Asai

BUTTER-YAKI

1 1/2 pints sliced mushrooms
1 1/2 quarts green onion, cut in
       1 1/2-inch pieces
  1/2 cup melted butter
    2 pounds sirloin steak, cut to ba-
       con thickness

Pan-fry mushrooms and onions in butter until tender. Add meat and cook to desired doneness.

Dipping sauce

   1 tablespoon Shoyu sauce
  12 lemon wedges—squeezed
 1/8 teaspoon Japanese wasabi
      (horseradish or hot mustard
      powder may be substituted)
   1 tablespoon, per individual,
      grated Japanese radish

Combine Shoyu sauce and lemon juice; add wasabi and grated radish to desired taste.

Serve sauce in individual bowls as a dip for Butter-Yaki.

Serves: 6

Yamato Restaurant
San Francisco, California
Chef: Joe Ishizaki

TEMPURA

Batter

     Vegetable oil
   2 egg yolks
   1 pint water
   3 cups pastry flour
   1 tablespoon baking powder

Fill skillet with 2 inches of vegetable oil and heat to 350°. The temperature of the oil is one of the most important parts of making tempura. Beat eggs, baking powder and water together. Mix water and flour to thickness of pastry cream. Dip ingredients one by one in batter and fry 1 1/2 minutes on each side. Be sure not to add too many ingredients at one time, for this will tend to drop the oil temperature. Drain and serve piping hot.

The most popular kind of tempura ingredients are shrimp or prawns, but the Japanese people are equally fond of many other foods fried in this way, such as seafood of every type and vegetables in season.

Sauce
 1/2 cup dashi (consommé)
 1/4 cup shoyu
   2 teaspoons sugar
      Pinch of Aji-no-moto

Combine these 4 ingredients. Heat and serve with above.

Serves: 4

Wine: Sake (rice wine)

*The Inn of the Eight
Immortals
Falls Church, Virginia
Chef: William Mon*

SWEET AND SOUR SAUCE FOR PORK,
CHICKEN, SHRIMP OR FISH

1	pint white vinegar
1/2	cup water
6	ounces tomato catsup
1	tablespoon tomato paste
3/4	pound granulated sugar
1/2	teaspoon salt
1/2	fresh lemon (juice and residue)
2	tablespoons salad oil
3	tablespoons cornstarch (dissolved in water)
1/2	cup pineapple chunks
1	cup mixed pickle chunks

In a 2-quart aluminum or stainless steel deep saucepan put all ingredients except pineapple, mixed pickles and cornstarch. Stir and bring mixture to boil and simmer about ten minutes or until sugar is melted. Thicken the mixture to a light consistency with cornstarch batter. Keep mixture under low fire and stir constantly until boiling. Add pineapple and mixed pickle chunks and stir the mixture well until boiling again. Turn off fire. The sauce is now ready to serve on top of pork, chicken, shrimp or fish.

To Prepare Pork, Chicken, Shrimp and Fish

10	ounces lean pork
10	ounces chicken, boned
10	shrimp, peeled and deveined
10	ounces fish fillet
2	cups flour
2	eggs

Cut lean pork and boned chicken into 1/2-inch cubes. Leave medium-size shrimp whole and fish fillets in convenient sizes. Dip each in a batter of flour, eggs and water, and deep-fry until brown or done. Then drain them free of oil.

Serves: 6

---

*The Oriental Restaurant
Charlotte, North Carolina*

ORIENTAL SPECIAL EGG FOO YUNG

2	eggs
1/4	cup chopped green scallions
1/4	cup shredded cooked chicken
	Salt and pepper
	Frying oil
1/2	cup chicken broth
1	tablespoon cornstarch
1	tablespoon soy sauce
1/4	cup each sliced cooked chicken and Chinese barbecued pork

Beat eggs. Add scallions, bean sprouts, shredded chicken, salt and pepper. Mix well. Scoop up large ladles-full of mixture and drop into hot oil (about 300°). When browned on bottom, turn with spatula and allow the other side to brown. Mix cornstarch and soy sauce with chicken broth. Cook until thickened. Place sliced chicken and Chinese barbecued pork on top of vegetable and shredded chicken mixture. Pour cornstarch, soy sauce and chicken broth mixture over egg foo yung and serve with a side dish of cooked rice.

Serve: 1

Wine: Rhine

Ruby Foo's Restaurant
Montreal, Canada
Chef: Peter Wai

FOUR SEASONS

2 ounces pork tenderloin
2 ounces chicken (white meat)
4 ounces shrimp
1 teaspoon soya bean sauce
1 teaspoon Geneva gin
1 teaspoon (canned) oyster sauce
4 ounces lobster meat
6 ounces fresh baak-choy and celery
3 ounces canned water chestnuts
3 ounces canned bamboo shoots
4 ounces fresh pea pods
2 ounces fresh mushrooms
Salt
1 teaspoon cornstarch

Sauté pork tenderloin, chicken and shrimp with soya bean sauce, gin and oyster sauce. Add lobster meat.

In separate pan steam your vegetables for 5 minutes with a pinch of salt. In a serving dish, place your meat and seafood mixture. Add your vegetables on top, and before serving mix 1 teaspoon of cornstarch with water and stir until it thickens, and pour over your completed dish.

Serves: 4

Wine: Alsatian

Hawaiian Village
Tampa, Florida
Chef: Joe King Sui

STEAK KEW

12 (1-inch) sirloin steak cubes
1 tablespoon peanut oil
1 pinch ground garlic
1 pinch salt
1 tablespoon oil
2 ounces water chestnuts, sliced
2 ounces bamboo shoots, sliced
2 ounces Chinese black mushrooms, sliced
4 ounces bock-choy, sliced
2 cups chicken soup stock
1 tablespoon oyster sauce
1/2 teaspoon Accent
1 tablespoon cornstarch

Sauté steak cubes in hot peanut oil, add pinch of ground garlic and salt. Remove from fire when sautéed to taste.

In another pot, heat 1 tablespoon oil, add water chestnuts, bamboo shoots, black mushrooms, bock-choy and stir. Add 2 cups chicken soup stock, cover and simmer. When cooked, add 1 tablespoon oyster sauce, 1/2 teaspoon Accent and 1 tablespoon cornstarch mixed with water to thin. Stir gently. Add steak from first pan, stir in pea pods. Remove from fire.

Serves: 2

Wine: Sherry

King Dragon
New York, New York
Chef: Dick Fong Suey

STEAK PORK À LA KING DRAGON

8- to 10-pound loin of pork (about
   16 chops)

Remove ribs and fat around the eye of the loin. If loin is too long, cut in half. Marinate loin (see included ingredients for marinade) few hours or overnight. Preheat the oven to 350°. Place loin on rack in an open, shallow roasting pan. Turn loin occasionally and maybe lower heat so as not to burn. Roast 45 minutes to an hour depending on the thickness of the loin. While roasting, prepare vegetables and get ready for the final sauce.

Marinade for pork
   1 cup Hoy Sen sauce
   2 tablespoons honey
   2 teaspoons salt
   1 cup tomato-shade coloring
   3 tablespoons sherry wine

Vegetables
   1/2 teaspoon corn oil
   1/2 teaspoon salt
   1/2 pound snow pea pods
   1 can water chestnuts
   1/2 pound Chinese baak-choy
   24 dried whole black mushrooms

Presoak dried black mushrooms, 2 hours, in warm water. Cut bamboo shoots and baak-choy in chunk sizes. Wash all vegetables thoroughly. Put corn oil in preheated pot. Add salt. Put all combined vegetables into pot and stir 15 seconds. Add 1/2 cup water and cover pot 3 to 5 minutes. Pour cooked vegetables on serving platter, spilling out all juice. Slice cooked loin at angle, 1 inch apart. Lay sliced loin on bed of cooked vegetables.

Final sauce
   1 cup chicken broth
   4 tablespoons Chinese oyster
      sauce
   1 teaspoon cornstarch

Dissolve cornstarch in 3 tablespoons water. Bring chicken broth and oyster sauce to boil. Slowly pour dissolved cornstarch into pot until thickness desired. Pour final sauce over whole dish and serve.

Serves: 6

Trader Vic's
Scottsdale, Arizona
Chef: Gerald Young

SWEET AND SOUR SHRIMP

   1 pound fresh shrimp or prawns
   4 tablespoons flour
   4 tablespoons cornstarch
   1/2 teaspoon salt
   1/4 teaspoon MSG
   2 tablespoons water
   1 egg, beaten
      Oil for frying, safflower or peanut
   2 cups sweet and sour sauce (see
      index)

Wash, peel and devein shrimp. Dry thoroughly in paper towels. Mix flour, cornstarch, salt, MSG and water together and add beaten egg. Mix lightly and dip shrimp in batter. Fry in oil that has been preheated to 370° until they are brown on both sides. When golden brown drain on paper towels. Serve with sauce mixed-in.

Serves: 4

Meat Entrées

Jasper's Restaurant
Kansas City, Missouri
Chef: Manual Lervonles

SPAGHETTI À LA CARBONARRA

1	ounce corn oil
4	strips bacon, cut julienne-style
3	ounces prosciutto ham, cut julienne-style
1/2	large onion, cut julienne-style
2	ounces cream sherry
1/2	pound butter
1	pound spaghetti, cooked and drained
15	egg yolks

Heat corn oil in heavy skillet, add bacon and ham, sauté until bacon is almost crisp.

In another heavy skillet, cook onion slowly, until golden brown then add to ham and bacon. Add sherry and simmer a minute or two. Remove skillet from fire, add butter, let butter melt while skillet is off the flame. Add the spaghetti and return to flame, toss all together quickly. Add egg yolks and toss again for a minute or two. Remove from flame and serve while steaming hot.

Serves: 4

Wine: Soave Bolla

Ruby Foo's Restaurant
Montreal, Canada
Chef: Peter Melcetei

LE FILLET DE BOEUF SAUTÉ EN CASSEROLE

24	ounces beef tenderloin, cut into 1-inch cubes
	Salt and fresh ground pepper
6	ounces melted butter
2	tablespoons dry shallots, chopped fine
6	ounces red Bordeaux
1	cup baby carrots, pre-cooked
1	cup frozen peas, pre-cooked
1	cup mushroom caps, pre-cooked
1 1/2	cups Parisienne potatoes (scooped balls)
1	tablespoon parsley, chopped
8	ounces demi-glacé (brown gravy)

Season meat pieces with salt and fresh ground pepper and brown them in casserole with butter. Add chopped shallots, brown lightly, pour in wine and reduce to half. Simmer for 5 minutes. In a separate frying pan, sauté in butter: carrots, peas, mushrooms, demi-glacé and Parisienne potatoes. Combine meat and vegetables and serve.

Serves: 4

Wine: Red Bordeaux

The Golden Ram
Miami, Florida
Chef: Emmanuel
  Styleanonthakis

PASTITSIO
(Baked Macaroni with Meat Filling)

    1   pound macaroni
    1   medium onion, chopped
  1/2   pound butter
1 1/2   pound ground meat
  1/2   can tomato paste
        Cinnamon and nutmeg
        Salt and pepper
    4   ounces grated cheese

Cook macaroni in boiling salted water and drain.

Proceed as follows: sauté chopped onion in a little butter, add ground meat and stir until brown, add tomato paste thinned with a little water. Add seasoning —salt, pepper, cinnamon and nutmeg— to taste. Cook until meat is done.

Melt butter and pour 1/2 over drained macaroni, mixing carefully. Spread 1/2 of macaroni on bottom of 9″ × 13″ pan. Sprinkle some of the grated cheese on top. Spread entire meat sauce over the macaroni and cover with remaining buttered macaroni as top layer. Add rest of cheese. Over this pour cream sauce and bake in moderate oven for 40-45 minutes. Cut in squares and serve.

Cream sauce
  1/4   pound butter
    5   tablespoons cornstarch or flour
    1   quart milk
        Pinch of salt
    4   eggs, beaten

Place butter in saucepan and brown slightly, add the cornstarch or flour and milk, stirring all the while. Cook over a low flame until thickened. Add salt and remove from fire. When cooled, add the beaten eggs and mix well. Spread cream sauce over the macaroni and sprinkle with remaining grated cheese. Then bake as directed, above.

Serves: 4

Dominique Restaurant
Dallas, Texas
Chef: Lonell Jones

TOURNEDOS DOMINIQUE

  1/4   pound butter
    6   prime fillets of beef (4-6 ounces each)
  1/2   cup roasted peppers
    1   cup sliced mushrooms
    6   ounces white wine
    6   ounces beef stock or bouillon
    1   tablespoon roux (2 tablespoons flour, 1 tablespoon butter— kneaded together to form several small balls)
    2   ounces brandy

Melt some of the butter in heavy skillet— sauté meat until medium-rare—remove meat from skillet, set aside, but keep warm. Add rest of butter, peppers, mushrooms, wine, stock and roux—simmer for 15 minutes. Add brandy. Pour sauce over meat on hot serving platter and serve with wild rice.

Serves: 6

Wine: Pommard—1964

Log Cabin
Indianapolis, Indiana

SHISH KEBAB ON A FLAMING DAGGER

12 (2 1/2-ounce beef tenderloin
   tips
1/2 cup red wine
   4 medium tomatoes, sliced (3
     slices per serving) from top to
     bottom
   4 medium onions, sliced (3 slices
     per serving) from top to
     bottom
   2 green peppers, cut in quarters
     Parmesan cheese
   4 slices pineapple
   8 breaded onion rings
   8 breaded mushrooms
     Garlic if desired
1/2 ounce 151-proof rum to flame

Marinate tenderloin tips 30 minutes in
red wine. For each shish kebab, skewer 1
piece of meat, 1 slice tomato, 1 slice
onion, 1/4 pepper, 1 meat, 1 tomato slice,
1 slice onion, 1/4 pepper, 1 meat. Save
center slices of tomato and onion to be
grilled and put on plate for garnish.

Dust tomato slices with Parmesan cheese.
Grill pineapple slices. Garnish Thermo
platter with grilled tomato, onion, pineapple, fried onion rings and fried mushrooms. Broil steak to order. Season with
garlic if desired. Flame at table.

Serves: 4

Wine: Red

Fan and Bill's Restaurant
Atlanta, Georgia

PRIME FILLET À LA MAISON

  English muffin, toasted
1 6-ounce piece of prime fillet,
  completely trimmed of fat and
  broiled to individual taste—
  rare, medium, well-done
1 thick slice Bermuda onion sprinkled with sweet basil and
  broiled
1 thick slice beefsteak tomato
  sprinkled with anise spice
  Béarnaise sauce

Using 1/2 of an English muffin as a base,
stack in layers, the beef fillet, slice of
Bermuda onion, slice of tomato and cover
all, liberally with Béarnaise sauce.

Place on serving plate and surround with
petite vegetables (peas, baby carrots,
small white onions, potatoes, etc.)

Béarnaise Sauce
2 egg yolks
1 tablespoon tarragon vinegar
2 tablespoons heavy cream
  Dash salt and cayenne pepper
2 tablespoons fresh herbs,
  chopped
1 small clove garlic, very finely
  chopped

Place all ingredients in top of double
boiler over low flame, simmer slowly,
stirring constantly, until sauce thickens to
custard-like consistency.

Serves: 1

*Great Wall Mandarin
Restaurant
Miami, Florida
Chef: Shiu Ming*

MONGOLIAN BEEF

1/2 quart light cooking oil
14 ounces sliced flank steak in bite-size pieces, 1 1/2-inch strips
1 cup leeks, coarsely chopped
1/2 cup bamboo shoots
15-20 (2-inch) carrot slices or sweet red pepper (added for color)
1/2 ounce garlic, finely chopped
1/2 ounce ginger, chopped
1/2 ounce sesame oil
Rice for 2, about 1 1/2 cups

Pour cooking oil in hot skillet, 350°. Quickly mix meat with vegetables and saute together approximately 1 minute. Remove meat and vegetables. Remove oil, leaving small amount to cook with. Add garlic and ginger together with meat, vegetables and sauce. Cook in skillet, adding sesame oil, for 1 minute or until sauce thoroughly coats meat and vegetables. Remove all ingredients and serve with rice.

Mongolian sauce
1/2 tablespoon cooking sherry
2 teaspoons sugar
2 tablespoons soy sauce
1/2 cup chicken broth

Combine ingredients. Heat and use as directed, above.

Serves: 2

Wine: Sake

*Mario's
Dallas, Texas
Chef: William McKnight*

SALTIMBOCCA ALLA ROMANA

1/3 cup butter
8 (3-ounce) slices veal, pounded thin
2 cups chicken stock or broth
1/2 cup cup white wine
1/4 cup tomato sauce
1/16 cup lemon juice
Salt and pepper to taste
Roux: 2 tablespoons flour, 1 tablespoon butter kneaded together to form several small balls
8 (1-ounce) slices Mozzarella cheese
8 thin slices prosciutto ham

Preheat oven to 375°.

Melt butter in heavy skillet. Dust veal slices with flour and sauté until lightly browned. Remove veal slices and place pieces side by side in a shallow baking dish. In the skillet used to brown the veal, pour chicken stock, white wine, lemon juice, tomato sauce and salt and pepper to taste, simmer about 10 minutes. Add roux to thicken sauce. Place 1 slice of cheese and 1 slice ham over each cutlet. Bake in 375° oven until cheese melts, then top with the sauce, and serve.

Serves: 4

Wine: Soave Bolla

MR. McNAMARA'S
PIER I RESTAURANT
HAMPTON, VIRGINIA
*Mr. McNamara's
Seafood Fra Diavolo*

CHESHIRE INN
ST. LOUIS, MISSOURI
Prop: Stephen J. Apted
Champignons Parisienne

CAMELOT RESTAURANT
MINNEAPOLIS, MINNESOTA
Prop: Hans Skalle
Chef: Jage Eriksen
Roast Norwegian Reindeer

Sam's Gourmet Restaurant
Winston-Salem, North Carolina
Chef: Sam Pappas

SAM'S SIRLOIN TIPS — SAUTÉED IN WINE AND FRESH MUSHROOMS

- 1 ounce margarine
- 7 ounces lean top sirloin beef, cubed and trimmed of all fat
- 2 ounces mushrooms, sliced
  Salt and pepper
- 2 drops liquid Maggi or Gravy Master
- 1 1/2 ounces dry sherry wine
- 4 toast wedges

Heat a heavy skillet to about 500°—add the margarine. When pan is hot enough, add the meat which you let stick to the skillet. (Do not let the meat burn but allow to cook very thoroughly on all sides. This method will leave a base for your juice, later). After the meat is well-browned all around, add the mushrooms, salt and pepper and Maggi or Gravy Master. Leave skillet on flame 1 more minute. Stir and scrape skillet well to release all the meat crusts. As you remove it from the flame, pour in the wine (do not return it to the flame). The wine and beef-flavor stock will automatically produce enough juice for 1 portion. Serve as soon as possible in a hot casserole garnished with the toast wedges.

Serves: 1

Wine: Red—Bordeaux or Burgundy

Salerno Restaurant
Richmond Hill, New York
Chef: Sal Seiroco

VEAL ROLLATINE

- 8 small slices veal cutlet (from the fillet)
- 8 small slices proscuitto ham
- 8 very thin slices Mozzarella cheese
- 1/4 cup olive oil
- 1/2 cup Marsala wine
- 1/8 teaspoon salt
- 1/8 teaspoon freshly ground black pepper
- 1 teaspoon chopped parsley
- 1 teaspoon grated Parmesan cheese
- 1/2 pound sliced fresh mushrooms or 8-ounce can
- 1/4 cup butter

Pound cutlets very flat with a mallet. Place 1 slice each of ham and Mozzarella, also grated Parmesan cheese, parsley and ground pepper on each slice of cutlet. Roll each cutlet up individually, using toothpicks to secure together.

Put oil in heavy skillet, heat, then brown the rolled cutlets on all sides turning very gently until well-browned. Put the sliced mushrooms in another small skillet with small amount of oil. Sauté for 10 or 15 minutes. Remove the excess oil from the pan, add the butter and the wine to the mushrooms, season with salt and pepper. Let cook for about 5 minutes.

Serve with the sauce and a potato croquette.

Serves: 4

Wine: Marsala

The Pen & Pencil
New York, New York
Chef: Attilio Delsignoie

SLICED TENDERLOIN SAUTÉ

Tenderloin

    5 tablespoons butter
   12 slices (about 4-ounces each)
       prime beef tenderloin, 1/2-
       inch thick

Place 5 tablespoons butter into each of 2 large frying pans — heat until butter is well-melted (over a medium-high flame). Cook tenderloins when butter is just slightly browned (3 minutes on each side for medium-rare). Place on hot serving plates and cover with hot sauce.

Tenderloin Sauce

    2 ounces fresh mushrooms, sliced
  3/4 pint red wine
    2 tablespoons butter
    1 tablespoon flour
    1 medium-size onion, chopped
    1 carrot, chopped
    2 tablespoons butter (additional)
       Pinch of thyme
    2 bay leaves
       Salt and pepper to taste

Soak sliced mushrooms in the red wine for 2-3 hours then cook them until tender in the same wine in which they were soaked. Melt 2 tablespoons butter in saucepan and brown flour in butter. Dilute this with 1/2 pint of the hot mushroom stock and simmer for 25 minutes.

Meantime, sauté the chopped onion and carrot in 2 tablespoons butter, remove mushrooms from the stock and sauté along with the onion and carrot, adding the thyme and bay leaves. Simmer for a few minutes until slightly browned. Remove the mushrooms and mix them back into the thick brown mushroom stock. Season to taste and simmer, gently, for 5-10 minutes.

Serves: 4

Wine: Gevrey-Chambertin
(1959)

The Three Farthings
New York, New York
Proprietor: Ernest Short

CHICKEN CORDON BLEU

    2 pounded boned chicken breasts,
       (4 ounces each, about
       5″ x 4″)
  1/4 pound Swiss cheese
  1/4 pound prosciutto ham
       Flour
       Beaten egg
  1/2 cup bread crumbs
       Oil

Lay each chicken breast out flat and put equal amounts of cheese and ham in center. Roll and insert toothpick to hold. Lay on a sheet pan carefully, and partially freeze until firm enough to handle. Then roll in flour, dip in beaten egg and roll in bread crumbs. Deep-fry in a pan which has enough oil to cover. Brown and finish baking in a 350° oven for 10 minutes. Serve with mushroom gravy on top.

Serves: 2

Villa Pierre Restaurant
Glen Cove, New York
Chef: Louis Bernard

NOISETTE OF VEAL CHATELAINE

2 tablespoons butter
1 1-inch thick loin veal chop, dusted lightly with flour
1 cup white wine
1/2 cup shallots
1/4 pound mushrooms or 3-ounce can mushrooms (sliced or caps)
1/4 pound or small can shelled chestnuts
  Few small white onions, boiled
2-4 tablespoons meat stock or bouillon
  Pepper and salt to taste

Melt butter in heavy skillet. Add chop when pan is hot, sauté until well-browned on both sides (about 10 minutes). Add white wine, shallots, mushrooms, small onions and chestnuts. Simmer for about 20 minutes. Add meat stock or bouillon and stir in well.

Serves: 1

Wine: Chablis or Soave Bolla

Aux Anciens Canadiens
Quebec, Canada
Chef: Irene Gauthier

RAGOUT DE PATTES ET BOULETTES

6 full pieces of pig's knuckles
1 minced onion
1 tablespoon salt
1/2 tablespoon pepper
1 1/2 pounds ground pork
1 onion, minced
1 teaspoon salt
1 pinch pepper, 1 pinch powdered nutmeg
1/2 cup crumbs
1 egg
1 1/2 cups brown flour
1/4 teaspoon powdered cinnamon
1/2 teaspoon powdered cloves

Place in an uncovered pan, pig's knuckles and minced onion, add about an inch of cold water to the pan. Brown in moderate oven (350°) about 1 hour. Remove from oven and drain the meat. Discard the liquid.

Put your pig's knuckles in 2 1/2-quart covered casserole, add salt and pepper, cover with cold water. Bring to a boil and skim it. Simmer for 1 hour or until the meat is very tender. Mix together ground pork, minced onion, salt, pepper, nutmeg, crumbs and egg. Shape in 1-inch balls and roll in brown flour. When your pigs knuckles are cooked—to have a thick gravy, add 1 1/4 cups brown flour diluted in a little cold water. Stir well. Add cinnamon and cloves. Dip your meat balls and cook for another 1/2 hour, at a low heat.

Serve this ragout with boiled potatoes and marinated beets.

Serves: 6

Wine: Châteauneuf-du-Pape, Chapoutier

Cy Bloom's Place in the Alley
Baltimore, Maryland
Chefs: Vincent Magnani and
Hans Ruppenthal

VEAL CUTLET "CORDON BLEU"

2 (6-ounce) veal cutlets
4 slices imported Swiss cheese
2 slices ham
2 cups bread crumbs
2 raw eggs
Sufficient oil for frying

Pound the veal cutlets as flat as possible without breaking them. On one half of the meat place 1 slice of cheese, 1 slice of ham and a second slice of cheese. Fold second half of meat over the first and bread the cutlet on both sides. Dip into beaten eggs and brown in hot skillet. When meat is brown, place on a metal tray and bake in a 400° oven for 10-15 minutes. Serve with lemon wedges and fresh parsley.

Serves: 2

Hugo's Gourmet Dining Room
Hyatt House Hotel
Seattle, Washington
Chef: Josef Sin

MIGNONETTE OF VEAL PRINCE ORLOFF

2 (3 1/2-ounce) veal tenderloins
Soubise (white onion sauce)
1 slice Frigrasse truffle

Cut veal tenderloins into fillets. Sauté in pan. Top lightly with Soubise sauce, also a slice of Frigrasse truffle. Cover again with Soubise sauce and glaze under salamander.

Serves: 1

Wine: Gewurztraminer Sichel

The Cloister
Buffalo, New York

CLOISTER DELIGHT

1 pound Italian sausage
1 pound spinach, precooked
1 pound raised dough
  Olive oil
  Salt and pepper
  Oregano

Cook sausage in oven until medium-done. Dice sausage. Precook spinach. Roll out dough to make a large pie. Dress pie lightly with olive oil, spread spinach evenly over pie, sprinkle with chopped sausage and add seasoning as desired. Roll pie into a loaf similar to a jelly roll. Bake loaf in oven until golden brown. Serve in 1-inch slices.

Serves: 4

Wine: Chablis

Miller Bros
The Hilton Inn
Baltimore, Maryland

VEAL CUTLET FORT McHENRY

2 ounces crab meat
  Fresh white bread crumbs
  Tarragon
  Parsley
  Sherry
1 egg yolk
2 3-ounce veal cutlets

Crab meat, bread crumbs, tarragon, parsley, sherry and egg yolk should be blended and stuffed between the 2 veal cutlets. The lightly breaded cutlet is then sautéed.
Serve with lemon butter.

Serves: 2

Georges Rey
    Restaurant Français
New York, New York
Chef: André Ledoux

FLEMISH CARBONNADES OF BEEF

2	pounds lean beef
	Salt
	Pepper
	Clarified dripping
1/4	pound butter
4-5	large onions, chopped
	Bouquet garni
1	bottle beer
	Brown stock
4	ounces brown roux (see index)
2	ounces brown sugar

Cut the meat into thin slices, season with salt and pepper, and brown quickly in a little dripping. Remove to a casserole. Add a little butter to the pan if necessary, add the chopped onions and brown lightly then put with the meat in alternate layers, with the bouquet garni in the center. Add the beer and stock to the sediment left in the pan, bring to boiling point and thicken with the roux. Lastly add the sugar. Pour over the meat in the casserole, cover and cook in a slow oven for 2 1/2-3 hours.

Note: The carbonnade is usually served in the casserole as it is, but if preferred the onion may be removed.

Bouquet Garni
Tie together 3 sprigs parsley, 1/2 bay leaf, 1 sprig fresh thyme and 2 cloves.

Serves: 2

Gaddi's
Kowloon, Hong Kong
Chef: Rolf Heiniger

VEAL KIDNEYS IN PEPPER SAUCE

1 1/2	pound veal kidney trimmed and thinly sliced
	Salt and pepper to taste
	Flour for dusting
5	tablespoons olive oil
3	tablespoons fresh butter
2	teaspoons shallots, chopped
1/2	teaspoon garlic, chopped
2	dessert spoons crushed black peppercorns
3	tablespoons brandy
1/2	pint brown sauce
1/4	pint whipped cream
	Chopped parsley

Slice kidneys thinly, sprinkle with salt, pepper and a little flour and fry them quickly in fairly hot olive oil for about 1 minute on each side. Pour off the oil and add 2 tablespoons of butter, the shallots, the garlic and peppercorns. Sauté the kidneys in this mixture for a further 1-2 minutes, then pour on the brandy and ignite it, shaking the pan gently until the flames die down. Remove the kidneys to a serving dish and keep warm.

Add the brown sauce and whipped cream to the residue in the pan and stir and mix well until hot. Pour this sauce over the kidneys and sprinkle with chopped parsley. Serve with rice or noodles.

Serves: 4

Wine: Clos de Vougeot
Chateau de la Tour
1964

*Sheraton-Rolling-Green
Motor Inn
Andover, Massachusetts*

INDIVIDUAL BEEF WELLINGTON

- 1 (6-ounce) well-trimmed fillet
- 1 ounce butter
   Salt and freshly ground black pepper
- 1 small shallot, diced
- 1 ounce Burgundy wine
   Pâté feuilletee (puff paste)
   Egg white
   Bread crumbs
- 2 ounces duxelles (see index)
   Duchesse potatoes for border (see index)
- 1 broiled tomato
   Parsley sprig
   Bordelaise sauce

Sauté fillet in butter in well-heated skillet, (very quickly) on both sides to a golden brown. Season with salt and fresh ground black pepper. Add shallot and sauté. Déglace with red wine. Put fillet aside, pour juice over it and let stand.

Roll out pâté, cut into 4″ by 4″ square, brush the edges with egg white. Sprinkle some bread crumbs into the middle to absorb the meat juice. Place fillet on the pâté, top with duxelles. Fold pâté over the fillet making sure it is completely covered. Decorate the top with cutouts from the leftover pate. Brush completely with egg white and bake in 350° oven for 20 minutes.

Pipe border of Duchesse potatoes on serving platter. Brown under broiler. Set fillet on platter, garnish with broiled tomato and parsley sprig. Serve with Bordelaise sauce on the side.

Bordelaise Sauce
- 1/2 cup dry red wine
   Add 1 cup brown sauce

Simmer for fifteen minutes, add peppercorns, 1/2 teaspoon lemon juice and some chopped parsley.

Serves: 1

Wine: Macon, Beaujolais or rosé

---

*The Pub
Coral Gables, Florida*

BARBEQUED SPARERIBS

- 10 strips baby back ribs
- 2 tablespoons Hoisin sauce marinade
- 1 #10 can tomato puree
- 1 pint water to rinse can
- 4 ounces lemon juice
- 2 ounces soy sauce
- 2 ounces white vinegar
- 1 ounce tomato red color
- 1 1/2 pounds sugar
- 1/2 pound salt
- 1/2 tablespoon Accent
- 1/2 small garlic

Preparation: day before serving, combine all ingredients—except the ribs. Mix well until all dry ingredients are blended into marinade. Place ribs in marinade.

Cooking: lay ribs out on flat sheet pans, rub well with small amount of extra sauce. Put into very slow oven, 250° to 275°, (time approximately 2 1/2 hours). Check for tenderness. Some larger ribs will require additional time. This marinade should be enough for 10 strips of back ribs.

Serves: 4

The Cove
Los Angeles, California
Chef: Helmut Moser

SCHNITZEL BLACK FOREST

    12 (3-ounce) medaillons of veal
    12 slices zucchini
        Flour
     4 eggs
     2 ounces grated Parmesan cheese
     3 ounces ''jus'' (pan drippings
          from rib roast best)
        Juice of 1 lemon
        Salt
    12 ounces sliced mushrooms
     6 ounces butter
 1 1/2 ounces Chablis

Salt the veal and zucchini slightly. Roll them in flour and dip them in the raw egg which has been beaten into a batter. Then sauté them to a golden brown. Place the veal and the zucchini alternately on a platter, 3 per serving. Sprinkle with the Parmesan cheese and brown slightly under the broiler. Add the "jus" and the lemon juice equally to each serving.

Salt the mushrooms slightly and sauté them in butter, adding the Chablis. Distribute evenly over each serving. Garnish with watercress.

Serves: 4

Wine: Zeller Schwarze Katz

William Tell Restaurant
Vancouver, British Columbia
Chef: Christian Thoeny

ESCALOPES DE VEAU À LA CRÈME AUX
MORILLES

     1 ounce cottonseed oil
    24 ounces tenderloin of veal (12
          escalopes of 2-ounces each,
          flattened)
        Salt, pepper, flour
 1 1/2 ounces butter
     5 ounces morels, fresh or canned
     1 ounce finely chopped onions
     6 ounces dry red wine
     6 ounces Bordelaise sauce (see
          index)
     8 ounces whipping cream
     1 ounce brandy
     2 parsley branches

Put cottonseed oil in medium-heated frying pan. Season escalopes slightly with salt and pepper and turn in flour. Then put in frying pan and sauté until golden brown. Set aside and keep warm.

Put butter in same frying pan, add onions and morels and sauté. (Do not brown onions.) Then add red wine, Bordelaise and whipping cream and bring to boil. Let simmer for 1 minute, season to taste and add brandy. Pour sauce over escalopes. Serve with noodles or spetzlis, white asparagus tips and grilled tomatoes.

Serves: 4

Wine: Gewürztraminer or
Riesling

Mister A's
San Diego, California
Chef: David Segal

MISTER A'S SPECIAL

Puff Paste
    3 3/4 cups sieved flour
    1 1/2 teaspoon salt
    1 1/4 to 1 1/2 cups water
    1   pound butter

Place flour on a board in a circle, making a well in the middle. Put salt and water into the well. Knead the dough until it is smooth. Roll into a ball and let stand for 25 minutes. Roll the paste into a sheet about 8 inches square and of uniform thickness. Put butter, which is of the same consistency as the paste, in the middle of the sheet. Fold the ends of the paste over the butter, enclosing it completely. Let it stand for 10 minutes in a cold place.

Roll the paste into rectangle (24″ long, 8″ wide and 1/2″ thick.) Fold the ends over to meet in the center. Fold in 1/2 to make 4 layers. Let stand in cold place for 10 minutes. Roll dough again into a rectangle, (24″ long, 8″ wide and 1/2″ thick). Fold the ends over to meet the center. Fold in 1/2 to make 4 layers. Let stand in cold place for 10 minutes. Roll dough again into a rectangle, fold as before and chill for 10 minutes. Roll dough again into a rectangle, fold as before and chill for 10 minutes. Roll dough again into a rectangle, fold as before and chill for 10 minutes. Roll dough again into a rectangle, fold as before and chill for 10 minutes. Repeat 4 more times—the rolling, folding and chilling processes.

Duxelles
    1   pound mushrooms
    1   medium onion, chopped
        Butter
    6   chopped shallots
        Salt and pepper
        Nutmeg
        Chopped parsley

Thoroughly clean and trim 1 pound fresh mushrooms. Chop fine, wrap in towel to extract as much moisture as possible. Lightly brown 1 medium-sized onion in butter. Add shallots, salt, pepper, pick of nutmeg and mushrooms. Stir over brisk fire until all moisture has completely evaporated. Sprinkle with well-chopped parsley.

Périgueux Sauce
    2   tablespoons raw truffles
    2   tablespoons butter
        Salt and pepper
    2   tablespoons Madeira wine
        Brown beef stock

Cook diced raw truffles in butter. Season with salt and pepper and remove from pan. Add 2 tablespoons of Madeira wine to the juice in the pan. Stir in one cup of concentrated brown beef stock. Simmer. Strain. Return truffles to sauce; add Madeira wine. Keep hot but do not allow to boil.

Souffléed Potatoes
    1   Idaho baking potato
        Frying oil
        Salt

Peel Idaho baking potato and trim surface so that it is smooth and regular. Cut into long narrow slices about 1/8″ thick. Wash potato in cold water and dry thoroughly.

Preheat fat to 275°. Drop a few slices of potato at a time into fat. When potato slices begin to puff, remove, drain and cool at least 5 minutes. The final frying may follow immediately or later in the day. Fat should be preheated to 400°. Put a few slices at a time into basket. Potatoes will puff into small oval-shaped balloons. Brown on all sides. Remove from fat. Sprinkle with salt and serve immediately.

Prepare Puff Paste

Mix duxelles of mushrooms. Spread layer duxelles on puff paste. Place 14 ounce tenderloin on duxelles, cover with puff paste. Spread layer of pâté de foie gras on top of tenderloin. Pull puff paste up to cover meat completely. Top with another strip of puff paste. Mold, score and seal. Glaze with beaten egg. Bake in 425° oven for 20-25 minutes for medium-rare serving.

Serves: 2

Ethel's Hideaway
Palm Springs, Florida
Chef: Fred Magnabiban

BEEF STROGANOFF WITH RICE

2 pounds beef tenderloin
1/2 pound mushrooms
2 cloves garlic, chopped
3 cups white sauce (see index)
2 cups heavy sour cream
4 teaspoons red wine
Salt and pepper to taste

Cut tenderloin into strips 1 inch long and 1/2 inch wide. Brown both sides. Add garlic and mushrooms and red wine. When mushrooms are done, add white sauce, red wine and sour cream. Simmer 5 minutes and serve with rice.

Serves: 4

Wine: Lancer's rosé

Marriott Motor Hotel
Washington, D.C.

CHARCOAL FLAMED BROCHETTE OF BEEF

1 1/2 to 1 3/4 pounds beef tenderloin
1/2 pound fresh mushrooms, about 1-inch round
2 whole green peppers
1/2 pint basket large cherry tomatoes
4 bacon slices
1 to 1 1/2 cups sherry mushroom gravy

Cut the tenderloin into even-size cubes of about 1 inch (1 1/2 pounds of meat should give you about 20 to 25 cubes, enough for 4 brochettes).

Wash, seed and remove the membranes of 2 whole green peppers. Cut into 8 squares, about 1-inch in size. Place pepper squares into boiling water and let them stand for about 10 minutes—don't cook. Then drain off the water.

Cut the stems from the fresh mushrooms even with the bottom of the cap. Slice stems to make smaller pieces. Sauté both the stems and caps in a little butter only until wilted. Fry the bacon until half done. Drain and cut each slice into 4 squares.

Place the ingredients onto the skewer in the following order: mushroom, tenderloin, cherry tomato, mushroom, tenderloin, bacon, pepper, mushroom cap, tenderloin, tomato, pepper, bacon, mushroom, tenderloin, tomato, bacon, mushroom, tenderloin.

Salt and pepper to taste. Charcoal broil from 5 to 15 minutes, according to your liking.

For the gravy, add the sautéed mushroom stems to any good beef gravy; mix and, just before finished, add 2 tablespoons of sherry wine.

Serves: 4

Le Manoir
New York, New York
Chef: Alain Sajac

MOISETTE DE VEAU

Butter
4 to 6 veal scallops, pounded thin
Flour
Salt and pepper
2 tablespoons butter
1/2 pound mushrooms, chopped
1/2 cup (approximately) calvados or mellow apple-jack
1 cup heavy cream

Melt butter in heavy skillet; flour the veal, and season with salt and pepper. Brown veal in butter until golden (takes only a few minutes), remove to platter. Sauté mushrooms in butter and glaze, return veal to pan, heat the calvados in a separate container, then pour over veal. It should ignite. (If it does not, ignite with match). Let liquor burn off, then add cream, stirring constantly. Lower flame, let heat through, then serve immediately. Serving suggestions: serve over hot rice.

Serves: 4

Keen's English Chop House
New York, New York
Chef: Paul Henning

ENGLISH BEEF AND KIDNEY PUDDING

2 pounds chuck beef
1 pound beef kidneys
1 piece beef suet, approximately size of a large egg
1 large onion, coarsely chopped
1 cup rich beef stock
Salt, pepper, pinch of cayenne
1 teaspoon Worcestershire sauce
1 pie crust

Cut beef chuck and 1 pound beef kidneys into 1 1/2-inch cubes. In a stew kettle, fry out a piece of beef suet the size of a large egg and when the fat is rendered, remove the suet cracklings from the kettle. Fry in the fat, 1 large onion, coarsely chopped. When the onion has taken on a little color, add the beef and the kidneys and brown them thoroughly, stirring almost constantly. Moisten with 1 cup rich beef stock. Season to taste with salt, pepper, a pinch of cayenne, and Worcestershire sauce. Stir the mixture well, cover saucepan, and simmer over a very low flame for about 1 3/4 hours, or until the meat is tender. (If the liquid in the pan should be too thin, thicken it with flour mixed to a smooth paste with water.) There should be a good amount of sauce. If necessary, add more stock to the liquid in the saucepan, but not before the meat is tender.

Line a dome-shaped earthenware casserole with a flaky pie crust dough and fill with the meat and sauce which have been slightly cooled. Bake in a very hot oven for about 12 minutes until crust is done. Turn out onto a large plate with the unbroken pie crust dome on top. Pour a thick brown gravy over the dome and serve piping hot.

Serves: 4

Wine: Full-bodied red

L'Aiglon Restaurant
New York, New York
Chef: Nick Marioni

VEAL CHOP À L'AIGLON

    4   (6-ounce) veal chops, pounded
        to 1/8-inch thick
    1   egg
    1   cup bread crumbs
 1/2   cup clarified butter
 1/2   pound green noodles
        Mornay sauce
        Grated Parmesan cheese

Bread chop with egg and bread crumbs. Cook in clarified butter until golden brown.

Boil some green noodles, strain them dry and then mix in melted butter.

Place chop on top of green noodles and cover with Mornay sauce, and sprinkle grated Parmesan cheese over the sauce.

Broil until golden brown and serve piping hot.

Mornay sauce
    3   ounce melted butter
    2   ounces flour
    1   pint milk
    3   egg yolks
    3   ounces whipped cream

Take melted butter and flour and cook for 10 minutes, stirring constantly. Add boiling milk and stir with whip until creamy—about 8 minutes. Remove from fire, add the egg yolks and stir for 4 minutes. Let this cook for 15 minutes and add 3 ounces whipped cream.

Serves: 4

Rainbow Room
New York, New York
Chef: Serge Prat

VOL-AU-VENT OF SWEETBREADS À L'ORANGE

    2   pair sweetbreads
    2   carrots
    2   onions
        Stalk of celery
        Parsley
    2   leaves each of thyme and bay
        leaf
        Vegetable oil
        Butter
        Juice and rind of 1 orange
        Juice and rind of 1 lemon
    4   teaspoons orange liqueur
    1   cup heavy cream
    4   vol-au-vent (puff pastry—see
        index)

Blanch the sweetbreads by placing them in a casserole filled with cold water. Bring to boil, cook for 3 minutes and cool off under cold water immediately. After cooling, clean sweetbreads, removing bad parts. Place on bed of vegetables (carrots, onions, celery, etc. that have been cut small) and herbs. Sprinkle with 2 soup-spoons of oil and season to taste. Bake in oven at 350° for about 35 minutes or until light golden brown on both sides. Remove and cool slightly.

Sauté sweetbreads few minutes in skillet with 2 tablespoons of butter; add very fine julienne of orange and lemon peels. Flambé with orange liqueur. Add juice of 1 orange and 1 lemon. Reduce amount of liquid to about one-fourth. Add heavy cream and simmer until sauce has regular consistency. Serve in vol-au-vent.

Serves: 4

Le Trianon
San Francisco, California
Chef: Paul C. Du Four

SUCKLING WILD BOAR FOR 8

20 pound boar
2 parts red wine
1 part honey
1 part melted butter
1/2 part lemon juice
Salt
Pepper
Bay leaves or wild laurel

For the sauce, use 2 parts red wine, 1 part honey, 1 part melted butter, 1/2 part of lemon juice. Season with salt and freshly ground pepper and add a few bay leaves or wild laurel. Cover with sauce and add more as you go.

Start the roast at 450° and reduce to 350° after 20 minutes, and cook 2 hours, not stuffed. Cover ears and tail with foil while cooking so they will not burn. (Better to over-cook!) If you use a spit, have boar about a foot above coals and baste with sauce as you go.

Serves: 8

West Side Room
Los Angeles, California
Chef: Walter Roth

VEAL TENDERLOIN CASSIMIR

2 (4-ounce) veal tenderloins
Butter
2 fresh artichoke bottoms
1 ounce creamed morels
2 stuffed butterfly prawns (fish and almond mousse)
2 ounces Foyot sauce (Béarnaise with meat glaze—see index)

Sauté tenderloin in butter. Fill cooked artichokes with creamed morels, place tenderloins on top, then the stuffed broiled prawns and cover with Foyot sauce. (Béarnaise with glacé de viande)

Fish Almond Mousse
8 ounces prawns
1 8-inch fresh fillet of sole
3 ounces almonds
Dash of Worcestershire sauce
Lemon juice
Salt and pepper
2 sprigs of fresh parsley
Sweet cream
Butter

Grind ingredients, except cream, through a fine blade. Let stand for 1/2 hour. Work in sweet cream to a fine paste. With a pastry bag, mount on flattened prawns, sprinkle with butter and broil.

Serves: 1

Wine: Johannisberger Riesling

The Coachman
San Francisco, California
Chef: Malcolm Stroud

STEAK AND KIDNEY PIE

1/2 pound beef kidney
1 pound top round beef steak
2 tablespoons butter
1 large onion, thinly sliced
2 1/2 tablespoons flour
1/2 teaspoon salt
1 teaspoon Monosodium glutamate
1/8 teaspoon pepper
2 cups beef broth
1 tablespoon tomato paste
Flaky pastry

Trim off and discard fat from kidney and steak. Cover kidney with cold water. Then heat to boiling; drain and cool. Cut beef steak and kidney into 1 inch cubes and brown in butter. Add thinly sliced onion, browning lightly. Stir in flour, salt, Monosodium glutamate and pepper. Add broth and tomato paste. Heat to boiling, stirring until smooth. Bake in slow oven (300°), 2 to 2 1/2 hours, until meat is tender. Remove from oven. Increase heat to 425°. Turn meat and sauce into shallow 8 1/2-inch baking dish. Cover with flaky pastry, pinching edges against sides of dish. Cut small hole in pastry to allow steam to escape. Return to oven and bake 15 minutes or until brown.

Flaky Pastry
- 1 cup sifted flour
- 1/2 teaspoon salt
- 3 tablespoons shortening
- 2 tablespoons firm butter
- 2 to 2 1/2 tablespoons ice water

Combine flour with salt. Finely cut-in shortening and butter. Moisten with ice water, roll out to 6″ × 10″ rectangle. Cover with 2 tablespoons firm butter cut in wafer-thin slices. Fold in thirds and roll out to rectangle as before. Fold and roll again. Wrap in foil and chill several hours or overnight.

Serves: 4

Wine: English ale or Beaujolais

The Vineyards
Southfield, Michigan
Chef: Señor Maximillian Gonzalez

SWEET AND SOUR PORK ROAST

4   #1 center cut pork roasts

Place pork in roasting pan, bone side down, and brown in oven at 450° for 30 minutes.

Remove from oven when well-browned and transfer to deeper baking dish. Pour sweet and sour sauce over pork and bake for 2 1/2 hours at 300°, or until pork is tender. Baste occasionally. Serve on platter with generous amount of sauce ladled over pork. Garnish with a baked apple.

Sweet and Sour Sauce
- 2 cups sugar
- 1 cup distilled vinegar
- 2 tablespoons chopped green pepper
- 1 teaspoon salt
- 1 cup water
- 4 teaspoons cornstarch
- 2 teaspoons paprika
- 2 teaspoons chopped parsley

Mix sugar, vinegar, green pepper and salt with 1 cup water. Simmer 5 minutes. Combine cornstarch and 2 tablespoons cold water, add to mixture. Cook and stir until sauce thickens. Let cool. Before serving, strain out vegetables. Add paprika and chopped parsley.

Serves: 4

Wine: 1967 Pouilly-Fuissé

The Tower
Los Angeles, California

ESCALLOPINES DE VEAUX AUX CEPES

- 12 (1 1/2-ounce) slices leg of white veal, pounded very thin and dipped lightly in flour
- 6 teaspoons butter
- 2 teaspoons finely minced dry shallots
- 1 cup sliced imported cepes
- 1 1/2 cups dry white wine

Season the 12 slices of leg of white veal. Brown the veal on both sides in butter and add finely minced dry shallots. Add cepes and wine. Cook for about 6 minutes. Arrange the escallopines on a heated platter. Pour sauce over meat.

Serves: 4

Wine: White Burgundy

La Rue
Los Angeles, California
Chef: Andre Pister

COTE DE VEAU "VAL SUZON"

6 medium veal cutlets, approximately 8 ounces each
Salt
Seasoning
Flour
Butter
1 ounce brandy for flaming or marc de bourgogne
2 cups Poivrade sauce (a reduced venison marinade)
1 cup double cream (40%)
2 tablespoons butter (additional)
6 slices (goose liver) fois gras
6 slices of truffle for garnish
6 fresh artichoke bottoms, precooked
1/2 pound chestnut puree
6 halved hearts of celery, braised
Dauphine potatoes
6 small vol-au-vent (see index—puff pastry)
1 small jar currant jelly

Salt, lightly season and flour the veal. Cook on slow fire in butter until half-cooked, browning each side. Pour off butter and flame with brandy. Add the cream and the Poivrade sauce. Cook slowly for another 10 minutes.

Place veal on a silver platter and pour the sauce on top. Put 1 slice fois gras and 1 slice truffle on top of each cutlet. Garnish the platter with artichoke bottoms stuffed with chestnut puree, braised celery and Dauphine potatoes. The vol-au-vent are filled with currant jelly and served with the veal.

Serves: 6

Wine: Nuit-Saint-Georges

Gene Boyle's
Clifton, New Jersey
Chef: Russell Albinson

MEDAILLONS OF PRIME FILLET ROTINI, BOUQUETIERE

1/4 pound margarine
6 shallots, chopped fine
2 cups sliced fresh mushrooms
1 tablespoon Fereze-Vinagre Superior
2 jiggers rich Burgundy wine
Pinch chervil
Pinch tarragon
2 cups diced plum tomatoes and juice
2 quarts veal and beef stock
Salt and white pepper to taste
1 ounce Accent
3 tablespoons arrowroot
6 (3 1/4 inch) slices fillet mignon, slightly seasoned with salt and pepper
Vegetable oil
Saucepan adequate for all ingredients

Melt 3 tablespoons margarine, add shallots, simmer and stir approximately 3 minutes. Add mushrooms and Vinagre Superior, Burgundy, chervil and tarragon. Sauté, stirring constantly, for 5 minutes, then add chopped tomatoes and juice. Simmer 10 minutes then add veal and beef stock, simmer 30 minutes. Add salt and pepper according to taste and Accent.

Put 3 tablespoons arrowroot in bowl, add enough cold water to make a smooth but thick roux, bring other mixture to a fast boil and add arrowroot very slowly, stirring constantly for 5 more minutes. Then take off the stove.

Sauté the medaillons in a very hot skillet using a little vegetable oil. Turn over rapidly, place on platter, then lace the meat with Rotini Sauce.

The bouquetière should be arranged to have the best colorful effect. It should consist of pommes Parisienne (petite pan-browned white potatoes) and a macedoine of colorful vegetables such as broccoli, pearl onions, grilled tomato stuffed with petite pois (baby peas), carrots à la Vichy, asparagus spears.

Serves: 2

Sid Allen's
Englewood Cliffs, New Jersey
Chef: Rogello Serrono

MEDAILLONS DE FILLET MOSCOVITE

1	ounce shallots
2	tablespoons butter
2	(6-ounce) beef fillet steaks
1	ounce vodka
1	cup brown sauce
1	teaspoon heavy cream
1	teaspoon Beluga caviar
2	rounds of white toast

Sauté shallots in butter, add fillets and sauté for approximately 5 minutes on each side (medium-rare). Add vodka to hot pan and permit to flame. When flames cease, add the brown sauce and heavy cream. Remove from fire and add caviar.

Put fillet on plate for serving. Put toast on top of fillet and spoon sauce over top.

Crisp hash-browned potatoes are recommended as garnish.

Serves: 2

Wine: Nuits-Saint-Georges

Space Needle Restaurant
Seattle, Washington
Chef: Wolfgang Fillinger

TICINESE SAUCE

1/4	cup chopped onions
1	garlic clove, mashed
2	ounces butter
1/4	cup diced ham
1/4	cup diced raw pork
1/4	cup diced celery
1/4	cup diced carrots
1/2	cup Burgundy wine
1/2	cup tomato paste
1	herb bunch (parsley sprigs, thyme, 1/2 bay leaf, 1 clove)
3/4	teaspoon oregano
4	ounces fresh mushrooms, diced
1 1/2	teaspoons chicken concentrate
1	pint Madeira sauce
3	anchovy fillets, chopped
2	cups peeled and diced fresh tomato

Sauté onions and garlic. Add ham, pork, celery and carrots. When vegetables are softened, add red wine and reduce two-thirds. Add tomato paste, anchovy fillets, herb bunch, oregano, mushrooms, chicken concentrate, Madeira sauce and simmer 15 minutes. Remove herb bunch, add tomato and season to taste.

Madeira Sauce

1	cup brown sauce, boiled to reduce to 3/4 cup
1/4	cup Madeira wine (dry sherry can be used if you prefer)

Heat together, add one tablespoon butter, don't let boil. You may add drippings from the meat pan to mix in.

Serves: 2

Le Chambertin
New York, New York

LE BOEUF BRAISE CHAMBERTIN
(Short Ribs of Beef Chambertin)

          6   pounds short ribs of beef
              Salt and pepper
              Flour
      1/4   pound diced salt pork
          3   carrots, diced
          2   cloves garlic, minced
          2   tablespoons green peppers,
                  diced very fine
          3   onions, diced
          1   cup celery, diced
          2   shallots, minced
      1/4   cup brandy
          3   cups Burgundy wine
              Beef stock
          3   sprigs parsley
          1   bay leaf
          3   sprigs fresh thyme
          2   teaspoons Worcestershire sauce
          1   cup (6-ounces) sautéd fresh
                  mushrooms, sliced
        12   small white onions, boiled

Cut short ribs into serving-size pieces. Sprinkle with salt and freshly ground pepper; dredge with flour. Place in greased shallow baking pan, roast at 500° until meat is brown.

In a large deep saucepan, brown diced salt pork. Remove and reserve crisp pieces of pork. Sauté in remaining fat until tender and golden: 3 carrots, garlic, green peppers, onions, celery and shallots. Add the browned cubes of beef. Add brandy and set aflame. Bring Burgundy wine to a boil, and set aflame. When flames go out, pour wine over beef. Add enough beef stock to cover the meat. Tie together sprigs parsley, bay leaf, sprigs fresh thyme and place in pot with meat. Cover and cook in 350° oven for 2 hours, or until beef is tender. Remove lid; skim off excess fat. Remove meat pieces, keep hot.

Press the sauce through a sieve and add Worcestershire sauce. Pour sauce over meat. Add sliced, sautéd fresh mushrooms and small white onions. Reheat. Sprinkle top with crisp pork pieces.

Wine: Red Burgundy (Gevrey-Chambertin)

Le Trianon
San Francisco, California
Chef: Paul C. Du Four

WILD BOAR BARBECUE OR SUCKLING
WILD BOAR ROAST

          1   (100-pound) boar
          2   parts red wine
          1   part honey
          1   part melted butter
      1/2   part lemon juice
              Bay leaves or wild laurel
              Salt
              Pepper

Basting sauce for 100-pound roast: 2 parts red wine, 1 part honey, 1 part melted butter, 1/2 part lemon juice. Season with salt and freshly ground pepper and add a few bay leaves or wild laurel. Start the roast in a 300° oven or a charcoal barbecue with coals banked low. (It will take approximately 5 1/2 hours to barbecue a 100-pound young wild boar.) Brush on the basting sauce, liberally, every 15 minutes, and turn the meat at the same time. During the last 45 minutes, lower the meat close to the coals in order to thoroughly crisp the skin which is delicious to eat with the meat.

[Not recommended for small dinner parties. *S.L.*]

Serves: 50

Smoke House
Encino, California
Chef: Samuel R. Haroway

JULIENNE OF BEEF, SAUTÉ VALENCIA

1 pound steak meat, cut in thin
   strips
1 medium onion, cut in strips
1 bell pepper, cut in strips
1 large tomato, quartered
1 cup mushrooms, sliced
1 ounce Burgundy wine
   Salt and pepper to taste

In skillet sauté meat until brown. Add vegetables and cook until they are tender. Add wine, salt and pepper to taste. Serve over rice.

Serves: 4

Gallatin's
Monterey, California
Chef: Alfred McCulloch

IMPERIAL SIBERIAN WILD BOAR

[Another boar recipe hardly for an intimate dinner soirée, but it makes great reading. *S.L.*]

Wash Boar and dry well—rub insides with garlic clove and brush with brandy. Stuff pig (stuffing recipe given later) loosely and skewer opening and lace well. Truss fore legs and hind legs forward separately, making sure they are close under the body. Rub a generous amount of butter on pig and make a few slashes on pig's back, so as to enable fat to drip into pan.

Place a block of wood in pig's mouth (to be replaced by apple later) and cover ears with foil to prevent burning. Baste frequently with pan juices to which has been added 1 cup hot water. If pig browns too fast, cover with foil. Roast pig about 3 to 3 1/2 hours according to size. Meat must be tender and well done. (400°—5 to 6 hours, large pig; 7 to 9 hours).

When pig is done, remove and place carefully on heated platter and surround with watercress. Brush pig lightly with butter until skin is shiny. Surround pig with baked apples. Place on inch-thick cranberry rings. Stuff apertures of apples with whole cooked cranberries. Place apple in pig's mouth and place large green olives with red pimento centers in pig's eyes. Wire clusters of red maraschino cherries together, leaving wire loop to fit around pig's ears. Hide wires around ears with small wreath of watercress. Make a saddle blanket to fit pig's back of wired leaves and then attach (by wires) clusters of maraschino cherries to blanket wherever your fancy dictates. Place large clusters of maraschino cherries around platter to alternate between apples and cranberries and then wire a big fat satin bow on the pig's tail.

Stuffing: Moisten 2 1/2 cups of soft bread crumbs in dry white wine. Add 1 tablespoon each, finely chopped parsley, chives and chervil, 3 grated onions, 1/2 small grated clove of garlic. Salt and pepper to taste. Add 1/2 teaspoon, each, of thyme, mace, sage, nutmeg and marjoram. Next add 1/4 cup of butter and 3 chopped hard-cooked eggs. Then cook this mixture in 1/4 cup of butter over low flame, stirring constantly with wooden spoon for 7 minutes. Cool and then stuff the pig and sew up the opening securely. Do not stuff too full but leave some space for swelling and expansion.

An 80-pound pig will serve 10 people nicely. A nice accompaniment for this dish is a spinach soufflé.

Wine: Beaujolais

Le Manoir
New York, New York

VEAL SCALLOPS BOHEMIENNE

      Butter
    4 to 6 veal scallops, pounded thin
      Salt and pepper
      Flour
    2 tablespoons butter
  1/2 pound mushrooms, chopped
  1/2 cup calvados or mellow apple-
      jack
    1 cup sour cream

Melt butter in heavy skillet; flour the veal, and season with salt and pepper. Brown veal in butter until golden (takes only a few minutes), remove to platter. Sauté mushrooms in butter and glaze, return veal to pan, heat the calvados in a separate container, then pour over veal. It should ignite. If it does not—ignite with match. Let liquor burn off, then add sour cream, stirring constantly. Lower flame, let heat through, then serve immediately. Serving suggestions: serve over hot rice.

Serves: 4

Venetian Room
Fort Lauderdale, Florida
Chef: Maurice Bossi

MANICOTTA

    1 quart Ricotta cheese
    4 eggs
    4 tablespoons chopped parsley
      Pepper to taste
      Salt
    1 pound noodles (lasagne wide)
      Tomato sauce
      Grated cheese

Mix well together for filling: Ricotta cheese, eggs, parsley, salt and pepper.

Cook noodles until tender. Drain and cool. (If you wish to make your own noodle dough see recipe below). Cut in 3-inch lengths, stuff with a tablespoon of filling then roll them. Place in a buttered casserole. Pour tomato sauce on top, sprinkling grated cheese on top before baking. Bake 10 to 15 minutes in a medium oven.

Noodle dough
  1 1/3 cups flour
      1 egg
      1 egg yolk
    1/2 teaspoon salt
      1 teaspoon oil

Work mixture together until dough is in a ball and comes away from hands without sticking. Roll with rolling pin until dough is paper thin. Keep rolling pin well sprinkled with flour to prevent sticking. Dry for about 30 minutes. Before it turns stiff, cut into lasagne-width.

Serves: 2

The Windsor
Los Angeles, California
Prop: Ben Dimsdale
Chef: Louis O. Baumann

TOURNEDOS OF BEEF QUEEN OF SHEBA

    1 large eggplant
      Flour
      Butter
    8 large mushroom caps
      White wine
      Lemon juice
   16 jumbo asparagus tips
  1/2 cup shallots, finely chopped
    4 ounces brown stock
    1 ounce Burgundy
  1/4 pound prosciutto ham, sliced
      thin
      Salt and pepper
    8 tenderloin medaillons, defatted

Peel eggplant and cut into 1/2 inch slices. Pass through flour gently and sauté in butter until golden brown. Sauté mushrooms in butter and a little white wine with a dash of lemon juice. Place asparagus tips in boiling water 5 to 8 minutes. Sauté shallots 1 minute, adding 4 ounces brown stock; bring to simmer and add Burgundy wine. Warm prosciutto (to be placed on eggplant slices). Salt and pepper medaillons of beef and pass lightly through flour; sauté to degree desired.

Place medaillons of beef on top of eggplant and ham slices and cover with simmering sauce—capping with mushrooms. Pyramid asparagus tips on sides.

Serves: 4

Fouquet's
Paris, France
Prop: Jean Drouant
Chef: Andre Fevre

MEDAILLON DE VEAU COPPELIA

1 (12-ounce) veal steak
  Salt and pepper
2 teaspoons butter
2 small onions
  Some laurel leaf
  Some sprigs of thyme
1 tablespoon whiskey
2 tablespoons champagne
1 artichoke heart
1 cup asparagus tips
  Red pepper

Dissolve a teaspoon of butter in a saucepan and add the veal seasoned with salt and pepper. Cook in covered pan for 20 minutes adding 2 small onions, 1/2 a laurel leaf and a sprig of thyme.

Remove the veal and keep hot in another closed dish. Skim off the butter from the remaining cooking juices and add the whiskey and champagne. Thicken with a spoon of butter. Boil for 2 or 3 minutes and strain. Pour over the veal.

Garnish with an artichoke heart warmed with butter and filled with asparagus tips. Place a small red pepper on top and serve with tiny baked potatoes.

Serves: 1

Wine: Red Bordeaux

Space Needle Restaurant
Seattle, Washington
Chef: Wolfgang Fillinger

VEAL CUTLET VALDOSTANA

  10 2-ounce veal slices
  10 thin slices prosciutto ham
2 1/2 ounces fontina cheese
     Flour
   1 egg
 1/2 cup milk
   2 cups fresh bread crumbs
 1/2 cup Parmesan cheese
   4 ounces butter
 1/2 cup sauterne wine
     Ticinese sauce (see index)

Flatten slices of veal as thin as possible. In the center of each, place a thin slice of prosciutto ham, a thin slice of fontina cheese, then cover with ham slice and second veal slice. Press cutlet edges together, then dip each shaped cutlet lightly in flour, then egg wash and bread crumbs that have been mixed with Parmesan cheese. Fry in butter until golden brown.

Place in casserole 1 ounce Ticinese sauce, lay cutlet on top and cover each cutlet with a soup spoon of sauce. Sprinkle with Parmesan cheese and butter. Bake for 20 minutes.

Serves: 6

O. Henry's Steak House
New York, New York

O. HENRY'S FAMED SPARERIBS BARBECUE
SAUCE

5	or 6 stalks of celery
3	green peppers
3	cloves garlic
1/2	cup vegetable oil
4	pounds canned peeled tomatoes
1/4	pound tomato puree
2	pounds dry hot peppers
4	bay leaves
1	tablespoon black pepper
3	tablespoons salt
3	tablespoons sugar
3	tablespoons dry mustard
2	tablespoons chili powder
2	tablespoons Worcestershire sauce
1	tablespoon Tabasco sauce
1	tablespoon cloves, ground
2	cups cider vinegar

Finely chop celery, peppers, garlic. Pour vegetable oil into frying pan. When hot, add chopped vegetables and brown them lightly. Strain the canned tomatoes through cheesecloth (or put through a blender until no lumps remain). Mix thoroughly with tomato puree in large saucepan. Add contents of frying pan and all other ingredients listed. Stir to eliminate lumps. Simmer the sauce for 1 1/2 to 2 hours over low heat, adding a little water to retain proper thickness and stirring occasionally. Strain once more through cheesecloth or put in blender.

Serves: 8 to 10

Danny's
Baltimore, Maryland
Prop: Danny Dickman

STEAK DIANE FLAMBÉE

2	ounces butter
4	ounces mushrooms, sliced
2	tablespoons shallots, chopped fine
1/2	teaspoon chives, chopped
1	teaspoon parsley, chopped
1/4	teaspoon Worcestershire sauce
1	tablespoon Sauce Robert (commercially prepared)
1/4	teaspoon salt
1	teaspoon freshly ground pepper Twin mignonettes of beef
2	ounces beef stock
2	ounces cognac
1	ounce dry sherry

Melt the butter in the blazer of a chafing dish. Add sliced mushrooms and shallots; sauté for 5 minutes. Add chives and parsley. Then add Worcestershire sauce, Sauce Robert, salt and pepper and simmer well over the flame for 15 minutes. In another skillet sauté twin mignonettes of beef in butter. When done to a medium turn, add cognac and set aflame. When the flame is extinguished, add sherry.

Serve Steak Diane on a heated platter, and spoon sauce on top. Ring platter with wild rice and serve.

Serves: 1

Wine: Mouton Baron-Philippe 1964

Paul Young's Restaurant
Washington, D.C.
Prop: Paul Young
Chef: Nino Lonzo

TOURNEDO JETÉE PROMENADE

5 pounds veal bones, cut into small pieces of perhaps 3-4 inches in length
1 large onion
3 branches celery
1 bunch leek (green stems only)
1 garlic clove, crushed
1 cup tomato paste
1 cup flour
1 gallon water
   Demi-Glacé

In roasting pan brown the veal bones for about 1/2 hour. (This will also develop free fat). Make a mirepoix (mixture) of the onion, celery (cut into rough chunks) and the leeks. Add, together with the garlic, to the bones in the roasting pan. Brown approximately 20 minutes longer. Add the tomato paste and continue to brown another 10 minutes. Add the flour and stir well. Add the water and bring to a boil. Scrape the bottom and sides of the pan and transfer all the ingredients to a soup pot and simmer for 2 hours. Strain through a cheesecloth. Yield: approximately 2 quarts.

Perigord Sauce
2 quarts demi-Glacé
2 tablespoons truffle essence
1/2 cup Madeira wine
1 ounce black truffles, coarsely chopped

Place all the ingredients in a saucepan and stir well. Keep hot.

Béarnaise Sauce
1 teaspoon shallots, chopped
1 teaspoon tarragon, chopped
1/2 teaspoon salt
1/2 cup white vinegar
4 egg yolks
1 cup butter, melted

Boil the shallots, tarragon and salt in the vinegar for 5 minutes. Strain into a mixing bowl. Set the bowl into a hot water bath (not over a flame) and add the egg yolks. Whip briskly to a thick foam. Slowly add the melted butter a little at a time while still whipping. Keep whipping until sauce thickens. Do not refrigerate or keep hot.

Tomato Concassee
2 cups tomatoes, peeled, drained and roughly crushed
1 garlic clove
1 tablespoon olive oil
   Salt and pepper to taste

Cook garlic lightly in the olive oil. Remove the garlic. Add tomatoes. Let boil 5 minutes. Add salt and pepper to taste. Keep hot.

Tournedos
6 artichoke bottoms, warmed
6 fillet mignons, approximately 9-ounces each
3 tablespoons Perigord sauce
2 tablespoons Béarnaise sauce
6 spoons tomato concassee

When the sauces are ready, sauté the fillet mignons to desired doneness. Remove to platter, or individual plates, and spoon Perigord sauce over each fillet. Spoon Béarnaise Sauce over each fillet. Place an artichoke bottom (hollow side up) on top of each fillet and fill each one with a spoonful of tomato concassee.

Serves: 6

Wine: Mazis-Chambertin 1961

Empress-of-China
San Francisco, California
Chef: Warren Kwok

EMPRESS BEEF

- 1/2 pound sirloin steak, cut into shoestring strips
- Vegetable oil
- 1/4 teaspoon salt
- 3 stalks celery, coarsely chopped
- 1 small can button mushrooms, thinly sliced
- 1 large white onion, thinly sliced
- 1/2 small can water chestnuts, coarsely chopped
- 1/4 pound snow peas, or substitute French-cut stringbeans
- 1 tablespoon cornstarch
- 5 tablespoons soy sauce
- 1/2 tablespoon sugar
- 1/2 cup water

Brown the beef with several tablespoons vegetable oil and 1/4 teaspoon salt in a hot skillet. Add onions, celery, mushrooms, snow peas and chestnuts and stir slowly for a few minutes over the hot fire.

Then cover the pan, turn down the fire and simmer for about 3 minutes. Just before serving, stir in a thickening made up of the cornstarch, sugar, soy sauce and water.

Serve immediately with fluffy steamed rice.

Serves: 2

Doros
San Francisco, California
Chef: Paolo Bermani

TOURNEDO OF BEEF ETRUSCAN

- 6 tournedos of beef
- 6 slices of marrow
- Salt and pepper
- Round croutons
- 2 cups demi-glacer
- 3 ounces brandy
- 1/2 cup melted clear butter

Sauté tournedos of beef in melted butter until cooked as desired (medium or rare). Place on croutons and set aside.

Remove excess butter from skillet, add 3 ounces brandy and let flame. To this add two cups demi-glacer.

Separately poach the slices of marrow in boiling water for 2 or 3 minutes. Strain and add to sauce in skillet. Let simmer for additional 2 minutes. Pour over tournedos and serve.

Serves: 6

Wine: Chianti Ruffino

The Newporter Inn
Newport Beach, California
Chef: Oscar Zink

OSCAR'S RACK OF LAMB

4   pound lamb rib
    Salt and pepper
8   small tomatoes
8   small pearl onions
4   carrots, sliced
8   asparagus
1   cup string beans
1   mushrooms
1   cup chicken or beef stock

Trim meat off the bone about 1 to 1 1/2 inches. Season lamb rack with salt and pepper. Roast at about 325° to 350°. (Medium-rare—approximately 25 minutes; medium—approximately 30 minutes; well-done or medium-well-done—approximately 40 minutes).

Remove and place on platter. As garnish, use broiled tomatoes, pearl onions, carrots, asparagus and string beans—set these around lamb rack. On meat side of lamb rack, arrange mushrooms (about 1-2 per person).

Empty fat from roasting pan and add water or chicken or beef stock and make gravy.

Serves: 4

Alta Vista
Manila, Philippines

ROAST SMOKE PORK LOIN

1   6-pound pork loin roast (10-12 ribs)
1   cup pineapple juice
1/2   bottle beer
1 1/2   teaspoons prepared mustard
2   pieces whole cloves
1 1/2   cups brown sugar

Place smoked pork loin in uncovered roasting pan, fat side up. Over it pour pineapple juice and beer.

Spread prepared mustard and brown sugar evenly on the roast. Stick in the cloves.

Roast at 425° until brown sugar is caramelized, about 45 minutes. Turn it over, bone side up. Baste the roast with the liquids. Then reduce heat to 325° and roast until done (185° interior temperature for a total roasting time of approximately 2 hours). Baste while roasting, once every 20 minutes.

When done, arrange pork on large platter. Around it place candied sweet potatoes and garnish with fried pineapple slices and cherries. Serve with chutney sauce.

Chutney Sauce
1   cup mango chutney, chopped
1   cup roast drippings, with beer-pineapple marinade

Mix above ingredients and simmer until thick.

Serves: 6

L'Auberge
Los Angeles, California
Chef: Raymond Dreyfus

COTELITTE OF LAMB BONNE AUBERGE

8 double loin lamb chops, French trimmed and lean, (about 3/4 to 1 inch thick with only 1 rib bone)
2 or 3 ounces sherry (optional)
Puree Soubise
Mornay sauce

Sauté lamb chops in pan on medium-high heat. Cook to taste with a little seasoning. Turn to high heat and pour in 2 or 3 ounces of good dry sherry (optional).

Arrange chops on platter, top with one tablespoon of puree Soubise on each, 1/2 spoon of Mornay Sauce and glaze under broiler.

Mornay Sauce
4 ounces butter
5 ounces flour
1 pint milk
2 tablespoons onion, chopped and slightly cooked
Salt and pepper
Grated nutmeg, bay leaf, thyme, parsley
3 ounces Gruyère cheese
3 ounces grated Parmesan cheese

Heat 4 ounces of butter in pan. Add flour while mixing with a wooden spoon. Cook slowly for 5 minutes, stirring.

Boil milk and mix into butter-flour mixture until smooth. Add 2 tablespoons of onion, chopped and slightly cooked in butter, salt and pepper, touch of grated nutmeg and bay leaf, thyme and parsley tied in a bouquet garni. Let simmer 45 minutes, stirring occasionally. Pass through fine strainer.

Mix in good Gruyère (Swiss cheese), grated Parmesan, and mix well while still warm, with 6 ounces of butter.

Serves: 4

Swiss Chalet
San Juan, Puerto Rico
Chef: Hans Moosberger

ÉMINCÉ OF VEAL ZURICHOISE

1/2 cup clarified butter
36 ounces thinly sliced lean veal, minced
1 onion, finely chopped
6 ounces fresh mushrooms, sliced
1 cup dry white wine
2 tablespoons flour
2 cups heavy cream
Salt and pepper
Chopped parsley

Heat frying pan with clarified butter, sauté minced veal over open fire to a light brown. Remove meat from pan. Add to pan: some butter, chopped onions, sliced fresh mushrooms, sprinkle with flour, white wine and heavy cream, cook until sauce is thick. Add sautéed veal, and salt and pepper to your taste. Do not boil, as meat gets tough. Sprinkle with chopped parsley when served.

The meat is served with Swiss home-fried potatoes (roesti) and salad.

Serves: 2

Quo Vadis
New York, New York
Chef: Eugene Bernard

CARRE D'AGNEAU NICOISE

- 1 rack of lamb, cut and trimmed
  Salt and pepper
- 1 small onion, diced
- 1 small carrot, diced
- 1 branch celery, diced
- 1/2 teaspoon thyme leaves
- 1/2 bay leaf
- 1/2 teaspoon rosemary
- 1/2 glass dry white wine
- 1/4 pint brown sauce
- 1/2 cup fresh bread crumbs
- 2 tablespoons parsley
- 1 shallot, finely chopped
- 2 medium potatoes
- 1/2 pound French string beans
- 1 medium-size tomato

Season lamb with salt and pepper. Roast for 35 minutes in 350° oven. Before removing, add onion, carrot, celery, thyme, bay leaf and rosemary. When ready, remove meat from pan, pour off excess fat, add wine and allow to reduce. Add brown sauce, allow to cook 5 minutes, then strain.

Mix bread crumbs, parsley and shallot, cover rack of lamb with it. Sprinkle some melted butter over it, return rack of lamb to oven for 5 minutes or until brown.

Cook and sauté potatoes, string beans and tomato. Arrange meat in serving dish with vegetables surrounding it.

Serves: 2

Swiss Chalet
San Juan, Puerto Rico
Chef: Hans Moosberger

OLD FASHIONED BASLER SAUERBRATEN

- 4 1/2 pounds bottom round of beef
- 2 large carrots, diced
- 2 large onions, peeled and diced
- 1 garlic clove, chopped
- 1 stalk of celery, diced
- 1/2 cup red vinegar
  Salt
  Bay leaves and rosemary
- 2 cups red wine
- 1/2 cup cooking oil
- 3 tablespoons flour
- 1 tablespoon tomato paste
- 2 teaspoons sugar
- 8 cups beef stock (consommé)
  Dry raisins

Wipe meat well with damp cloth, place in a deep mixing bowl, add cut vegetables, vinegar, spices, red wine until meat is covered. Leave meat in marinade, for at least 4 days, in cool place.

Remove meat from the marinade, dry, then brown it well on all sides in hot oil. Sprinkle with flour and tomato paste and let it brown with some sugar. Add vegetables and liquid in which meat has been marinated, add some red wine and beef stock, mix well and cook, covered, until meat is tender (2-3 hours).

Remove meat and strain sauce. Cook the sauce until slightly reduced. Slice the meat in thin slices and serve covered with the sauce (add some dry raisins to the sauce).

The sauerbraten is served with buttered spetzli and braised red cabbage.

Serves: 4

The Empress
London, England
Chef: Gino Scandolo

TERRINE DE FAISAN

1   pheasant
1   pound minced veal or venison
1   pound minced pork
1/2 pound minced chicken livers
1/2 pint double cream
3   tablespoons each brandy and sherry
1   teaspoon salt
1   dessert spoon ground black pepper
4-5 crushed juniper berries
3-4 garlic cloves
1/2 pound pork fat
     Foie gras and truffles (canned)
1/2 bay leaf
     Lard

Completely bone the pheasant. Set aside the wings and breast to be cut into thin slices and steeped in the brandy.

Mince the remainder of the pheasant meat and mix with all the other minced items in a large bowl; blend together thoroughly. Add double cream and sherry and mix again. Season to taste—average for this quantity: 1 dessert spoon salt, 1 spoon ground black pepper, 4-5 crushed juniper berries, 3-4 cloves of garlic. The seasoning must be tested before cooking.

Line a round or oval dish with thin slices of pork fat. Put a layer of the minced ingredients at the bottom of the dish. On this arrange some of the sliced pheasant, alternating with thin slices of foie gras and truffles. Cover this with another layer of the minced ingredients and continue to fill the dish to within 1/8 inch of the rim, ending with a layer of minced ingredients. Top with 1/2 a bay leaf.

Fold inward the overlapping ends of pork fat. Stand dish in water and cook for 1 1/4 hours in 400° oven. It ought to come out pink. Leave the mixture to cool under a light weight, overnight. When cold, turn it out. Dry with a cloth and then return it to the dish which must, meanwhile, have been lined with a layer of lard 1/8 inch thick. (The lard must be well set before the mixture is put into the dish.) Finally, pour lard, which is almost cold, on top of the terrine so that it is completely sealed.

Serves: 4

Tony's
Houston, Texas

SLICED FILLET NINO

8   (1/2-inch) thick cuts of prime beef tenderloin
1   cup sliced fresh mushrooms
3   tablespoons butter
1   cup quartered artichoke hearts, pre-fried
1   tablespoon garlic, finely chopped

Sauté meat and mushrooms in butter over medium-heat until desired degree of rare, medium or well-doneness is achieved. Add garlic and artichokes, shortly before meat is cooked to taste, so that they will be thoroughly heated.

To serve, place 2 pieces of the meat on each serving plate and top each with some of the mushroom and artichoke hearts mixture.

Approximate cooking time: 18-20 minutes.

Goes very well with fettuccine noodles, gnocchi or flavored rice pilaff.

Serves: 4

Wine: Red Bordeaux (Sainte-Julien—Sainte-Emilion)

Top of the Tower Restaurant
Kansas City, Missouri
Proprietor: John Wallace

AUSTRIAN SAUERBRATEN

3	ounces granulated sugar
1 1/4	pints water
2/3	cup cider vinegar
1/4	teaspoon black pepper
2	ounces salt
2	ounces chopped onion
1	tablespoon mixed spices.
1 1/2	pounds beef shoulder, rolled and tied

Combine sugar, water, vinegar in warm water until sugar is dissolved. Add salt, black pepper, chopped onions and mixed spices to marinade. Pour over meat and bring to a boil. Let boil 20 minutes. Remove from fire and let stand in refrigerator for 1 week. Stir marinade daily during pickling period.

Roasting instructions
After meat has marinated for 1 week, place in roasting pan (covered) for 1/2 hour or until browned, uncover last 5 minutes.

Remove meat and thicken marinade with roux of flour and oil. When thickened, add meat and simmer until meat is fork tender.

Serves: 4

Camelot Restaurant
Minneapolis, Minnesota
Proprietor: Hans Skalle
Chef: Jage Eriksen

ROAST NORWEGIAN REINDEER

10	pound leg of reindeer or venison Knuckle of veal
1	large onion
4	medium-size carrots
2	stalks of celery
1	small bunch parsley
3-6	bay leaves
1	pound salt pork for larding Salt and pepper
1/4	pound Norwegian goat cheese
1/2	cup lingonberries
1/4	pound butter
1/4	pound flour
1/2	pint whipping cream

Remove shank bone of leg and saw or chop into 2-inch pieces. Add knuckle of veal preferably cut in same manner. Brown in skillet. Add vegetables, 3 quarts of water and bring to a moderate boil. (Cook for 2 or 3 hours, reducing liquid to half.)

Lard roast with one-half finger-size pork. Rub with salt and pepper. Sear in iron skillet, sealing in juices. Put into roasting pan. Add meat stock. Baste occasionally. Allow 20 to 24 minutes per pound.

For extra flavor, almost a must, at the end add Norwegian goat cheese and lingonberries. Use roux to make sauce (1/4 pound butter and 1/4 pound flour), add pan drippings and strain. (But first let roux cook well.) To sauce add 1/2 pint whipping cream. Strain through cheesecloth and serve with meat. Wild rice goes well with this and turns it into a gourmet treat.

Serves: 10

Las Novedades
Tampa, Florida
Chefs: Lee Mendoza and
Nelson Cruz

FILETE SALTEADO "EMPERATRIZ"

1/2	cup olive oil
2	tablespoons butter
3	medium-size potatoes, cubed
1	small onion, minced
1	small bell pepper, finely chopped
1	bay leaf
1	garlic clove, minced
1/4	cup mushrooms, sliced
1	cup smoked ham, cubed
2	Spanish sausages (chorizos), sliced thin
1/4	scant teaspoon nutmeg
1/4	cup tomato sauce
1/4	cup good Burgundy wine
1/2	teaspoon hot sauce
3	(7-ounce) prime fillets
	Sprinkle of dry sherry
1 1/2	cups long grain white rice
1	tablespoon salt (for rice)

Heat oil and butter in skillet. Add cubed potatoes and brown. Remove with slotted spoon to oven-proof casserole. Remove all grease from skillet except 4 tablespoons. Add onions and pepper; sauté until transparent. Add bay leaf and garlic; cook 5 minutes. Combine hot sauce with mushrooms, ham, sausages, nutmeg, tomato sauce. Add to sauté and cook another 5 minutes at moderate heat. Pour contents of skillet over potatoes in casserole. Sprinkle all with Burgundy wine. Stir carefully, cover casserole and place over low heat.

Clean sauté skillet and add 2 tablespoons more of grease. When grease is hot, add cubed fillets and sear quickly. Add to casserole and mix thoroughly but carefully. Sprinkle with dry sherry and pars-ley, cover, and place in preheated oven at 325° for 20 minutes. Garnish with pimento strips.

To prepare white, long grain rice: fill a 2-quart pot three-quarters full of water. When water boils briskly, add 1 tablespoon salt and the rice. Cook uncovered, at a brisk boil for 20 minutes. Remove pot from heat and place under running water to cool slightly. Strain and serve with Salteado, artistically presented.

Serves: 2

Wine: Brillante rosado,
Bodegas Bilbaina
(Spanish wine)

Auberge le Vieux St. Gabriel
Montreal, Canada
Chef: André Carpenter

BOEUF GABRIEL

3	pounds beef cubes
	Butter
1 1/2	pounds chunks of fat
2	finely chopped onions
1	pound minced mushrooms
12	to 13 ounces red wine
	Bay leaves
	Salt and pepper
3 1/2	ounces beef consommé

Sauté beef in a deep casserole with butter. Sauté the fat chunks with mushrooms and onions then add to the beef. Add the red wine, bay leaves, salt and pepper. Mix in the consommé. Cover and simmer 1 1/2 hours.

Serves: 6

Wine: Beaujolais or
Anjou de Neuville

Swiss Chalet
San Juan, Puerto Rico
Chef: Hans Moosberger

VEAL CUTLET TICINESE

    Frying oil
1   onion, chopped
1   garlic clove, finely chopped
2   pounds fresh ripe tomatoes, peeled and diced
12 veal cutlets, lean and tender
    Salt, pepper, flour, rosemary, sage
24 ounces processed Swiss cheese
1   cup dry white wine

To prepare sauce: heat oil in pan, add onions, garlic and diced tomatoes. Cook for about 10 minutes with seasoning.

Fry the cutlets, which have been prepared with salt, pepper, rosemary, sage and flour, quickly, in hot oil, until brown.

Place the cutlets on the tomato sauce in gratin platter (2 cutlets each), cover with 2 slices of cheese and bake in oven with a little white wine until cheese melts.

Can be served with buttered rice and vegetables.

Serves: 6

Biggs Restaurant
Chicago, Illinois
Chef: Dennis Michaloh

FILLET OF BEEF WELLINGTON

4   pounds beef fillet
1   stick butter
    Salt
    Ground pepper
1   bay leaf
1/2 cup sliced celery
1   cup sliced carrots
1/2 cup sliced onion
1/3 cup chopped parsley
1/2 teaspoon crumbled dried rosemary
    Pâté de foie gras (canned)
    Pie pastry
    Milk
1   cup veal stock
1/4 cup additional pâté de fois gras
1/4 cup chopped mushrooms

Spread meat generously with butter. Sprinkle with salt and pepper. Spread vegetables, bay leaf and rosemary over bottom of a shallow baking pan and place roast on top. Cook in a preheated oven (450°) for 40 to 50 minutes. Remove from oven and allow to cool completely.

When cold spread pâté de fois gras over entire roast. Roll pastry 1/8-inch thick and wrap around roast. Trim edges of pastry, moisten and seal edges together. Place in a baking dish with sealed side down. Brush milk on crust and prick. Bake until browned about 15 to 20 minutes. Remove to platter to keep warm.

Add veal stock, 1/4 cup of fois gras and chopped mushrooms to roasting pan. Simmer to sauce consistency about 10 to 15 minutes. Slice beef and serve with sauce in sauceboat.

Serves: 6

Maisonette
Cincinnati, Ohio
Prop: Lee Comisar

MEDAILLONS DE VEAU PIERRE

  12 medaillons of veal (veal escal-
       lopine), 2- to 3-ounces each
       (preferably from the tenderloin
       or loin of veal)
       Salt and pepper
       Flour for dredging
   2 tablespoons butter
   3 shallots or 1/2 onion, chopped
   1 cup Chablis wine
1 1/2 cups heavy or whipping cream
   1 tablespoon fresh or dry tarragon,
       chopped
   2 ripe avocados, peeled and diced
   6 average slices imported Swiss
       cheese

Have the butcher cut and flatten the medaillons very thin. Salt and pepper the medaillons on both sides then dredge in flour. Pre-heat a heavy-bottom skillet or saucepan with 2 tablespoons butter. In hot butter sauté the medaillons on both sides until golden brown. Remove medaillons onto serving platter and keep hot. Turn broiler on very hot.

Remove excess fat from skillet. In same skillet add chopped shallots or onions, cook for 10 seconds then add Chablis wine and reduce it until only one-quarter its original volume. Then add heavy cream and reduce again to one-half its volume or until sauce coats the spoon. Taste for seasoning, then add chopped tarragon and diced avocado and cook 2 more minutes. The sauce should be viscous but not too thick or thin. The quality of cream used is very important. If the sauce is too thin, thicken with 1 teaspoon cornstarch, dilute with wine. The reducing is done on a very high heat.

Pour sauce over medaillons, arranging Swiss cheese on top of the veal to cover all the meat. Place platter under hot broiler and let cheese melt until it becomes very soft, about 2 minutes at most. Serve at once with boiled potatoes or noodles.

Serves: 4

Wine: Le Montrachet, Comte
Lafon

Old Farm's Inn
Avon, Connecticut
Chef: Gaspare Cuchiarra

VEAL PORTERHOUSE — À LA OLD FARM'S
INN

   2 cups flour
   4 veal porterhouse steaks from the
       loin of the veal
   4 tablespoons oil
   1 shallot or onion, finely chopped
   2 ounces Madeira wine
   1 quart veal stock or canned
       bouillon

Flour the veal steaks — sauté in hot oil in heavy skillet until brown on both sides. Remove steaks from pan and set aside.

Sauté shallot in same pan until light brown, add the flour and wine — stir thoroughly until all is a nice light brown then add the veal stock, stirring well until sauce is thick. Simmer for 20 minutes.

Place veal steaks in shallow casserole — pour sauce over meat and cook in 350° oven for 30 minutes.

Serves: 4

Wine: Brolio Bianco (Ricasoli)
or Vouvray

Karl Ratzch's Restaurant
Milwaukee, Wisconsin
Chef: Raymond Drews

BEEF ROULADEN

4 pieces thinly sliced round steak
1 large dill pickle
2 medium-size green peppers, cut
     in strips
2 strips bacon
2 large onions
   Salt and pepper
   Cooking oil and fat
3 tablespoons Maggi bouillon
     granules
   Flour
   Accent
1 cup Burgundy wine (optional)

Season meat. Roll up each piece of meat with 1/4 dill pickle, strip green pepper, 1/2 strip bacon and large piece of onion in center, salt and pepper. Brown in oil and fat. Add 3 tablespoons Maggi bouillon granules and rest of green pepper and onion, finely chopped. Allow to simmer until meat is done.

Remove meat from pan and thicken gravy with flour or roux. Season gravy to taste with salt and pepper and Accent. If you wish, you may add 1 cup of Burgundy wine at this point. Place rouladen back into gravy and heat through.

Serves: 4

Wine: Any full red Pommard

Mon Cher Ton Ton
Tokyo, Japan
Chef: Masaki Muramato

GARLIC STEAK

1 tablespoon green pepper
1 teaspoon onion
1 clove garlic
1/2 teaspoon mustard
1 tablespoon catsup
2 teaspoons A-One sauce
4 teaspoons Pilin sauce
5 teaspoons lemon juice
1/2 teaspoon Tabasco
1/2 teaspoon sugar
   Dash salt
1/2 clove garlic for steak
   Salt for steak
3 1/2 pounds sirloin steak

For steak sauce: cut green peppers and onions into chunks. Scrape and cut garlic and then scorch. Batter mustard, then mix up the rest; catsup, A-One sauce, Pilin sauce, lemon juice, Tabasco, sugar, salt and the green peppers and onions.

Broil steak: cut 1/2 clove of garlic and scorch. Scatter salt over the meat and leave it about 1 minute, then turn it over and put scorched garlic on it. Cover with lid of the pan and broil until just before smoke. Then drop the heat down for about 1 to 2 minutes. Take off the scorched garlic from the meat and then cut the meat into about 15 medium-square pieces and broil them again, but not till scorch. Eat with scorched garlic before the steak gets cold.

Serves: 4

Wine: Château Haut-Brion

Marie Schreiber's Tavern Chop House in the Statler-Hilton Cleveland, Ohio

FILLET OF BEEF WELLINGTON

     5   pounds tenderloin of beef
     1   teaspoon dry English mustard
         Larding pork
     5   tablespoons butter
   1/2   pound mushrooms, finely
         chopped
   1/2   small garlic clove, crushed
   1/3   cup sherry
     4   chicken livers
     1   tablespoon tomato puree
     1   tablespoon meat extract
     3   truffles, finely chopped
     1   sheet puff pastry (or rich pie
         crust) (see index for puff
         pastry)
         Egg white

Sprinkle tenderloin of beef with dry English mustard. Tie larding pork over it and roast for 25 minutes in a hot oven (400°). Let the fillet cool. Remove the larding pork. Skim the pan juices.

In 5 tablespoons of butter sauté, for 5 minutes, mushrooms, tomato puree, meat extract, truffles, garlic, sherry and chicken livers. Mix well and remove pan from heat.

Roll out a sheet of puff paste or rich pie crust, large enough to enclose the fillet. Lay the cold fillet in the center of the puff paste or pie dough and pile mushroom mixture on and around it. Carefully wrap the fillet in the puff paste or pie dough, turning in the ends, and press all edges together firmly. Lay the fillet seam side down on a baking sheet and paint the dough with egg white. Cut decorative shapes from puff paste or pie dough—leaves, circles or stripes—to form braids.

Paint the cutouts with egg white and affix them to the top of the fillet. Bake in a hot oven (425°) for 25 to 30 minutes or until pastry is golden.

To the reserved pan juices add 1/2 cup each of beef stock and sherry and 1 tablespoon chopped tarragon and heat the sauce for 5 minutes. Arrange the fillet on a serving platter and carefully slice it. Keep the crust intact around each slice.

Serves: 8

CHRISTOPHER INN

COLUMBUS, OHIO

Chef: Kenneth L. Garver

Chinese Pepper Steak Christopher Inn Style

DYNASTY

HONOLULU, HAWAII

Chef : Kurt Wuest

Tournedos Marco Polo

THE MATADOR
RESTAURANT

WEST LOS ANGELES,
CALIFORNIA

Prop : William D. Fremont

Paella A La Valencia

Sign of The Dove
New York, New York
Chef: Peter Mischke

LAMB CHOP FLORENTINE

2 lamb chops (fat free)
2 onions
1 cup spinach
Salt and pepper
4 pastry leaves
1 egg

Salt lamb chops and brown them in pan on hot stove. *Do not overcook; leave rare.* Let them cool. Then sauté slightly 1 teaspoon fine-chopped onion in pan. Do not brown. Then sauté 6 soupspoons fine-chopped spinach (must be dry) in pan with chopped onion until hot. Add pepper and salt to taste.

Separate pastry leaves, 2 for each chop. Fold each set of 2 leaves 4 times. On top of folded leaves place mixture of onion and spinach. Then place lamb chop on top. Cover chop with balance of spinach and onion. Fold 4 corners together with bone of chop staying outside folds.

Brush top with egg wash (whipped egg) and bake in 450° oven for 15 minutes.

Serve with carrots and Fondant potatoes.

Serves: 1

Coach Inn
Fort Washington, Pennsylvania

CALVES' SWEETBREADS À LA MAISON

6 pair fresh jumbo sweetbreads (the best sweetbreads are from a young calf—and the bigger the sweetbread, the younger the calf)
1 gallon water
1/2 cup flour
4 eggs, beaten
12 ounces butter
3 cups English beef tea broth or beef stock
3 level teaspoons sugar
10 teaspoons cider vinegar
1 bunch fresh parsley, chopped fine
3 ounces celery
3 ounces onion
1 bay leaf

Start sweetbreads in cold water and bring to a boil, cook for 20 minutes—let cool in stock. Clean fat and connective tissue from sweetbreads. Cut sweetbreads in half. Flour them well. Dip in egg batter, sauté them in butter until a golden brown, then divide into shallow casseroles.

Add flour to remaining butter—stir well over flame until flour and butter are completely mixed and flour is cooked—3 to 4 minutes. Add broth or beef stock—sufficient to make a thickened smooth sauce. Add celery, onions and bay leaf. Add sugar and vinegar and simmer for 1-2 minutes. Take off flame—mix 1 ounce of butter into sauce and pour over sweetbreads. Garnish with fresh chopped parsley.

Serves: 6

Wine: Chilled Moselle

Laffite
Denver, Colorado

CANNELLONI FILLING

2 tablespoons olive oil
1/2 cup finely chopped onion
1 teaspoon finely chopped garlic
1 (10-ounce) package frozen chopped spinach, defrosted, squeezed completely dry and chopped again or about 3/4 cup or 3/4 pound fresh spinach, cooked, drained, squeezed and finely chopped
2 tablespoons butter
1 pound beef round steak, ground twice or 1 cup finely chopped left-over beef
2 chicken livers
4 tablespoons freshly grated imported Parmesan cheese
2 tablespoons cream
2 eggs, lightly beaten
1/2 teaspoon dried oregano, crumbled
   Salt and freshly ground black pepper

Heat the olive oil in an 8 or 10-inch enameled or stainless steel skillet. Add the onions and garlic, and cook over moderate heat, stirring frequently, for 7-8 minutes until they are soft but not brown. Stir in the spinach and cook, stirring constantly, for 3-4 minutes. When all of the moisture has boiled away and the spinach sticks lightly to the pan, transfer it to a large mixing bowl.

Melt 1 tablespoon butter in the same skillet and lightly brown the ground meat, stirring constantly to break up any lumps. Add the meat to the onion-spinach mixture. Then melt 1 more tablespoon of butter in the skillet and cook the livers, turning them frequently, for 3-4 minutes until they are somewhat firm, lightly browned but still pink inside.

Chop them coarsely. Then add them to the mixture in the bowl along with 5 tablespoons of grated Parmesan, 2 tablespoons of cream, the eggs and oregano. With a wooden spoon, mix the ingredients together, gently but thoroughly. Taste and season with salt and pepper.

Serves: 2

La Scala Restaurant
Hollywood, California

STEAK AND PEPPERS AU COGNAC

4 (16-ounce) lean New York steaks cut in 1″ x 1″ pieces
3 ounces clarified butter
3 shallots, chopped fine
2 large bell peppers, roasted and peeled
1/2 teaspoon oregano
1 teaspoon chopped chives
   Salt and pepper
4 ounces cognac

In a large heavy frying pan, heat the butter. Add the meat and quickly sauté enough to brown the meat slightly. Immediately discard excess butter and add shallots, bell peppers, salt and pepper, butter, oregano and chives and mix well.

Flambé with cognac and serve. (The meat should be cooked medium-rare.)

Serves: 4

The Abbey
Atlanta, Georgia
Chef: Andre Maison

BEEF STROGANOFF

Oil
2 pounds defatted beef tenderloin
3 tablespoons claret wine
1 teaspoon white wine
1/8 teaspoon garlic
Pinch of white pepper
1 teaspoon finely chopped shallots
1/2 cup sour cream
6 tablespoons brown sauce (brown gravy)
1 cucumber sliced 1/4 inch thick
1/3 pound fresh mushrooms
Salt to taste
1 tablespoon butter
1/4 teaspoon Worcestershire sauce

Heat iron skillet dry until very hot, put oil into hot skillet turning until it is lightly coated with oil. Put meat into pan turning vigorously until lightly brown. Add wine, garlic, butter, Worcestershire sauce, pinch of white pepper and shallots. Add sour cream, stir gently so as not to bruise the meat with the spoon. Pour the brown sauce into the skillet, stirring gently; turn off the fire, add cucumber and mushrooms, salt to taste and stir gently again. Serve on a bed of buttered Polish egg noodles.

Serves: 6

Wine: Chaffagne Montrachet

Cafe De Paris
Chicago, Illinois
Chef: Pat Nuti

GRENADINES DE BOEUF À LA MARCHAND

2 pounds tenderloin tips trimmed fat-free
4 1/2 tablespoons butter
1/2 cup Madeira wine
Marchand sauce
4 slices white toast, crust removed
Chopped parsley
1 tablespoon melted butter

Tenderloin tips should be sliced on the bias. Heat 3 1/2 tablespoons of butter to smoking point in a large frying pan and sauté tenderloin tips quickly. Brown nicely but do not cook well-done. Mix cooked tips (draining butter) with the Madeira wine and Marchand sauce. Bring quickly to boil without scorching and remove from heat.

Serve in individual casseroles. Dip small toast points in 1 tablespoon of melted butter and chopped parsley and insert deeply in each casserole, parsley end out. Note: casseroles should be piping hot with adequate underliners for service.

Marchand de Vin Sauce

6 cups Burgundy wine
1 teaspoon crushed peppercorns
6 shallots, chopped fine
4 large mushrooms, chopped fine
3 tablespoons butter

Boil Burgundy wine and crushed peppercorns until reduced to one-third in volume. Strain out the peppercorns and add the shallots and mushrooms. Cook a few minutes and then cool. When ready to use add 3 tablespoons of melted butter.

Serves: 4

Wine: Pommard Chanlins

Marchi's Restaurant
New York, New York

LASAGNA

Pasta

    3   eggs
    1   cup water
  1/2   teaspoon salt
    4   cups flour
        Melted butter
    1   pound thinly sliced mild Provo-
        lone cheese
  1/4   pound grated Parmesan cheese

Place 3 whole eggs, water and salt in a large mixing bowl. Stir the ingredients well and continue to do so until all the flour has been sifted in. Remove the dough from the bowl and knead for 5 minutes. Roll the dough into thin sheets and cut into strips about 3 to 4 inches wide. Place the strips in 6 quarts boiling water and add 1 tablespoon salt. Boil for 10 minutes. Place pot under cold water tap and permit water to run until the pasta has cooled. Drain.

Sauce

    4   thin slices salt pork
  1/4   cup butter
    1   cup chopped onion
    1   cup chopped carrots
    1   cup chopped celery
  1 1/2 cups chopped tomatoes
  1/2   pound ground pork
  1/2   pound ground beef
  1/2   teaspoon salt
  1/8   teaspoon pepper
    2   cups water
    4   bouillon cubes dissolved in 5
        cups boiling stock or water
  1/2   cup white wine

Place salt pork and butter in a large sauce pan and cook over medium flame for 10 minutes. Then place onions, carrots, celery, tomatoes, ground beef and pork, salt and pepper in pan and cook until meat is browned. Add 1 cup of water and stir until it has been absorbed. Repeat this procedure with the second cup. Add the boiling water or stock containing the bouillon to the mixture and simmer for several hours until the sauce reaches a desired consistency. Wine may be added 10 minutes before serving to enhance flavor.

Place a little melted butter and sauce in the bottom of a 12″ x 12″ baking pan to keep the pasta from sticking. Place a layer of pasta in the pan and cover with a layer of Provolone cheese. Then ladle in some sauce on top of the cheese. (Divide the sauce in half. Add 1 cup water to 1/2 the sauce and use for ladling. Save the rest for topping.) Repeat this procedure until the pasta is used up. Bake in preheated oven at 350° for 1 hour. Cut into squares, top with sauce and Parmesan cheese and serve.

Serves: 8

Il Sorrento
Dallas, Texas

SCALLOPINE SORRENTINA

1 1/2   pounds veal leg, boned
        Salt and pepper to taste
        Flour as needed
3   ounces butter
1   clove garlic, minced
1/2   cup sauterne wine
1/2   cup tomatoes, crushed
1/2   cup chicken stock
        Pinch oregano and sweet basil
1   small eggplant, sliced and fried
1/4   pound Fontina cheese, sliced

Slice veal very thin and pound well. When ready to cook, season with salt and pepper and dip in flour. Melt butter in large skillet. When hot, place veal cutlets in skillet and brown thoroughly on both sides. Add minced garlic. Add sauterne wine and cook over high fire. Add crushed tomatoes, stock and seasoning. Place slices of fried eggplant on each veal cutlet and top with slices of Fontina cheese. Simmer for 5 minutes. Place on platter and garnish with buttered egg noodles.

Serves: 6

Wine: Soave Bolla ·

Renaissance
Newark, New Jersey
Chef: Phil Stevos

RACK OF LAMB

        Rack of lamb consisting of 8 to
            9 chops and weighing about
            2 1/2 pounds
1   clove garlic
2   teaspoons salt
1   teaspoon fresh ground pepper
1   teaspoon crushed rosemary
1   small onion, chopped
2   stalks of celery, chopped
1   carrot, chopped

Preheat oven to 475° (3/4 hour).

Combine salt, pepper and rosemary. Rub rack of lamb with garlic and season with mixture. Cover ends of chop bones in strips of foil to prevent from charring. Place the rack of lamb in a shallow roasting pan and add chopped vegetables around rack. Roast at 475° for 20 minutes and reduce to 400° for 1 hour. (Basting lamb every 15 minutes will enhance flavor.)

When rack is done, carefully place on platter, remove the foil and let rack of lamb set 15 minutes to make carving easier.

To carve rack of lamb, remove the eye leaving the ribs without meat. Carve the eye of the rack on a bias and serve the ribs of rack on side of plate.

Serves: 2

The Blue Horse
St. Paul, Minnesota
Prop: Clifford Warling
Chef: George Wandzel

ROAST FILLET OF BEEF—PERIGUEUX

1/2	pound beef tenderloin per person
1/3	cup flour
	Salt, pepper and Accent
1/2	cup butter or cooking oil
1/3	cup fine minced onions
1/3	cup fine minced celery
1/3	cup fine minced carrots
1	clove garlic (optional)
2	cans undiluted beef consommé
1	teaspoon tomato paste
1/3	cup Madeira wine
	Watercress
	Diced goose liver paté
	Truffles

Dust meat in flour and season it with salt, pepper and Accent. Sear meat in butter or oil until brown on all sides. Remove meat from pan. Add to the drippings: onions, celery, carrots, (garlic optional) and sear. Into this, add flour which has been browned in a pie tin in a 350° oven. To this roux, add beef consommé and tomato paste. Let simmer for 8-10 minutes, stirring occasionally.

Place beef tenderloin in a small roaster and strain sauce over the meat. Loosen scrapings with Madeira wine and strain into roaster. Roast the meat to desired doneness. Place roast on a platter, garnish with watercress and decorate with diced goose liver paté and truffles. Keep sauce warm and add chopped truffles. Serve sauce in a sauceboat.

Serve with fonds d'artichauts Princesse (Artichoke bottoms with asparagus tips and Hollandaise sauce) and pommes Parisienne Rissoles, (small round-shaped potatoes, rissoled in butter with chopped parsley).

Serves: 6

Keyaki Grill, Tokyo Hilton
Tokyo, Japan
Chef: Paul Mueller

THE EMPEROR'S PEPPER STEAK

	Salt
2	(12-ounce) tenderloin steaks
1	tablespoon crushed black pepper
	Butter
1	tablespoon chopped onions
1 1/2	ounces old brandy
1	cup brown sauce (demi-glacé)
2	ounces heavy cream

Salt the steaks and bread them with the crushed black pepper. Fry them in butter until dark brown, add the onions, fry them slightly. Add the brandy and flame the steaks. Add the brown sauce and the cream, stir, simmer the steaks slowly until they are medium or well-done, or how you like them.

Serve with buttered rice and green peas.

Serves: 2

Wine: Red Bordeaux or rosé

St. Clair Inn
St. Clair, Michigan

IRISH LAMB STEW WITH DUMPLINGS

2 1/2 pounds boneless lamb stew in
      3/4-inch cubes
   1 large onion, chopped coarse
      Salt and pepper
   1 large bunch carrots, cross-cut
      3/8 inch thick
   1 tablespoon chicken base
   3 drops egg-shade color
   1 pound frozen peas, cooked
      separately
      Biscuit mix for 6 or 7 dumplings

Cover lamb cubes with water. Bring to a boil, skim off top and add onions, salt, pepper and cook for 45 minutes. Add carrots and continue to cook until meat is tender and carrots are done.

Drain off stock, add 1 tablespoon chicken base and 3 drops egg-shade color. Bring stock to a boil and thicken to about the consistency of medium cream sauce. Pour over meat and carrots. Add peas and taste for seasoning.

Make 6 or 7 dumplings and serve 1 dumpling with each serving of lamb stew.

Serves: 6

Villa Fontana
Orange, California
Chef: Wilfred C. Mattice

ROAST RACK OF SPRING LAMB MASCOTE

   2 pound rack of lamb
      Salt and pepper
      Garlic
      White Burgundy wine sauce

Served with: Tomatoes farcie
              Fresh string beans sauté au
                Beurre
              Spears of broccoli
                Hollandaise
              Diced potatoes and arti-
                chokes (bottoms sautéed
                in butter)

Lightly salt and pepper the lamb and rub it lightly with garlic. Cook at 425° for 20 minutes per pound for rare, 30 minutes per pound for medium, or 40-45 minutes per pound for well-done. Glaze with white wine sauce and serve.

Wine sauce
   1 tablespoon chopped onions
1 1/2 tablespoons flour
 1/2 cup veal stock
 1/2 cup white wine

Stir onions and flour into pan drippings until smooth. Add veal stock, wine and salt as needed.

Serves: 4

*Wine: Château Les Carmes
Haut-Brion*

King Cole
Dayton, Ohio

FILLET WELLINGTON

        6   pounds tenderloin (remove all
              fat)
            Salt and pepper
        2   pounds mushrooms
    1/2   pound morels, chopped very
              fine
        4   ounces shallots, chopped
            Nutmeg
            Thyme
            Garlic
        1   pound goose liver
            Puff paste (see index)

Take tenderloin with all fat removed, season with salt and pepper and brown on all sides, but leave the fillet raw inside.

Take mushrooms and morels, chop very finely and sauté them with chopped shallots. Season with salt, pepper, nutmeg, thyme and a touch of garlic. Mix goose liver into this paste. If fresh goose liver is not available use pâté de fois gras.

Roll out puff paste about 1/8 inch. Place fillet on pastry and encase it with the paste and mushrooms, then fold the puff paste completely around the fillet and make a small hole on top so the steam can escape.

Bake for 40 minutes in oven about 350-375°. If it browns too much cover with foil to protect.

Serve with Madeira sauce, braised celery and hollowed tomatoes stuffed with peas.

Serves: 6

Italian Village
Chicago, Illinois

SALTIMBOCCA ALLA ROMANA

        8   small veal cutlets
        2   cups flour
        2   cups Parmesan or grated Moz-
              zarella cheese
            Small leaf of fresh sage or dried
              sage leaves
        8   slices of prosciutto
        3   tablespoons melted butter
        1   cup chicken broth
        1   cup white cooking wine
    1/2   cup chopped parsley

Flatten 8 small cutlets to a thickness of less than 1/4 inch. Flour veal lightly and brown on both sides. Remove from pan.

Add grated Parmesan or grated Mozzarela cheese and small leaf of fresh sage (or sprinkle lightly with dried sage leaves). Attach prosciutto (the size of the veal slice by threading veal with toothpick).

Sauté the meat in 3 tablespoons melted butter. Pour off excess fat, and add chicken broth and white cooking wine. Simmer for 5 to 6 minutes.

Sprinkle lightly with chopped parsley.

Serves: 4

Wine: Soave or Verdicchio

Riviera Hotel
Las Vegas, Nevada
Chef: Raymond MacCurtin

ESCALOP OF VEAL ORLOFF

Flour
2 ounces clarified butter
2 4-ounce battened veal cutlets
3 ounces crab legs
3 ounces cooked asparagus
4 ounces Foyot sauce (canned)
1 ounce Russian caviar

Flour veal cutlets, season lightly. Heat frying pan, add butter. When hot, add veal cutlets, cook 1 1/2 minutes each side. Remove from pan and place on serving platter.

Add a little more butter to pan and heat asparagus and crab legs separately. Arrange on top of veal, alternating asparagus and crab legs. Cover all of this lightly and evenly with Foyot sauce (lukewarm). Just before serving place caviar in center.

Serve with artichoke bottoms stuffed with chopped spinach (Pernod flavored) and O'Brien potatoes.

Serves: 2

Elizabethan Room
Kahler Hotel
Rochester, Minnesota
Chef: Charles Case

ESCALLOPES OF VEAL, NICOISE

1 1/4 pounds veal scallops
2 eggs
3 ounces flour
1 teaspoon salt
1 tablespoon parsley, chopped
2 tablespoons Parmesan cheese, grated
2 cloves garlic, finely chopped
1 tablespoon onion, finely chopped
1 tablespoon green pepper, finely chopped
2 ounces olive oil
1 teaspoon dried basil
6 ounces tomato sauce
1/2 cup ripe olives, pitted
1/8 bunch parsley, chopped
4 slices eggplant

Dip the veal scallops in flour, then in beaten egg and in flour seasoned with salt, chopped parsley, grated Parmesan cheese and the garlic. Sauté the onion and green pepper in enough oil to cover the bottom of the skillet. Cook for 3-4 minutes. Add the veal scallops and sauté them very quickly until nicely browned. Add the basil, tomato sauce and pitted black olives. Cook mixture with the meat for 3-4 minutes. Remove the scallops to a hot platter, pour the sauce over them and sprinkle with chopped parsley. Serve with sautéed eggplant slices.

Serves: 4

Prince Albert Rotisserie
Hotel Inter-Continental
Manila, Philippines

FLAMED TENDERLOIN STEAKS PATRICIA

　8　(4-ounce) tenderloin steaks,
　　　　flattened
2 1/2　ounces dairy butter
　2　shallots, chopped
　10　fresh mushrooms, sliced
　3　tomatoes peeled, chopped
　　　　juiceless
　1　crushed garlic clove
　3　teaspoons parsley, chopped
　3　ounces Irish whiskey
　4　tablespoons demi-glacé
　　　Salt and pepper from mill

Pan-fry seasoned steaks in clarified butter to medium-rare. Place steaks in serving dish. Add shallots and mushrooms to the butter, half cook them, add tomatoes, herbs, garlic. Let simmer for 5 minutes, return steaks to pan, pour whiskey over, flame and finish the sauce with the demi-glacé.

Suggested garnishes: rice pilaff, home fried potatoes, broccoli, French beans or leaf spinach

Serves: 4

Wine: Saint-Emilion
(Bordeaux)

Court of the Two Sisters
New Orleans, Louisiana

TOURNEDOS CREOLE STYLE

1　(9-ounce) fillet, cut in half
　　　horizontally
1　tablespoon butter
2　green onions, chopped fine
1　whole fresh medium tomato;
　　　skin, remove seeds and chop
1　teaspoon green pepper,
　　　chopped fine
1　small piece of bay leaf (about
　　　1/4 inch)
1　tablespoon sliced mushroom
2　ounces dry red wine
　　Salt and pepper to taste

Sauté fillet in butter on both sides for 2 minutes. Remove from pan. Add green onions, sauté lightly. Then add tomato, green pepper, bay leaf, mushrooms and red wine. Simmer over low flame for 15 minutes or until sauce is reduced one-half. Return fillets to skillet and sauté a few minutes longer.

Can be served with rice or pasta.

Serves: 2

Amelio's
San Francisco, California
Chef: Pierre Joris

VEAL ALL'AGRO DI LIMONE

1 pound veal
1 cup flour
1 tablespoon olive oil
1 cube butter
  Lemon juice
  Chopped parsley
2 ounces white wine

Cut tender slices of veal, pound them thin to 3″ x 4″. Dip in flour. Heat olive oil and butter, put in veal slices and brown on both sides. Remove veal and set aside. Pour in lemon juice and chopped parsley; shake pan then add 2 ounces white wine while still shaking pan. Gradually add another cube of butter until it is completely blended with all ingredients to serve as a sauce.

Arrange the veal slices on a hot platter. Pour the lemon sauce over the veal, garnish with slices of lemon.

Serves: 4

Wine: Soave Bolla

Bayou Belle
Bridgeton, Missouri
Chef: Eugene Alexandre

SLICED BEEF TENDERLOIN
(Old French Market Style)

1/3 medium onion, chopped very fine
1/2 teaspoon shallot, chopped fine
1/3 teaspoon garlic, chopped very fine
1/8 pound mushrooms, sliced
2 3/4 ounces butter
1/8 cup flour
1 1/3 cups beef stock or broth
1/2 cup stewed tomatoes
  Salt and pepper
1 1/4 pounds beef tenderloin, sliced
1/2 cup Burgundy wine

Sauté onions, shallots, garlic and mushrooms in 1/2 of the butter. When light brown in color, sprinkle flour over, very gradually, stirring.

Add beef stock, tomatoes, salt and pepper to taste.

Sauté beef in remaining butter in separate pan, browning both sides. Add wine and let simmer 2 or 3 minutes. Add the above sauce and bring to boiling point.

Serves: 2

Topinka Country House
Detroit, Michigan
Proprietor: Kenneth Nicholson

BRAISED SHORT RIBS OF BEEF
JARDINIÈRE

6	pounds short ribs of beef
	Salt and pepper to taste
1	stalk celery, coarsely chopped
1	clove garlic, minced
1/4	cup onions, coarsely chopped
1/2	cup flour
6	cups beef bouillon or consommé
1	cup stewed tomatoes
1/3	cup cooked green peas
1/3	cup carrots, cut into julienne strips
1/3	cup celery, cut into julienne strips

Preheat oven to 400°. Place short ribs in a roasting pan and sprinkle with salt and pepper. Bake uncovered, turning occasionally for approximately 15 minutes or until they are browned. Add the coarse-cut celery, onions and garlic and cook for 15 minutes longer. Sprinkle with flour and cook, shaking the pan occasionally, until the flour is browned. Add bouillon and tomatoes, cover the pan, reduce heat to 325°. Simmer until the meat is tender, approximately 2 hours.

Drain the sauce from the roasting pan into a saucepan and simmer for 5 minutes. Add julienne carrots, celery and the peas and cook for another 5 minutes or until the vegetables are tender.

Arrange ribs on a hot platter and spoon gravy over them to serve.

Serves: 6

Wine: Rosé

Dynasty
Honolulu, Hawaii
Chef: Kurt Wuest

TOURNEDOS MARCO POLO

8	(3-ounce) beef tenderloins
	Marinade for tenderloin: soy sauce, salt, pepper and squeezed fresh ginger
1 1/2	ounces clarified butter
8	round croutons toasted in butter
1/2	cup mushrooms, sliced
1/2	cup water chestnuts, sliced
1/2	cup bamboo shoots, cubed
3	ounces pea pods
3	ounces bean sprouts
	Salt
1/2	tablespoon oyster sauce

Marinate tenderloins for about 10 minutes. Sauté them in butter, medium-rare or the way you like them. Remove from pan and set aside. Using same pan, add pea pods, mushrooms, water chestnuts, bamboo shoots and bean sprouts. Steam constantly 2 minutes. Vegetables have to be crispy. Finish with oyster sauce and a touch of salt.

Place the tenderloins on croutons and the vegetables on top. Tournedos Marco Polo is served with Chinese fried rice.

Serves: 4

Cork 'N Cleaver Restaurant
Tucson, Arizona
Chef: Mike Ernst

STEAK "17"

3 large Bermuda onions
1/4 pound butter
1/4 pound fresh mushrooms, thick sliced
3-4 tablespoons cream sherry
    Dash salt
2 pounds top sirloin steak
    Splash cognac

Peel and slice 3 large white onions and sauté them, covered, over low heat in 1/4 pound of butter. Add generously thick sliced fresh mushrooms. Just before you serve this on your steak (which you always slice cross-grained, after char-broiling), add a generous touch of an inflammable cognac (it takes about 3 ounces to do the job well) and light, for a few moments to say the least, and for a minute at the most.

Serves: 2

Stouffer's 'Top' Restaurants
Cleveland, Ohio

TENDERLOIN OF BEEF MADEIRA

2 1/2 pounds beef tenderloin, trimmed
1/2 cup flour
1 teaspoon salt
1/4 teaspoon pepper
1/2 teaspoon dry mustard
    Dash garlic salt
1/4 pound butter
1 cup onions, chopped into 1/4" pieces
1 1/2 quarts hot beef broth
1/4 cup tomato paste
1/2 pound mushrooms (whole, if small; cut, if large)
3/4 cup pale dry Madeira wine

Cut trimmed beef tenderloin in thin slices. Mix flour, salt, pepper, mustard, and garlic salt together. Dip pieces of meat in this mixture to coat all sides lightly. Melt butter in skillet but do not burn. Add chopped onions and stir through butter. Then add pieces of meat, putting them in carefully by hand so they sauté evenly. Watch carefully and turn to brown both sides of meat. Add hot broth and tomato paste. Cover and cook gently over low heat for 35 minutes, or until meat is tender but not broken apart. The liquid should have reduced to the consistency of a thin gravy at this point. Add mushrooms and wine and cook again for 6-8 minutes, without cover. Serve slices of meat over cooked white rice. Spoon sauce on top, and garnish with chopped parsley.

Serves: 6

Chanhassen Dinner Theatre
Chanhassen, Minnesota
Chef: Thomas W. Middleton
(Sir Thomas)

SCALLOPINE CAPRICCIO—SIR THOMAS

2	tablespoons fresh butter
4	tablespoons chopped onion
1	cup cooked chopped mushrooms
1/2	cup sliced artichoke hearts
1	cup cooked asparagus tips
1	cup cooked green peas
1/4	cup white Chianti wine
12	(3-ounce) thin veal cutlets
	Salt and pepper
2	tablespoons fresh butter
1/2	teaspoon sage
1	cup thickened veal stock
1/2	cup Parmesan cheese

Sauté onions in butter until browned lightly, add mushrooms, cook for 3 minutes. Add sliced artichokes, cook for 3 minutes. Add asparagus tips, green peas and wine. Let simmer under low flame.

Pound veal cutlets to flatten. Season with salt and pepper. Place in pan after 2 tablespoons of butter and sage have been added. Brown veal cutlets for 8 minutes. Add 2 tablespoons wine and let cook until wine has reduced to half. Place over portioned vegetables—3 slices per person.

Add veal stock to pan with 2 tablespoons wine, when heated, serve over Veal Scallopine. Top with a very little Parmesan cheese.

Serves: 4

Wine: Barolo Piedmont, Mirafore

Trattoria Gatti
New York, New York
Chef: Attilio Vosilla

BEEF AND CHICKEN À LA GATTI

Chicken (Total Preparation Time—35 Minutes)

1/8	pound butter
3	tablespoons flour
1	(2 1/2-lb) chicken, boned
2	tablespoons onion, chopped
3	slices prosciutto ham, cut julienne
1/2	pound fresh mushrooms, sliced
1/2	teaspoon sage
2	bay leaves
	Salt and pepper
1	cup white wine
1	cup chicken or beef broth

Heat the butter in a saucepan. Flour the chicken and shake off the excess. When the butter is very hot, sauté the chicken in the butter until it is brown on both sides. Add onions, prosciutto, mushrooms, sage, bay leaves, salt and pepper and cook 10 minutes. Turn chicken, add white wine and cook 10 minutes more. Add broth, cover and cook 10 minutes more, or until chicken is tender.

Beef (Total Preparation Time—10-15 Minutes)

1/8	pound butter
3	tablespoons flour
4	slices (about 1 1/2 pounds) fillet mignon, cut 1 inch thick
2	shallots, chopped
	Salt and pepper
1	cup red wine
1	cup beef gravy
1	tablespoon Diable sauce

Heat the butter in a saucepan. Flour the meat and shake off the excess. When the butter is very hot, brown the meat in the butter about 2 1/2 minutes on each side. Add the shallots, salt and pepper and cook until the shallots are golden. Add the red wine and cook 5 minutes, or until the sauce gets syrupy. Add the beef gravy and Diable sauce and cook 5 minutes more.

Serves: 4

Wine: Soave Bolla

The Mövenpick Restaurants
Switzerland and Germany

TOURNEDOS MEDICI

1	tablespoon oil
4	(6-ounce) pieces tournedos
2	tablespoons butter
1/4	teaspoon rosemary leaves
1	tablespoon mustard
3	tablespoons shallots, finely chopped
2	tablespoons cognac
1/3	cup red wine
1/4	cup maderisé
1	cup mushrooms, raw, sliced
1/2	cup heavy cream
	Catsup to taste
1/2	teaspoon Worcestershire sauce
	Salt, pepper, paprika to taste
1	teaspoon French cognac

Heat oil in frying pan, sprinkle tournedos with salt and pepper and fry on both sides until rare, medium or well-done, as desired. Remove oil, add butter. Add rosemary leaves and crush them with a fork. Spread mustard on both sides of tournedos and move meat to the edge of frying pan. Add chopped shallots and turn until slightly yellow. Pour cognac over tournedos and ignite with a match. Ladle burning liquid over meat until flames are extinguished. Remove tournedos from pan and put them on a plate.

Pour red wine and maderisé in frying pan, bring to a boil and reduce 1/2 of the liquid. Reduce heat, add cream and sliced mushrooms and let simmer for about 4 minutes. Transfer the tournedos with meat juice back into frying pan, add catsup and Worcestershire sauce. Season with salt, pepper, paprika and add 1 teaspoon of French cognac for final touch. Dress tournedos on platter, pour sauce over them.

Serves: 4

Wine: Red Burgundy or
Bordeaux

La Groceria
Greenwich Village, New York
Chef: David Gould

SALTIMBOCCA ALLA ROMANA

	Flour as needed
	Salt and pepper
8	large veal scallopinis
8	slices prosciutto
1/4	pound butter
1 1/2	ounces dry white wine
1 1/2	pounds cooked spinach
	Sliced hard-boiled egg

Flour, salt and pepper the veal. Dip veal in flour. Attach prosciutto to veal with toothpicks. Sauté in pan with hot butter on fast fire.

Cook 10 minutes until veal is tender. When brown, add wine. Divide cooked spinach in 8 equal parts on a platter. Cover spinach with scallopini and prosciutto, embellish with sliced hard-boiled egg and sauce.

Serves: 4

Quo Vadis
Toronto, Canada
Chef: M. Michelangelo

ROULADE DE VEAU AU PARMESAN
(Stuffed Veal Rolls)

8 thin slices of veal
1/2 cup chopped ham
1/2 cup chopped mushrooms
2 ounces grated Parmesan cheese
2 ounces butter
1 ounce chopped parsley
1 cup bread crumbs
1/4 cup sherry
3 tablespoons flour
2 tablespoons olive oil
1/2 cup white wine
1 1/2 cups brown sauce
1/2 cup 35% cream

Flatten the veal slices as thinly as possible, season well. In a bowl mix the ham, mushrooms, cheese, 1 ounce butter, chopped parsley, bread crumbs and sherry, season well. Place the mixture equally on the veal slices. Roll in the flour.

Melt the butter slowly in a saucepan and add the olive oil. Slowly brown the rolls in it. When the rolls are brown throw away any excess fat. Add the wine to the rolls and let reduce for about 3-5 minutes, turning the rolls occasionally. Then add the brown sauce, cook slowly over a low heat for about 15-20 minutes, and just before serving add the cream. Serve with boiled noodles tossed in butter.

Serves: 4

Wine: Verdicchio

Aperitivo
New York, New York

SALSA BOLOGNESE

4 tablespoons butter
1/2 pound chopped beef
1 carrot, washed and chopped
1 stalk celery
1 onion, chopped
3 ounces prosciutto, chopped
1 pinch nutmeg
1 clove garlic, chopped
2 bay leaves
Salt and pepper to taste
1 cup dry red wine
1/2 pound tomato paste (prefer California tomato)
2 cups warm beef consommé

Melt the 4 tablespoons of butter in a heavy saucepan. Add chopped beef and brown. When the meat is browned add the carrots, celery and onions.

Sauté until onion is golden brown. Add prosciutto, nutmeg, chopped garlic, bay leaves, salt and pepper. Cook over low heat for 4 minutes.

Add red wine, cover and bring to a boil. Add tomato paste diluted with 2 cups of warm beef consommé. Cover and continue cooking for 2 hours stirring occasionally with a wooden spoon. (If sauce becomes too thick, add more consommé.)

Serves: 2

Vegetables

Golden Fox Steak House
Albany, New York
Chef: Vincent Figliomani

STUFFED BUTTERNUT SQUASH, FLORENTINE

2	butternut squash, about 1 1/2-pounds each
2	pounds frozen leaf spinach, Salt and pepper to taste
1/2	cup melted butter
1/2	cup flour
1 1/2	cups milk
1	egg yolk
	Sprinkle of Parmesan cheese
	Sprinkle of paprika

Take squash, wash and split in 4 pieces, take out all the seeds. Place pieces, skin side down, in a buttered sheet pan. Bake in moderate oven 45 minutes.

While this is baking, cook spinach, cool as soon as possible and drain. Arrange on cooked squash. Season with salt and pepper to taste.

In a saucepan put the melted butter and flour and make a smooth paste, add milk and slowly bring to boil, stirring frequently. Cook 5 minutes. Remove from fire, add egg yolk, stir constantly until smooth. Cover spinach-over-squash with sauce and sprinkle with cheese and paprika. Bake in medium-hot oven until browned.

Serves: 4

Dardanelles
New York, New York

ENGUINAR

6	medium artichokes
2-3	lemons, cut in half
	Salt
12	very small white onions
2	carrots
1	cup olive oil
3	cups water
1	teaspoon sugar

Peel artichokes until white petals show. Take 1/2 lemon and rub on each artichoke as soon as it is peeled. Then scoop up artichoke fuzz down to the meaty part. Also rub on lemon right away. (The lemon is used to stop the darkening of the artichoke.) Do not cut meaty part of artichoke. Peel the skin off each artichoke stem and lemon the skin. Drop the artichokes into a pan of salt, lemon water and sugar.

After all the artichokes are ready, put them, with their stems up, side by side in a pan and place onion in each hollow part. Place rest of onions and carrots into the pan. Add 1 cup olive oil and 3 cups plain water.

Serves: 4

Su Casa
Chicago, Illinois
Chef: Laura Valdoz

CHILE RELIENO
(Stuffed Pepper)

- 6 medium bell peppers
  Oil and vinegar
- 1 pound Monterey cream cheese
- 3 eggs
  Flour
  Cooking oil

Broil peppers evenly. Place in paper bag, close tightly. Allow to steam in closed bag for approximately 20 minutes. Remove from bag, peel outer skin. Cut 1/2 inch from stem end of pepper, remove seeds with spoon. Marinate peppers overnight in equal parts of oil and vinegar.

Next day: drain peppers and stuff with cream cheese. Separate eggs. Beat whites until stiff, fold in slightly beaten egg yolks. Roll peppers in flour, dip in egg mixture 1 at a time. Drop in deep frying pan with enough hot oil to cover. Brown evenly, remove and drain.

The sauce
- 1 medium onion, thinly sliced
- 3 tablespoons olive oil
- 1 clove garlic
- 3 #303 cans solid pack tomatoes (6 cups)
- 3 1/2 cups chicken stock
- 1/2 cup white wine
- 1 teaspoon oregano
- 1 bay leaf
- 3 teaspoons salt
- 1 teaspoon pepper

Fry onion and garlic in olive oil until onion becomes transparent. Strain tomatoes through sieve, combine with onion and garlic, add chicken stock and wine.

Add seasoning. Bring to boil, simmer for a few minutes. Correct seasoning if desired.

Twenty minutes before serving, place peppers in sauce and simmer until thoroughly heated.

Serves: 6

Venetian Room
Fort Lauderdale, Florida

EGGPLANT PARMIGIANA

- 2 whole eggplants
- 4 eggs
  Grated cheese
- 4 ounces olive oil
- 2 medium cans whole tomatoes
- 4 large slices mozzarella cheese

Bread sliced eggplant in eggs and then grated cheese. Sauté in oil. Brown both sides. Add tomatoes over the top then sliced mozzarella cheese and bake at 375° for 10 minutes or until mozzarella turns slightly brown. (Note that by breading in eggs it seals the eggplant so oil doesn't seep in.)

Serves: 4

Venetian Room
Fort Lauderdale, Florida

ZUCCHINI PROVENÇALE

2 medium cans whole tomatoes
Salt and pepper
3 tablespoons olive oil
1 large chopped onion
2 finely chopped garlic cloves
3 pounds sliced zucchini
Sprinkle of grated Parmesan cheese
Chopped parsley

Strain juice from tomatoes, reduce until thick. Add whole tomatoes, salt and pepper, and cook again until thick. In olive oil, sauté the onions and garlic. Sauté your zucchini in this mixture, add stewed tomatoes, sprinkle cheese over top and bake until top is brown and zucchini is done. Add chopped parsley before serving.

Serves: 6

The Blue Fox
San Francisco, California
Chef: Antony Penado

TOMATO TIMBALE

4 tablespoons butter
2 tablespoons finely minced onions
1/2 cup flour
1/2 teaspoon sweet basil
1/4 teaspoon nutmeg
1/2 cup sherry
1/2 cup chicken broth
1 1/2 cups (12 ounces) coarsely ground or chopped cooked broccoli
Salt and pepper to taste
8 medium-size tomatoes

Cook finely minced onions lightly in butter. Take off heat, add, all at once, 1/2 cup flour, sweet basil and nutmeg. Return to heat and add 1/2 cup sherry and chicken broth. Boil 1 minute, stirring well. Add cooked broccoli. Let cook 2-3 minutes. Add salt and pepper to taste.

Dip 8 medium-size tomatoes into boiling water and peel. Slice off 1/4 inch from bottom. Scoop out and drain well. Push tomato shells into buttered 5-ounce fluted individual molds or into small custard cups, pressing down well with palm of hand. Sprinkle with salt and pepper. Stuff with broccoli.

Bake in a pan of water in moderate 350° oven, 25 minutes. Invert, serve tomato-side up.

Serves: 8

Crest House
St. Louis, Missouri

GREEN BEAN CASSEROLE

1/4	pound margarine
3	tablespoons flour
1/2	teaspoon salt
1 1/2	pounds fresh or frozen green beans
2 1/2	cups whole milk
1/2	teaspoon white pepper
1 1/2	cups grated American cheese
4	tablespoons margarine
1	cup bread crumbs
1	teaspoon paprika

Melt margarine at low temperature, add the flour and stir until smooth. Cook about 3-5 minutes without browning and use wire whip.

Cook beans in small amount of boiling salted water, drain and set aside. Bring milk to simmering point, add salt and pepper and add grated cheese slowly, while stirring, to form a smooth sauce. Simmer 5 minutes longer. Cream sauce should be made in heavy saucepan so it will not burn. Combine green beans and cream sauce and pour into greased casserole dish.

For the topping, combine margarine with bread crumbs and paprika. Sprinkle topping over casserole. Bake at 350°, 15 minutes, until topping is browned.

Serves: 6

Blackhawk Restaurant
Chicago, Illinois

BLACKHAWK CREAMED SPINACH

2 1/2	ounces salt pork
1 1/2	ounces chopped onion
1 1/2	pounds finely ground frozen spinach
	Salt and pepper to taste
1/2	pint cream sauce (see index)

Grind salt pork fine and sauté until brown. Add chopped onion and sauté 20-30 minutes until brown. Add frozen spinach, salt and pepper to taste, and let come to a boil, stirring occasionally. Add cream sauce and cook about 35 minutes, stirring frequently.

Serves: 8

Salads, Dressings, Eggs and Sauces

David's Table
Buffalo, New York
Chef: Frank D. Insera

HOLLANDAISE SAUCE

- 3 egg yolks
- 2 tablespoons lemon juice
- 1 tablespoon boiling water
- 1/4 pound butter, melted
- Salt and cayenne pepper to taste

Combine the egg yolks and lemon juice in a pyrex or stainless steel mixing bowl. Beat together with a wire whip. Set the bowl over a pan of boiling water and continue to beat vigorously, until the egg yolks begin to thicken. Add the tablespoon of boiling water and continue to beat until the sauce has thickened again and has about doubled in volume. Remove the sauce from the water bath. Begin to add the melted butter, beating vigorously all the time. Continue until the butter has been incorporated into the egg yolks. Season sauce to taste with salt and cayenne pepper.

Yields: 2 servings

Le Profil
Denver, Colorado
Chef: Klaus Christ

CRAUTE AU CHAMPIGNONS
(Mushroom Toast)

- 1/2 onion, chopped
- Thyme
- 1/2 stick butter or margarine
- 1 1/2 pounds fresh mushrooms, sliced
- 2 tablespoons flour
- 1/2 cup white wine
- 1 cup brown sauce
- Salt and pepper
- 1 cup coffee cream
- 8 slices toast

Simmer the onions and the thyme in the butter until golden brown. Add the mushrooms and simmer for about 10 minutes. Mix in the flour and add the white wine, brown sauce, salt and pepper. Let simmer on low heat for about 15 minutes. Add cream slowly. Serve on toast.

Serves: 4

Yamato
Century Plaza Hotel
Los Angeles, California
Chef: Taijai Asai

CUCUMBER SALAD
(Sunomono)

1 1/4 quarts cucumbers, peeled and
       thinly sliced
  1 teaspoon salt
  1 cup cider vinegar
3/4 cup sugar
  1 teaspoon M S G

Marinate cucumbers in salt. Squeeze out excess liquid. Mix together remaining ingredients. Pour a little over cucumbers; squeeze out excess liquid. When ready to serve, add the remainder of the dressing to the cucumbers and put a small amount of cucumber salad in each individual bowl. Garnish with cooked crab, shrimp, abalone and tomato slice.

Serves: 6

Whipple House
West Branch, Iowa

WHIPPLE HOUSE SALAD

  1 (10 1/2-ounce) can condensed
      tomato soup
1 1/2 tablespoons unflavored gelatin
1/2 cup cold water
  2 (3-ounce) packages cream
      cheese
  1 cup mayonnaise
  1 cup diced celery
  2 tablespoons finely diced green
      pepper
  1 teaspoon chopped onion
1/2 cup sliced stuffed olives

Heat soup. Add gelatin which has been softened in cold water. Cool. Add other ingredients. Chill until firm.

Serves: 8 to 10

Mayfair Hotel
St. Louis, Missouri
Chef: John Johnson

MAYFAIR DRESSING

  1 button garlic
  1 rib celery
1/2 medium onion
  1 (2-ounce) can flat anchovies
  1 teaspoon ground black pepper
  1 heaping teaspoon Accent
1/2 teaspoon sugar
  2 tablespoons salad mustard
  1 tablespoon lemon juice
  2 cups salad oil
  3 eggs

You really should have a blender to do this dressing properly; it is the only way to produce the smooth, creamy emulsion that makes it perfect.

Peel and slice the garlic; scrape and slice the celery. Peel and slice the onion. Put these, together with the anchovies, mustard, lemon juice, and all other ingredients except the raw eggs, into a blender and whirl for about 2 seconds. Add the eggs and blend again for a few seconds.

Now add 2 cups salad oil a little at a time, blend between each addition, then blend a few seconds more after all the oil has been added.

This keeps well—for 2 weeks or so—in the refrigerator. Use on romaine, spinach, or head lettuce with crisp-toasted croutons.

Yields: 1 quart

L'Orangerie
New York, New York

SALADE NIÇOISE

        3   cans (6 1/2-ounces) tuna fish,
              drained and chilled
        2   cups cooked string beans, cut
              into 1-inch pieces and chilled
        1   cup potatoes, cooked, diced and
              chilled
      1/4 cup green pepper, diced and
              chilled
      1/2 cup celery, diced and chilled
             Salt and pepper to taste
             Oil and vinegar
             Lettuce leaves from 1 large head
       24 anchovy fillets, drained
       12 black olives, pitted
        2   hard-boiled eggs, shelled, quar-
              tered and chilled
             Tomato wedges, peeled and
              chilled

Combine tuna, beans, potatoes, celery
and green pepper in salad bowl; season
with salt and pepper. Toss with oil and
vinegar as desired. Arrange lettuce leaves
on serving plates; spoon salad onto lettuce. Arrange anchovy fillets and olives
over and around salad. Garnish with
quartered eggs and tomato wedges.

Serves: 6

The Fontainebleau
Miami Beach, Florida
Chef: William Fleischman

CHINESE SALAD

        2   large heads romaine lettuce,
              shredded
        1   cup canned bean sprouts
        1   cup canned water chestnuts,
              sliced fine
        1   cup bamboo shoots, cut julienne
        1   cup canned mushrooms, sliced
              fine
        1   cup tomatoes, chopped
        8   slices crisply cooked bacon,
              chopped fine
        2   tablespoons chopped green on-
              ions, sliced fine

Wash the shredded romaine and place
well-drained into a large salad bowl. In
small bouquets, on top of the romaine,
place the bean sprouts (well-drained),
water chestnuts, bamboo shoots and
mushrooms. In the center of the bowl, on
top of the romaine, place the chopped
tomatoes. Sprinkle the chopped bacon
and green onions over the entire salad.

Dressing

        1   cup mayonnaise
             Juice of 1/2 lemon
        2   ounces soy sauce
      1/2 teaspoon Accent

Combine the mayonnaise, lemon juice,
soy sauce and Accent in a bowl and mix
well. Pour dressing over the salad, toss
well and serve.

Serves: 8

Ports O' Call
Dallas, Texas
Prop: Alfred D. Ucci

MAUTE LUAU DRESSING

4	ounces celery salt
1 1/2	ounces cracked India pepper
2	ounces M S G
1/2	ounce garlic powder or puree of garlic
1	ounce dry powdered mustard
1	ounce shallots, minced fine
1 1/2	gallons salad oil
1	gallon sweet and sour mix (1 quart lime juice and 1 quart simple syrup)
3/4	pint capers
1/2	ounce onion juice

Combine all dry ingredients and blend well. Combine all wet ingredients and blend well. Combine the 2 mixtures and mix well.

Dressing must stand for a minimum of 3 hours before use so that all flavoring is blended.

LUAU TABLE

1	pound sliced fresh mushrooms, marinated in Luau dressing 3 hours
2	pounds fresh watercress, washed and cleaned
1	pound fresh pea pods, deveined, washed and cut in diagonals. (Chill in refrigerator, place on frozen plate upon serving—top with the fruit sections and dressing—serve with frozen fork.)
1/4	pound scallion tops, cut fine, chilled
2	pounds cooked shrimp, diced
2	pounds cooked lobster tails, cut into tiny medallions
2	pounds cooked crab legs, cut into small pieces
126	grapefruit sections
126	mandarin orange sections

Wash mushrooms thoroughly with stems on, slice thin and marinate in Luau dressing for 3 hours, remove. Add next 3 items to mushrooms and toss lightly. Add all seafood and toss lightly. Top each salad with 3 grapefruit sections and 3 mandarin sections. Lay 2 ounces of Luau dressing over all and serve.

Yields: About 12 portions

Willoway Manor
Naperville, Illinois

CAHIO BEAN SALAD

1	(#2) can green beans
1	(#2) can wax beans
1	(#2) can kidney beans
1/4	cup chopped onions
1/2	cup chopped celery
2 1/2	cups sugar
1 1/2	cups white vinegar
1	tablespoon salt
1/4	teaspoon white pepper
1/4	celery salt
1/2	cup oil

Place all 3 beans into large bowl—save liquid drained from beans. Mix all other ingredients with liquid from beans. Pour over beans. Cover and place in refrigerator for at least 24 hours to marinate.

Serves: 10 to 12

L'Orangerie
New York, New York

SALADE NICE-PLACE

    1   pound cooked shrimp, coarsely
        chopped and chilled
    1   cup cooked mussels, chilled
  1/2   pound cooked lobster, cut into
        chunks and chilled
    1   pound cooked crab meat, mem-
        branes removed and meat
        chilled
  1/2   cup celery, diced and chilled
        Salt and pepper
    2   cups mayonnaise
    2   tablespoons Dijon mustard
        Shredded lettuce
    2   hard-boiled eggs, shelled, quar-
        tered and chilled
        Tomato wedges, peeled and
        chilled
        Watercress
        Chopped chives

Combine shrimp, mussels, lobster, crab meat and celery. Season with salt and pepper. Combine mayonnaise with mustard, toss through seafood mixture. Arrange lettuce in serving bowl or on individual plate; spoon on seafood mixture. Garnish with quartered eggs, tomato wedges and watercress. Sprinkle chives over all.

Serves: 6

100 West
Kansas City, Missouri
Chef: Troy Bedford

100 WEST SAUCE

    1   cup Midget Jack cheese
    3   teaspoons blue cheese crumbles
        or bleu cheese bulk
    1   pound ground beef

Melt desired amount of diced Midget Jack cheese in a double boiler until smooth.

Add 1/2 the amount of blue cheese, stirring until blended. Pour in a metal container to keep warm. (Hold until ready to serve.)

When hamburger is finished, pour 1 1/2 teaspoons of Bleu cheese over top of hamburger, place on bun and serve.

Serves: 2

David's Table
Buffalo, New York
Chef: Frank D. Insera

LOBSTER BISQUE SAUCE

  1/4   pound melted butter
    2   tablespoons paprika
    2   cups flour
    1   can lobster bisque
  1/2   cup cream sherry

Melt butter. Add paprika and flour to make roux. Add lobster bisque and cream sherry and let cook together for 20 minutes. Strain sauce through a fine sieve.

Serves: 2

Seven Eagles Restaurant
Desplaines, Illinois

CAESAR SALAD À LA SEVEN EAGLES

     Salt
     Fresh ground pepper
3   cloves garlic
15   anchovy fillets
1/4 teaspoon dry mustard
1/4 teaspoon Worcestershire sauce
5   sprigs watercress
     Parmesan cheese
1   lemon
3   tablespoons wine vinegar
8   tablespoons olive oil
3   eggs (place in bowl of hot water)
3   heads romaine lettuce
     Croutons
6   slices Italian bread, sliced about
         1/4 inch
     Creamed butter
1   garlic clove
     Olive oil
     Lemon juice
     Meat, poultry or seafood
         (optional)

Start with large wooden salad bowl. Add salt, pepper and garlic to bowl. Mash ingredients into side of bowl, with large spoon, until paste is formed. Add anchovies and, again, mash with spoon to form paste. Then add dry mustard, Worcestershire sauce, watercress and 1 teaspoon Parmesan cheese. Mix coarsely until watercress is mashed. Add juice of lemon squeezed either through cheesecloth or linen napkin. Add wine vinegar and olive oil. Using both a large spoon and fork in same hand, mix all ingredients using a beating motion. Separate eggs, add just the yolks to salad and again mix, using both spoon and fork in a beating motion.

Cut romaine lettuce in coarse pieces, dry in linen cloth and add to bowl. Toss gently from the sides of bowl upward until completely mixed. Add croutons and 4 tablespoons Parmesan cheese, toss gently. Place salad on chilled plate or bowl, add fresh ground pepper and cheese to each serving.

To prepare croutons: spread each bread slice with creamed butter. Make garlic paste using garlic clove, olive oil and lemon juice. Spread garlic paste on bread. Toast in pan over low heat for 5-10 minutes until golden brown. Cut into small squares, add to salad.

Seven Eagles suggests that you add your favorite meat, poultry or seafood after the croutons, again gently tossing until mixed.

Serves: 6

Danny's
Baltimore, Maryland

CAESAR SALAD

1   garlic clove
3   ounces olive oil
6   ounces romaine lettuce inside
         leaves, washed
1/2 teaspoon Lea and Perrins sauce
     Dash salt
1   teaspoon freshly ground pepper
1   raw egg
1   lemon
2   ounces croutons (see index)
2   ounces Parmesan cheese
4   large flat Spanish anchovies

Mash completely 1 clove of garlic in mortar using pestle. Mix with olive oil and pour over romaine lettuce in wooden salad bowl. Add Lea and Perrins sauce, salt and pepper.

Add egg and toss lightly. Add juice of lemon and toss lightly. Add croutons and

---

Parmesan cheese and toss again. Cut anchovies up into bite-size pieces and add to salad. Toss salad and serve.

Serves: 2

L'Orangerie
New York, New York

LA "TALL SALADE"

    4 celery stalks, trimmed and
          quartered
    1 head Iceberg lettuce, trimmed
          and quartered
    6 scallions, trimmed
    8 carrot sticks, peeled
    8 white and red radishes, trimmed
    8 whole raw mushrooms, trimmed
    1 bunch fennel, green tops left on
    1 cup cauliflower, trimmed and
          cut into flowerets
    8 cherry tomatoes
    2 whole green peppers
    2 hard-boiled eggs, unshelled

Wash all vegetables thoroughly. Using wooden bucket filled with chipped or shaved ice as "bowl," plunge long vegetables vertically into center of ice. Arrange remaining vegetables around sides, alternating colors to resemble bouquet of flowers. Peel the eggs whole and center in bucket.

Serves: 4

Italian Village
Chicago, Illinois

INSALATA VERDE
(Italian Dressing for Green Salads)

    2 anchovy fillets
  1/2 teaspoon prepared mustard
    1 tablespoon wine vinegar or
          lemon juice
    1 tablespoon olive oil
       Garlic
       Salt and pepper

Chop and mash 2 anchovy fillets, combine with garlic, mustard, salt and freshly ground pepper, wine vinegar and olive oil.

    1 head of endive, leaves separated
          and cut lengthwise
    1 small head of fennel, cut in thin
          slices
    2 radishes, sliced

In a salad bowl combine the above ingredients, well-washed and cleaned. Pour the dressing over the salad and toss well.

Serves: 2

Smoke House
Burbank, California

GARLIC BREAD

  1/4 pound butter or margarine
  1/4 teaspoon granulated garlic
    1 loaf sour dough French bread
  1/2 cup grated American cheese

Soften butter and add garlic. Split bread lengthwise and warm in 375° oven. Spread bread with garlic butter and sprinkle with cheese, place under broiler until brown, slice and serve.

Serves: 4

The Cloister
Buffalo, New York

SADDLE DRESSING

1   head lettuce
2   tomatoes
1   teaspoon crushed garlic
1/2   cup 100% Italian olive oil
1/4   cup tarragon vinegar
2   eggs
1   teaspoon celery salt
1   teaspoon sweet basil
1   whole peppercorn
    Salt
    Italian grating cheese
1/4   pound dried bacon
1/2   cup minced onion

Break lettuce with hands, peel tomatoes, and cut in quarters. Rub bowl with crushed garlic. In a separate bowl, pour a liberal amount of olive oil; add tarragon vinegar proportionately; add eggs and seasoning to taste. Sprinkle with grated cheese. Pour dressing over salad and sprinkle with bacon, grated cheese and minced onions.

Serves: 4

Old House Restaurant
Louisville, Kentucky

OLD HOUSE EGGS BENEDICT

6   thin slices old Kentucky ham or baked ham
2   tablespoons butter
6   split toasted English muffin halves
6   poached eggs
    Famous Old House Hollandaise sauce, procured in all finer gourmet food shops (or see index)
    Cracked black pepper
    Chopped fresh or dried tarragon

Sauté ham in butter for 5 minutes until lightly browned. Place a slice of ham on each muffin half. Top with poached egg and liberally spoon Hollandaise sauce over it. Place on serving dish under broiler 1 minute. Remove from broiler and sprinkle, just before serving, with cracked black pepper and tarragon to taste. Excellent for lunch or late supper.

Serves: 6

Wine: Good French château

David's Table
Buffalo, New York
Chef: Frank D. Insera

BÉCHAMEL SAUCE

4   tablespoons butter
6   tablespoons flour
1   small onion
2   cups milk
2   cups chicken stock
    Salt, cayenne pepper and dry mustard to taste

Melt butter, add the flour and stir with a wooden spoon for 2-3 minutes to make a white roux. Scald the milk mixture and allow it to simmer with onion for a few minutes. Remove onion, add milk to the roux and beat vigorously with a wire whip. Return the sauce to the fire and cook for 2-3 minutes. Season sauce to taste with salt, cayenne pepper and dry mustard. Strain sauce through a fine sieve.

Yields: 16 ounces

SECTION THREE

Crêpes   *Soufflés*   *Desserts*

Crêpes

Señor Pico
San Francisco, California

GREEN ENCHILADAS WITH SOUR CREAM

2 cups cottage cheese
1 pound New York white Cheddar, shredded
1/4 cup cooked onions, chopped
1/4 cup crushed tostadas
2 tablespoons chopped olives
2 tablespoons chopped jalapeno chilies
1 teaspoon salt
1 teaspoon M S G
12 tortillas
Oil
Green Enchilada sauce
1/2 pint sour cream

Mix cheese, onions, tostadas, olives and chilies; add seasonings. Fry tortillas in oil until soft and pliable—not crisp. Drain and dip into Green Enchilada sauce, coating both sides completely. Place filling in center of prepared tortillas and roll. Place in greased baking dish with overlapped edges down.

Pour Green Enchilada sauce over rolled cheese enchiladas and bake in moderate oven until piping hot. Top with sour cream after removing enchiladas from oven.

Green Enchilada Sauce

2 cans cream of mushroom soup
2 small cans (3 1/2-ounces) Ortega chilies
1 large onion, chopped
1 clove garlic, minced
1 can chicken broth
1/2 cup raw spinach, pureed
1/2 teaspoon salt
1 teaspoon M S G
2 tablespoons flour

Puree mushroom soup, chilies, onion and garlic in blender. Add to chicken broth and bring to a boil. Add pureed spinach and seasonings and let simmer 10 to 15 minutes. Thicken with flour mixed with a little cold water. Stir into sauce and bring to a boil. Reduce heat and stir constantly to avoid lumping. Correct seasonings.

Serves: 6

The Empress
London, England
Chef: Gino Scandolo

CRÊPES DE VOLAILLE FLORENTINE

1/2	pint milk
1/4	pint water
6	ounces flour
2	eggs
1/4	ounce olive oil or melted butter
1/2	turkey breast or 2 chicken breasts
1/4	pint Béchamel sauce (see index)
1/4	pint double cream
	Glass white wine
	Seasoning
3-4	pounds leaf spinach
1	pint Mornay sauce with 2 eggs yolks added (see index)
2	ounces grated Parmesan cheese

To prepare the pancakes: pour the milk and water in a mixing bowl and whisk in the flour until there are no lumps. Fold in the beaten eggs and salt. Whisk in oil or butter and leave mixture for at least 2 hours before cooking. Make 12 pancakes and leave aside to cool.

Chop the white meat finely and mix with Béchamel, cream and white wine. Warm lightly but no more. Put a layer of cooked spinach in a fireproof serving dish. Fill the pancakes with the mixture and roll up. Place on top of the spinach. Coat with hot cheese and glaze slowly under the grill or on upper shelf of moderate oven long enough to let heat penetrate through to the spinach. Serve hot and well-browned.

Serves: 6

L'Orangerie
New York, New York

CRÊPES SUZETTE ORANGERIE

1	cup sifted all-purpose flour
1/2	teaspoon salt
1	tablespoon sugar
3	eggs, well beaten
2	cups milk
2	tablespoons melted butter
1	tablespoon cognac
2	oranges
10	lumps sugar
1/2	cup softened sweet butter
1	teaspoon lemon juice
1/4	cup Grand Marnier
1/4	cup cognac

Crêpes (allow 3 crêpes per person): sift together flour, salt and 1 tablespoon sugar into mixing bowl. Combine eggs, milk, melted butter and 1 tablespoon cognac. Stir in flour mixture. Allow batter to stand 1 hour to improve flavor and texture. Heat a 6-inch crêpe pan or skillet and brush bottom with melted butter. For each crêpe, pour in 2 tablespoons batter. (Spread batter evenly over bottom of pan). Cook, turning once, until nicely browned. Fold crêpes into quarters and keep warm.

Orangerie Sauce
Wash oranges well and dry thoroughly. Rub sugar lumps over skin of orange and then crush lumps into chafing dish. Squeeze juice from oranges into chafing dish. Add butter and lemon juice; cook, stirring constantly, until butter and sugar have melted. Add Grand Marnier and cognac; ignite and quickly pour over crêpes. Serve crêpes flaming.

Serves: 2

Camelot Restaurant
Minneapolis, Minnesota
Proprietor: Hans Skalle
Chef: Jage Eriksen

CRÊPES SUZETTE CAMELOT

- 2/3 cup flour
- 1 tablespoon sugar
  Pinch of salt
- 2 whole eggs and 2 yolks
- 1 3/4 cups milk
- 2 tablespoons melted butter
- 1 tablespoon rum or cognac

Sift together the flour, sugar and pinch of salt. Beat together 2 whole eggs and 2 egg yolks and add them to the dry ingredients. Add 1 3/4 cups milk and stir the mixture until it is smooth. Add 2 tablespoons melted butter and 1 tablespoon rum or cognac. Let the batter stand for 2 hours before using. To cook the crêpes, melt just enough butter in a hot pan to coat it thinly. Pour in a thin layer of crêpe batter. The crêpe should set and become brown in about 1 minute. Turn it over to brown the other side.

Sauce for crêpes

- 1/2 cup sugar
- 8 ounces fresh orange juice
- 1/8 pound sweet butter
  Peel of orange (include some of the yellow)
  Peel of lemon (include some of the yellow)
- 1 ounce Benedictine
- 1 ounce yellow chartreuse
- 1 ounce cognac

Caramelize sugar lightly, making sure it does not burn. Add orange juice, peel and butter. Reduce to about 1/3 of liquid. Then add crêpes one by one, turning them over so they are well saturated with the sauce. Fold or roll pancakes. Pour over 1 ounce each of Benedictine, yellow chartreuse and cognac. Ignite and serve quickly, pouring sauce over.

Serves: 4

David's Table
Buffalo, New York
Chef: Frank D. Insera

FRENCH CRÊPES

- 8 ounces crab meat, chopped
- 1/2 cup Béchamel sauce (see index)
- 2 crêpes (see index)
- 1/2 cup lobster bisque sauce
- 1 tablespoon Hollandaise sauce (see index)
- 4 tablespoons cream, whipped
- 1 tablespoon grated Romano cheese

Mix crab meat with Béchamel sauce. Place crab meat mixture in crêpe and fold crêpe. In a saucepan, add lobster bisque sauce, Hollandaise sauce and whipped cream. Stir until well-mixed. Place sauce over crêpes and sprinkle with cheese. Place under broiler until brown.

Serves: 1

Wine: Chablis

LA SCALA
HOLLYWOOD, CALIFORNIA
Steak and Peppers au Cognac

TRADER VIC'S
SAN FRANCISCO, CALIFORNIA
Prop: Victor J. Bergeron
Empress Chicken

THE NEWPORTER INN

NEWPORT BEACH, CALIFORNIA

Chef: Oscar Zink

Oscar's Rack of Lamb

L'Orangerie
New York, New York

CRÊPES DE VOLAILLE À LA REINE

    6   eggs, beaten
    2   cups milk
  1/4   cup melted butter
  1/2   teaspoon salt
    2   cups sifted all-purpose flour
    2   tablespoons butter
    3   cups cooked, diced chicken
    1   cup cooked, chopped
        mushrooms
    2   cups medium cream sauce (see
        index)
  1/4   cup dry sherry wine
    1   teaspoon salt
        Pinch cayenne pepper

To prepare crêpes: combine eggs, milk, 1/4 cup melted butter and 1/2 teaspoon salt in mixing bowl; fold in flour just until smooth. Heat and butter lightly a 5-inch crêpe pan or skillet. Pour in about 2 tablespoons batter, tipping pan so batter will cover bottom of pan evenly. Cook over medium heat until nicely browned, turn and brown other side. Stack crêpes and keep warm.

To prepare filling: melt 2 tablespoons butter in saucepan; add chicken and mushrooms and sauté lightly. Stir in cream sauce, sherry, salt and cayenne pepper, bring to boil. Adjust seasoning as desired and use as filling for crêpes.

Serves: 6

T. Pittari's
New Orleans, Louisiana

CRÊPES SUZETTE

    3   eggs
    3   ounces flour
  1/2   pint milk
    1   ounce kirschwasser
  1/8   pound butter
   12   tablespoons sugar
    2   oranges
        Lemon peels from 1 lemon
  3/4   ounce Cointreau
  3/4   ounce Grand Marnier
    2   ounces brandy

Beat eggs and flour until smooth. Add milk, keep the batter thin. Fry the pancakes paper-thin in a very small frying pan with butter. Do not lay cakes on one another. Do not fold them.

For the sauce, have the soufflé pan heated. Place sugar in pan. Heat well but do not scorch. Cut oranges and lemon peels and squeeze juice into mixture. Mix and let simmer for 10-15 minutes until sauce becomes a light syrup. Add Cointreau and Grand Marnier. Place cakes in sauce and cover with sauce on both sides. Fold each cake in 1/2 and then in quarters. Lastly pour the brandy. Tilt the pan and move rapidly, but gently, back and forth over the flame until the liquor ignites. Then level the pan and continue forward and backward movement until flame on cake dies. Serve the cakes, 2 to a person and pour remainder of the sauce over each serving.

Serves: 6

Georges Rey Restaurant
Français
New York, New York
Chef: André Ledoux

CRÊPES GEORGES REY

```
 9    tablespoons flour
 1    tablespoon sugar
      Pinch of salt
 3    eggs
 1    teaspoon melted butter
 2    cups milk
 2    tablespoons butter
 3    chopped shallots
 1    tablespoon chopped onion
 1    cup dry white wine
 1    cup tomato puree
 2    tablespoons Béchamel sauce
      (see index)
3/4   pound crab meat
 1    pint whipped cream
      Salt and pepper to taste
 1    cup Béchamel sauce (additional)
1/2   pint whipped cream (additional)
```

To 9 tablespoons flour add 1 tablespoon sugar and pinch of salt. Beat in eggs, 1 at a time, then add melted butter and milk. When batter is smooth, butter a 5-inch skillet or crêpe pan and pour a small amount of batter on the heated pan. Turn with spatula so it is cooked on both sides. Keep warm. (Makes 18)

Crab meat filling: in 2 tablespoons butter sauté chopped shallots and chopped onion. Then add 1 cup dry white wine, tomato puree, Béchamel sauce, crab meat, whipped cream and salt and pepper to taste. Bring to a boil and simmer. Then drop a spoonful of mixture on each crêpe and roll up around the filling.

To 1 cup of Béchamel sauce add 1/2 pint whipping cream, whipped. Mix and pour over crêpes. Place under broiler for a minute or so until sauce is browned.

Serves: 6

Quo Vadis
New York, New York

CRÊPES QUO VADIS

```
      Diced shrimp, lobster, scallops
       and crab meat for filling
      Curry sauce
 2    cups prepared pancake mix
 1    cup milk
 2    eggs
      Dash salt
 2    tablespoons melted butter
      Dash whipped cream
```

Sauté the seafood in butter. Add a light curry sauce and bring to boil for 5 minutes. Glacing: light cream sauce, 2 egg yolks cooked together and add some whipped cream. Fill pancakes with seafood, pour glacing over it and brown under flame.

Serves: 1

Bretton's Restaurant
Kansas City, Missouri
Chef: Gus Riedi

CRÊPES JOEL

```
 8    ounces flour
 1    pint milk
 4    egg yolks
 2    whole eggs
 1    ounce sugar
 2    ounces melted butter
 1    ounce cognac
 2    orange rinds
 1    lemon rind
      Vanilla ice cream
      Chocolate sauce
      Sliced almonds
```

Stir together the flour and milk. Mix the egg yolks, eggs, sugar, melted butter, cognac, orange and lemon rinds into batter, let stand about 20 minutes, then strain and make small crêpes. Prepare crêpes as for crêpes suzette, 2 per person (see index).

Place 1 crêpe on plate. On this crêpe put a scoop of vanilla ice cream. On top of this place the second crêpe. Prepare a chocolate sauce which is heated. In this sauce pour some rum, then flame and pour sauce over crêpes. Garnish with almonds.

Serves: 12

Wine: Champagne

Atlantis
San Diego, California

CRÊPE TUNA VERONIQUE

1	glass California white wine
2	tablespoons chopped shallots
8	ounces bay shrimp
1	pint white sauce
24	ounces tuna
	Lemon juice
2	minced shallots
1	cup oyster water
2	cups fish stock
2	tablespoons butter
2	tablespoons flour
1/4	teaspoon lemon juice
1 1/8	cups sifted flour
4	tablespoons sugar
	Pinch salt
3	eggs
1 1/2	cups milk
1	tablespoon butter
1	tablespoon cognac

Combine wine and shallots and bring to a boil; then add shrimp, simmer 5 minutes, blend into white sauce, stirring constantly until mixture boils. Add tuna and lemon juice, stir briefly. Stuff crêpe with combination, roll and garnish with white sauce.

To prepare white sauce: combine minced shallots and oyster water in large saucepan and bring to boiling point over high heat. Add fish stock to hot mixture, cover pan and remove from heat. Melt butter in another large pan and blend flour into melted butter to make a thick roux, stirring constantly, over medium-low heat, until mixture thickens. Add lemon juice, cover pan and remove from heat.

To prepare crêpes: sift into a bowl 1 1/8 cups flour, 4 tablespoons sugar and a pinch of salt. Combine beaten eggs and 1 1/2 cups milk and stir into the dry ingredients. Continue to stir until the batter is smooth. Stir in 1 tablespoon each of melted butter and cognac and let stand for 2 hours. In a frying pan, heat a piece of sweet butter the size of a small walnut. When the butter begins to bubble, pour in enough of the batter—about 1 generous tablespoon—to cover the bottom of the pan with a thin layer. Cook the crêpe for about 1 minute on each side. Flip it over and cook for another minute on the other side. Stack the crêpes flat, one on top of the other, until all are baked.

Serves: 6

Wine: Chablis

Cork 'N Cleaver Restaurant
Boulder, Colorado
Chef: Bob Gonzales

GONZALES TACOS WITH CHICKEN

Cooking oil
Canned, frozen or fresh tortillas
 (Get them fresh if you can)
Shredded chicken (see below)
Shredded lettuce
Little chopped Bermuda onion
Shredded mild Cheddar

Pour 1/2 inch oil into skillet. When the oil is hot, add a tortilla. It will go limp almost immediately. Fold it in half (remember to use tongs) keeping the edges of the tortilla apart, until it becomes crisp. Turn and lightly cook the other side. Paper towels are good drainers. Repeat until you have all the taco shells you'll need (figure 2-3 per person).

2 large whole chicken breasts
1 cup chicken broth
1 teaspoon salt

Place chicken in large skillet with broth and salt. Cover and simmer about 30 minutes (let it get tender). Let cool to finger temperature, remove skin and bones and shred the meat. Refrigerate until ready to use.

Fill each taco shell with shredded chicken, lettuce, Bermuda onion and Cheddar.

Ortega Chili Sauce
2 tablespoons onion, chopped
1 clove garlic, minced
1 tablespoon oil
3 cups tomatoes, peeled, seeded and chopped
1/2 teaspoon oregano
1/2 teaspoon salt
1 tablespoon canned green ortega chilis

Sauté the garlic and onion. After a few minutes, add the tomatoes, oregano and salt—let cook a few more minutes. Stir in the chopped chilis and remove from heat. Let cool before eating.

Serves: 4

The Forum of the XII Caesars
New York, New York
Chef: Claude Recher

THE CRÊPES OF VENUS WITH GINGER AND ICE CREAM

3 butter patties
5 teaspoons fine sugar
 Juice of 1 orange
 Crêpes (see index)
 Ginger
 Rum, Grand Marnier and brandy mixed to 2 ounces

Melt butter in crêpe suzette pan, add sugar. Cook until the sugar starts to brown. Squeeze the juice of 1 orange and mix well.

Prepare the basic crêpes and place crêpe in pan with sauce. Warm the crêpe. Place the ginger in the pan to heat. Fold crêpe in half. Place ginger on crêpe. Fold crêpe in half again making the crêpe folded in quarters. Remove pan from fire. Add 2 ounces of flaming mixture by premixing rum, Grand Marnier, brandy and flaming. Add ice cream on one side of dish.

Serves: 1

Au Bon Vivant
Manila, Philippines
Chef: Joel Gerodot

CRÊPE MONTAIGNE

  3 eggs
1/4 cup cooking oil
  1 cup all-purpose flour
  1 pint fresh milk
  1 quart cooking oil
  1 cup cooked mussel meat
  1 cup cooked shrimp, shelled
  1 cup fillet lapu-lapu, cut into small pieces
  1 cup smoked salmon, sliced
    French dressing
1/3 cup melted butter
1/2 cup parsley
    Salt and pepper to taste
  3 eggs, lightly beaten
    Bread crumbs
  1 piece American lemon

To prepare crêpes: in a large bowl beat the eggs lightly, add cooking oil, flour and 1/2 of milk. Blend well with a hand-beater until smooth. Add rest of the milk. Stir and strain. Preheat crêpe pan over low flame for about 3 minutes. Gradually pour some mixture just to cover surface, return to flame until dry, then turn pancake over. Continue making and set aside.

To prepare filling: preheat cooking oil. Combine mussel, shrimp, fillet of fish and salmon. Pour over French dressing and melted butter. Sprinkle parsley and season with salt and pepper. Mix well.

Fill the prepared crêpe by placing about 1/2 cup filling on one side, then fold crêpe to other side to secure filling. Soak crêpe in beaten eggs and roll out in bread crumbs. Fry slowly over low flame until golden brown. Flake parsley by frying gradually in hot oil. Use as garnish on top of Crêpe Montaigne with twists of lemon. Serve with Tartare sauce on side.

Tartare Sauce
    2 cups mayonnaise
2 1/2 tablespoons chopped parsley
2 1/2 tablespoons French capers
  1/2 cup chopped onions
      Cognac to taste, if desired

Combine all ingredients and stir.

Serves: 2

David's Table
Buffalo, New York
Chef: Frank D. Insera

CRÊPES A LA DAVID

1/2 cup flour
  1 cup milk
  2 tablespoons oil
    Salt and cayenne pepper to taste
  2 eggs
  1 egg yolk

Beat the flour, milk, oil, salt and pepper together. Add the eggs and the egg yolk and beat the batter until smooth. Let the batter rest for 1/2 hour in the refrigerator. Lightly grease an iron crêpe pan with oil and heat it over a high flame. Put about 3 tablespoons of the batter in the pan and quickly rotate the pan so that the batter coats the pan evenly and thinly. Brown the crêpe on one side, loosen the edge and turn the crêpe to bake on the other side.

Serves: 4

The Forum of the XII Caesars
New York, New York
Chef: Claude Recher

L'Etoile
San Francisco, California
Chef: Marcel Drozon

A BASIC CRÊPE MIX

3 3/4	cups sifted flour
1	cup minus 2 tablespoons fine sugar
	Pinch salt
1/2	teaspoon vanilla extract
8	whole eggs and 4 yolks
3	cups milk
2-3	tablespoons fresh thick cream
2-3	tablespoons cognac or other liqueur
2	tablespoons butter, heated to slightly nutty color

Combine the sifted flour, sugar, pinch of salt and vanilla extract into a bowl. Add 8 whole eggs and 4 yolks, one by one, working the batter with a wooden spoon. When this preparation is properly amalgamated, add 3 cups milk, cream and cognac to the batter. Add heated butter. Place crêpe in crêpe suzette pan on stove with moderate heat. The cooler the pan the thinner the pancake. Bake until light brown on both sides. Let cool.

Serves: 4

CRÊPES SOUFFLÉS JOYEUSE SOPHIE

1/2	pound butter
20	ounces flour
1	quart milk
11	ounces sugar
14	egg yolks
3	ounces Grand Marnier
14	egg whites
1	ounce sugar
6	French pancakes (crêpes—see index)

Melt butter, blend in flour, add milk and sugar and stir until mixture becomes thick. Blend in egg yolks and Grand Marnier. Whip egg whites, not too stiff, and add 1 ounce sugar. Fold egg whites into ingredients.

Take 6 French pancakes and put soufflé mixture into each pancake. Fold pancake in half. Place in oven at 450° for 15 minutes. Remove from oven and sprinkle with confectioner's sugar and serve.

Serves: 4 to 6

Wine: Château d'Yquem

Soufflés

L'Orangerie
New York, New York

SOUFFLÉ ORANGERIE GIVRE

- 8 large oranges
- 8 teaspoons currant jelly
- 8 egg yolks
- 1 cup sugar
  Grated rind of 2 oranges
- 2 ounces Grand Marnier
- 2 cups heavy cream, whipped
- 1 tablespoon sifted confectioner's sugar

Cut a slice across each orange about 1/4 from the top; scoop out oranges. Spoon 1 teaspoon currant jelly into bottom of each orange shell. In top of double boiler, beat egg yolks and sugar together over hot boiling water until thick and foamy. Remove from heat but continue beating until cool. Blend in orange rind, Grand Marnier and about 3/4 of the whipped cream. Spoon equal amounts of mixture into each orange shell; freeze. Sweeten remaining whipped cream slightly with confectioner's sugar. Just before serving, pipe or spoon rosette of sweetened whipped cream over each orange.

Serves: 4

Quo Vadis
New York, New York

SOUFFLÉ PRALINE AUX AMANDES

- 2 ounces flour
- 2 ounces butter
- 1/2 pint boiled milk
- 6 eggs
- 3 ounces almond paste
  Chopped almonds
  Vanilla sauce (prepared)

Work flour into the butter until you have a smooth paste; pour the milk into the paste. Add yolks of the eggs and continue stirring until you have a smooth batter. Add 3 ounces almond paste. Incorporate the whites of the eggs into mixture after you have beaten them to a firm stage with the sugar. Pour the batter into soufflé molds, which have been buttered and sprinkled with sugar and flour; add the almonds on top and bake in oven at 350° for 30 minutes. Serve with Vanilla sauce.

Serves: 2

Foyal Restaurant
Martinique, French West Indies
Chef: M. Provost

SOUFFLÉ FORT ROYALE

4 tablespoons butter
2 tablespoons flour
1 cup light cream
6 eggs
4 tablespoons sugar
5 tablespoons Grand Marnier
  Glazed oranges
8 ladyfingers

In a saucepan melt butter, add flour and cook for a short time until mixture colors. Add cream after it has been heated to a boiling point. Stir mixture constantly, cooking for 5 minutes. Beat 5 egg yolks and sugar. Stir this into mixture. Add Grand Marnier. Fold in 6 egg whites which have been beaten stiffly.

In a well-buttered and sugared soufflé dish pour in 1/2 of the mixture. Soak 8 ladyfingers in Grand Marnier and spread them out on the mixture. Spread chopped glazed oranges, soaked in Grand Marnier, over the ladyfingers. Cover with the other 1/2 of the mixture. Bake in hot oven at 450° for 10-12 minutes. Lower heat to 350° and bake for 20 more minutes.

Serves: 4

King Cole
Indianapolis, Indiana
Chef: Edmond Gass

SOUFFLÉ AUX FRAISES

1 cup half and half
2 ounces sugar
4 tablespoons sifted flour
4 egg yolks
3 ounces strawberry preserves
  Powdered sugar
1 pound fresh strawberries
6 egg whites
  Butter
  Vanilla Sauce (prepared)
  Kirschwasser

Bring to a slow rolling boil the half and half cream with 4 tablespoons sugar. Add the sifted flour and continue to cook. Stir for 3 minutes. Remove from stove and add egg yolks, strawberry preserves and fresh strawberries presoaked in 2 ounces sugar. Stiffly beat 6 egg whites and fold lightly into the above mixture.

Butter and sugar the inside surface of a soufflé ramekin before putting in the mixture. Place soufflé in 350° oven and bake for 20-25 minutes. Serve with Vanilla sauce flavored with kirschwasser.

Serves: 4

Desserts

The Quorum Restaurant
Denver, Colorado
Chef: Pierre Wolfe

STRAWBERRIES QUORUM

    2 cups fresh strawberries,
         cleaned, washed and
         quartered
1 1/2 jiggers kirschwasser
    2 teaspoons butter
    2 teaspoons sugar
         Juice of 1 orange
         Peel of 1 orange and 1 lemon
    1 jigger Cointreau
  1/2 jigger cognac
  1/2 jigger rum
         Vanilla ice cream

Soak quartered strawberries in kirschwasser overnight. Melt butter in chafing
dish. Add sugar and cook until lightly
browned. Add orange juice and the peels
of the orange and lemon. Add strawberries with kirschwasser and Cointreau and
heat thoroughly. Add cognac and rum
and set aflame before serving over vanilla
ice cream. Be sure to ladle all juices from
pan with strawberries over the ice cream.

Serves: 4

The Golden Lamb
Lebanon, Ohio
Chef: Erwin Pfeil

SHAKER SUGAR PIE

  1/3 cup flour
    1 cup brown sugar
         9-inch unbaked pie shell
    2 cups light cream
    1 tablespoon vanilla
    1 stick or 1/4 pound butter
         Nutmeg

Thoroughly mix the flour and brown
sugar and spread evenly on bottom of
unbaked pie shell. Add the cream and
vanilla. Slice the stick of butter into 12-
16 pieces and distribute evenly over the
top of pie. Sprinkle with nutmeg. Slowly
bake in oven at 350° for 40-45 minutes or
until firm.

Serves: 8

Lazy Susan Inn
Woodbridge, Virginia

DEEP-DISH CIDER APPLE PIE

      Pastry for 1 crust 8-inch pie
6   large cooking apples
1/4 cup butter or margarine
3/4 cup grated Cheddar cheese
3/4 cup flour
1/2 teaspoon powdered cinnamon
3/4 cup brown sugar
1/3 cup butter or margarine for streusel topping

Start oven, set at hot, 450°. Chill pastry-lined pan. Wash, pare, core and slice apples. Melt 1/4 cup butter in a sauce-pan, add apples and stir lightly until each slice is coated. Remove from heat. Arrange apples in pastry-lined pan. Sprinkle 3/4 cup grated Cheddar cheese over apples. Sprinkle streusel topping over apples.

To prepare streusel topping: sift together 3/4 cup flour, 1/2 teaspoon powdered cinnamon and 3/4 cup brown sugar. Cream 1/3 cup butter and work into the flour and sugar mixture. Bake in hot oven, 450°, for 15 minutes, then reduce temperature to 350° and bake 15-20 minutes longer.

Serves: 6 to 8

Les Champs
New York, New York,
Chef: Mike Fallon

MOUSSE DE SOLE

1   pound fillet of lemon sole
3   egg whites
3/4 pint heavy cream
1/4 teaspoon salt
      Pinch white pepper

Grind raw fillet of sole, add egg whites a little at a time, place in refrigerator and let rest for at least 2 hours. Then add heavy cream, salt and pepper by mixing with a wooden spoon. Place mixture in a buttered mold, 3/4 full. Set the mold in pan of water and cook in a moderate oven 30-35 minutes. When cooked, let set about 2 minutes, then turn out. Serve with lobster sauce, Newburg sauce or white wine sauce.

Serves: 5

Wine: White

Thwaites Inn
City Island, New York
Owner: Robert Borchers

RUM CREAM PIE

      Graham cracker pie shell
6   eggs, beaten
1   cup sugar
1   envelope gelatin
1/2 cup cold water
1   pint whipped cream
1   tablespoon dark rum
      Bittersweet chocolate

Make a graham cracker pie shell (or use prepared). Beat eggs until light in color.

Beat in sugar. Dissolve gelatin in 1/2 cup cold water. Place gelatin over low heat and bring to boil. When gelatin is dissolved, pour over sugar and egg mixture, stirring briskly. Let cool. Whip 1 pint cream until fairly stiff (careful not to make butter) and flavor with dark rum. Fold whipped cream into egg mixture which should be cool, but not set. Pour into the graham cracker pie shell. Sprinkle generously with bittersweet chocolate and serve cold.

Serves: 6

Farmer's Daughter
Orlando Park, Illinois
Chef: Deitrich Schroeder

IRISH WHISKEY PIE

1 tablespoon plus 1 teaspoon
   gelatin
   Pinch salt
1/4 cup milk
2 squares unsweetened chocolate
1/4 cup egg yolks
1/4 cup plus 2 tablespoons sugar
1/4 cup egg whites
2 tablespoons sugar
1/4 cup sliced almonds
2 tablespoons Irish whiskey
   9-inch baked pie shell
3/4 cup whipped cream
   Toasted almonds for garnish

Dissolve gelatin in cold water. Cook over double boiler until clear. Mix salt, milk, chocolate, egg yolks and sugar. Cook until chocolate and sugar are dissolved. Put in bowl. Add gelatin mixture. Chill over crushed ice until syrupy. Beat egg whites, adding 2 tablespoons sugar gradually. Fold in chocolate mixture to egg whites. Add nuts and whiskey. Fold until smooth. Pour into 9-inch baked pie shell. Top with whipped cream and sliced toasted almonds.

Serves: 6

Maison Lafite
New Orleans, Louisiana
Chef: Albert Sipin

MOUSSE AU CHOCOLATE

1/4 cup sugar
4 tablespoons dark rum
1/4 pound semisweet chocolate
2 egg whites
2 cups heavy cream

In a small saucepan, cook the sugar and rum over a very low heat until the sugar melts and becomes a syrup. Don't let it turn brown.

Break the chocolate into small pieces, melt in double boiler. When the chocolate is smooth add the syrup (syrup and chocolate should be about the same temperature). Stir vigorously with wooden spoon. If the mixture is too heavy, add lukewarm water until smooth. Beat the egg whites until they are stiff. Whip the heavy cream. Combine. Fold the chocolate into the mixture. Chill and grate some chocolate on top before serving.

Serves: 4

Wine: Château Coutet

L'Orangerie
New York, New York

HAZEL-NUT MOUSSE

2 cups milk
1 1/2 cups sugar
6 egg yolks
1/2 ounce granulated gelatin
1 cup roasted hazel-nuts
3 cups heavy cream, whipped

Boil the milk and 1/2 cup sugar. Once boiling, add milk to egg yolks stirring constantly. Return mixture back into saucepan and stir until it thickens over low fire, but do not boil or it will separate. Remove from fire. Soften gelatin in 1 spoon of cold water and add to mixture. Let it cool. Boil remaining sugar and 2 tablespoons water. When sugar is golden, add roasted hazel-nuts and mix well. Take off the fire and pour on oiled tray. Let cool until hard, then grind it coarsely. Mix in above mousse with 2 cups of whipped cream and fill into champagne glasses. Garnish top with remaining whipped cream and chill.

Serves: 4

Justine's Inc.
Atlanta, Georgia

LOTUS ICE CREAM

    2   cups almonds
        Grated rinds of 10 lemons
    2   cups lemon juice
    4   quarts heavy cream
    6   cups sugar
    2   tablespoons almond flavoring
    2   teaspoons vanilla

Brown 2 cups almonds in oven—then chop fine. To 4 quarts cream stir in sugar. Add almonds, grated lemon rind, the almond flavoring and vanilla. Stir in lemon juice and freeze.

Yields: 1 1/2 gallons

Stone Ends Restaurant
Albany, New York

SOUR CREAM PRUNE PIE

    2   cups cooked prunes
    2   eggs
  2/3   cup honey,
  2/3   cup sour cream
  1/4   teaspoon salt
    1   tablespoon lemon juice
        Pastry for 8-inch double-crust
        pie

Cut prunes from pits and into large pieces. Beat eggs lightly and blend in the honey, sour cream, salt and lemon juice until smooth and creamy. Add prunes. Pour into pastry-lined 8-inch pie plate. Cover with top crust. Flute edge and prick here and there with fork. Bake in 400° oven for 45 minutes until golden brown.

Serves: 6

Whipple House
West Branch, Iowa
Chef: Dietrich Schroeder

HEAVENLY CHOCOLATE PIE

    1   baked 8″ pie shell
    2   eggs, separated
  1/2   teaspoon vinegar
  1/4   teaspoon cinnamon
  1/4   teaspoon salt
  1/2   cup sugar
    1   (6-ounce) package semisweet-
        chocolate bits
  1/4   cup water
    1   cup whipping cream

Beat together egg whites, vinegar, cinnamon and salt until stiff but not dry. Gradually add sugar and beat until very stiff. Spread over bottom and sides of pie shell. Bake at 325° for 15-18 minutes and cool.

Melt chocolate bits over hot, not boiling, water. Blend in egg yolks which have been beaten with the 1/4 cup water. Stir until smooth. Spread 3 tablespoons of the mixture over the cooled meringue. Chill remainder of chocolate mixture. Whip cream until stiff. Add sugar and cinnamon. Spread 1/2 of this over the chocolate layer in the pie shell. Fold chilled chocolate mixture into remaining whipped cream. Spread over center of pie. Chill 4 hours before serving.

Serves: 6

Chalet Suisse
New York, New York
Executive Chef: Erwin Herger

SWISS ONION AND CHEESE PIE

    4 whole eggs
    1 pint milk
    1 pint light cream
       Salt, pepper, nutmeg to taste
       Pie crust for 11-inch plate,
          homemade or packaged
  1/2 pound Switzerland Swiss cheese
  1/2 pound Gruyére cheese
    2 large onions, sliced and sautéed
          in about 2 tablespoons butter

Blend together, to make custard, the whole eggs, milk, light cream, salt, pepper and nutmeg. Line an 11-inch pie plate with homemade pie crust or packaged mix. Grate and mix together the Swiss and Gruyère cheeses.

Preheat oven to 375°. Line pie plate with crust—add 1/2 of grated cheese, then sautéed onion on top and add rest of cheese until crust is completely covered. Add custard filling to within 1/4 of the rim of the crust. Place in preheated oven and cook for approximately 45 minutes until custard is set. Served with a salad this makes a light and lovely lunch or late evening supper.

Serves: 6

Wine: Light dry white—Chablis
or sauterne

Golden Fox Steak House
Albany, New York
Chef: Vincent Figliomeni

STRAWBERRY TART

    1 whole egg
    1 egg yolk
    3 tablespoons sugar
    3 tablespoons flour
    2 teaspoons softened gelatin
    1 tablespoon cold water
  3/4 cup hot milk
    2 egg whites, beaten stiff
  1/2 cup heavy cream, whipped
    2 tablespoons Jamaican rum
    4 baked pastry tart shells
          (prepared)
    1 quart fresh strawberries
    3 tablespoons red currant jelly
    1 tablespoon boiling water

In a saucepan beat 1 whole egg, egg yolk, sugar and flour until mixture is light and fluffy. Soften gelatin in cold water and dissolve in the hot milk. Add to the egg mixture and cook over moderate heat, stirring constantly until it is hot and thick, but be careful not to let it boil. Stir the mixture over cracked ice to let it cool quickly, then fold in the beaten egg whites, the whipped cream and rum. Turn the cream mixture into the baked tart shells and arrange large ripe strawberries, pyramid style, over the cream. Glacé with red currant jelly that has been melted and thinned with the boiling water.

Serves: 4

Wine: Champagne

Chez Vito Inc.
New York, New York
Chef: Mario Rasso

GATEAU D'AMOUR CHEZ VITO

12 eggs
1 cup sugar
1 cup flour
1 cup sweet butter
1 cup confectioner's sugar
2 cups chocolate pudding
1/2 cup Grand Marnier
1 pint heavy cream

Whip eggs and sugar until thick and foamy. When mixture clings to spoon, gradually add flour and continue to whip. Pour into a 14-inch round pan or 2 10-inch round pans which have been lightly buttered and sprinkled with flour. Bake 30-40 minutes in preheated oven at 300°. When baked, set aside and let cool.

In separate bowl whip the butter and confectioner's sugar until creamy and set aside.

Chocolate Pudding
8-10 egg whites
1 pound sugar
8 ounces bitter chocolate, melted
2-3 tablespoons whipped cream

(Make pudding according to directions on package and let cool or make your own favorite chocolate pudding or mousse.) Ours: whip whites of 8-10 eggs with 1 pound sugar until stiff but not dry. Add 8 ounces melted bitter chocolate and 2-3 tablespoons whipped cream.

After cakes have cooled, slice into 4 layers (3 layers if 14-inch pan is used) and cut into heart-shapes. Sprinkle each layer with Grand Marnier. Place 1 layer on plate and spread with butter cream.

Alternate rest of layers with chocolate pudding and butter cream. Whip the heavy cream until thick and spread over filled layers. Decorate to taste.

Serves: 16

Charles French Restaurant
New York, New York

COUPE ST. JACQUES

Fresh fruit salad
Kirschwasser
1 small scoop orange sherbet
1 small scoop lemon sherbet
1 small scoop raspberry sherbet
Fresh strawberries

Marinate any desired combination of fresh fruit salad in kirschwasser. Fill in champagne glass. On top put 1 small scoop each of orange sherbet, lemon sherbet and raspberry sherbet. Decorate with fresh strawberries. Sprinkle few drops of kirschwasser over it and serve.

Serves: 2

Villa Teo
Chapel Hill, North Carolina
Chef: Henri Paul Pellapiot

ZABAGLIONE

2   teaspoons unflavored gelatin
3   tablespoons cold water
9   large egg yolks
9   tablespoons sugar
1   cup Marsala wine
     Chantilly cream
6   glacé cherries
     Unsweetened chocolate

Soften gelatin in cold water and melt in double boiler. Whip egg yolks in another double boiler and slowly whip in sugar and wine. Beat vigorously until mixture is foamy and starting to thicken. Add the softened gelatin and continue beating while taking the mixture away from heat. Pour into custard cups and chill. Just before serving, garnish each portion with dollop of Chantilly cream, a glacé cherry and a few shavings of chocolate.

Chantilly cream
Whip 1 cup cream, fold in 2 tablespoons confectioner's sugar and 1/2 teaspoon vanilla.

Serves: 6

Masson's Restaurant Français
New Orleans, Louisiana

SABAYON

6   eggs, separated
3/4 cup granulated sugar
3/4 cup cream sherry wine
3/4 cup whipping cream, whipped
1   teaspoon vanilla extract

Separate eggs. Beat yolks with sugar until creamy. Add sherry and cook in double boiler until thick. Cool in mixing bowl for 10-15 minutes. Add beaten whipped cream. Beat egg whites with vanilla until stiff; fold into mixture. Divide into 6 ramekins and chill 2-3 hours.

Serves: 6

The Monks Inn
New York, New York

FONDUE AU CHOCOLAT

1   cup water
1/2 cup sugar
1   pound hard sweet Norwegian
       chocolate
3   ounces sweet Swiss chocolate
1   shot kirsch
1   shot cherry liqueur
3   teaspoons concentrated sweet
       milk

Boil for 15 minutes—1 cup water and 1/2 cup sugar. Add hard chocolate and, on very low flame, stir constantly until chocolate is melted. Add Swiss chocolate. Remove from fire and add kirsch, cherry liqueur and sweet milk. Serve on a fondue burner on a very low flame. Serve over day-old pound cake so it is crusty. Use fondue forks.

Serves: 4

*Mader's German Restaurant
Milwaukee, Wisconsin
Chef: Mrs. Catherine Mader*

SCHWARTZWALD TORTE
(Black Forest Cherry Torte)

6	eggs, separated
3/4	cup sifted flour
1/4	cup sifted cocoa
1/4	teaspoon salt
1 1/4	cups sugar
1	teaspoon vanilla
1	tablespoon water
1/4	cup sugar
1/4	cup brandy
2	cups whipping cream
1/4	cup confectioner's sugar
2	tablespoons brandy
	Shaved chocolate
	Maraschino cherries

Separate yolks from whites of eggs and allow both to warm to room temperature. Meantime, sift flour once, measure, add cocoa and salt and sift again. In small bowl of electric mixer, beat egg yolks until thick and lemon colored. Add 3/4 cup of the sugar gradually and continue to beat until egg yolks are thick and creamy, all has been added, and the entire mixture is thick. Transfer to large mixer bowl. Beat egg whites until frothy throughout then add 1/2 cup sugar gradually, beating constantly. Continue to beat until stiff peaks form. Fold into egg yolk mixture. Sift flour mixture gradually over egg mixture, folding gently but thoroughly. Add vanilla and blend. Turn into 2 deep 9-inch layer cake pans, the bottoms of which have been lightly greased and floured. Bake in a 350° oven about 25 minutes, or until cake tests done. Remove from oven and cool in pans 10 minutes.

Meantime combine sugar and water for glaze in small saucepan. Place over low heat and stir until sugar is dissolved. Remove from heat and cool slightly then add brandy. Cut cake layers from sides of pans and remove to wire cake racks. Brush brandy glaze over top of warm layers and allow to cool.

To make frosting: combine cream and confectioner's sugar and chill thoroughly. Beat until thick and light, then add brandy.

Spread whipped cream frosting on 1 layer of cake and top with the second layer. Use remainder of cream to frost sides and top. Sprinkle with shaved chocolate and garnish with well-drained maraschino cherries. Keep refrigerated.

Serves: 6

---

*Cambridge Inn
Paramus, New Jersey
Chef: Victor Sidone*

CRANBERRY RELISH

1	pound raw cranberries
2	whole oranges
1	whole lemon
2	pounds sugar
1	ounce brandy

Grind raw cranberries with whole oranges and lemon. Add sugar and brandy.

Serves: 6

Brennan's French Restaurant
New Orleans, Louisiana
Chef: Fernando Oca

BANANAS FOSTER

2 tablespoons brown sugar
1 tablespoon butter
1 ripe banana, peeled and sliced lengthwise
Dash cinnamon
1/2 ounce banana liqueur
1/2 ounce white rum
1 large scoop vanilla ice cream

Melt brown sugar and butter in flat chafing dish. Add banana and sauté until tender. Sprinkle with cinnamon. Pour in banana liqueur and rum over all and flame. Baste with warm liquid until flame burns out. Serve immediately over ice cream.

Serves: 1

Luchow's
New York, New York

ZWETCHGENKNODEL
(Bavarian Plum Dumplings)

20 small, fresh ripe blue plums or apricots
20 large sugar cubes
5 large potatoes, boiled and skinned
2 1/4 cups unsifted all-purpose flour
1 egg yolk
1 whole egg
2 tablespoons soft butter
1/3 cup sugar
1/4 teaspoon salt
Cinnamon and sugar

Using sharp knife, slit each plum and remove pit. Place sugar cubes inside each plum.

Finely grate potatoes into large bowl and gradually beat in flour a little at a time. Beat in egg yolk, egg, butter, sugar and salt: beat very thoroughly until dough loses most of its stickiness and resembles soft biscuit dough. Place on floured board and shape into a long roll about 2 inches in diameter. Cut into 20 slices, 1 inch thick. Pat each slice into large circle. Shape dough evenly and smoothly around plum. Place in deep boiling water—do not crowd—and boil, uncovered, 15 minutes. Remove and drain.

Serve as main course, accompaniment to poultry, or as dessert sprinkled with cinnamon and sugar.

Serves: 6

Giambelli Restaurant
New York, New York
Chef: Mario Boselli

STRAWBERRIES À LA GIAMBELLI

2	tablespoons sugar
1/4	orange, rind only
1/2	lemon, rind only
1/2	ounce lemon juice
2	ounces orange juice
1/2	pint fresh ripe strawberries
1	banana, ripe but firm
1/2	ounce orange Curaçao or Triple Sec
1	ounce Grand Marnier
2	teaspoons fine sugar
1	ounce brandy
	Vanilla ice cream
	Whipped cream

On a low flame, in saucepan, melt sugar with the orange and lemon rinds until sugar is blond-brownish color (caramelled). Add the fruit juices and stir until they are caramelled with the sugar. Add fresh fruits and cook 5-6 minutes until juice penetrates them (watch that the fruits do not burn). Add Grand Marnier and Curaçao and cook few minutes more. Sprinkle with fine sugar. Add brandy and slide pan around to enable brandy to flame.

To complete, serve with vanilla ice cream and whipped cream. The ice cream and whipped cream should be placed in cold dishes just before the brandy is added to the recipe.

Serves: 2

Marchi's
New York, New York

CROSTOLI

2	eggs
2	tablespoons sugar
1/2	cup butter, melted
1	glass milk
1	tablespoon rum or vanilla flavoring (optional)
4	cups flour

Place eggs in bowl with sugar and mix well. Add melted butter and milk and 1 tablespoon rum or vanilla flavoring, if desired. Sift in the flour and mix well until you have workable dough. Then roll out the dough as thin as possible. Cut into ribbons, 2 inches wide, and fry in oil until golden brown. To crown-shape the Crostoli, use pincers at each end and twist into a circle as they are taken out of the oil. Let dry and sprinkle with powdered sugar.

Serves: 8 to 12

Steer Palace
New York, New York

STEER PALACE BANANA MOUSSE

    1/2 cup sugar
      1 tablespoon cornstarch
         Dash salt
      3 large egg yolks
  1 1/2 cups light cream
    1/2 teaspoon vanilla extract
      4 ripe bananas mashed with juice
         of 1 lemon
      1 cup heavy cream, whipped

Combine first 3 ingredients in a saucepan or top of double boiler. Beat in egg yolks and 1/4 cup light cream. Heat remaining cream only until hot—do not boil. Add vanilla extract to the sugar and egg mixture. Stir and cook until custard is thick, over low heat or, if in double boiler, over simmering not boiling water. Cool, stirring frequently to prevent a skin from forming over the top. Blend with mashed bananas and fold in 1 1/2 cups whipped cream. Fill in champagne glasses. Garnish top with remaining whipped cream and chill for 1/2 hour before serving.

Serves: 6

Chanteclair
Indianapolis, Indiana

CAFÉ DIABLO À LA CHANTECLAIR

      6 regular cups of a first-class
         espresso coffee
      2 ounces Triple Sec liqueur
      2 ounces Courvoisier brandy
      1 ounce anise
     12 cloves
         Large orange rind
      2 cinnamon sticks

First prepare the coffee espresso; have ready in pot.

Pour liqueurs into large silver bowl. Place bowl over flame or richaud, allow to heat for 1 minute. Flame inside of bowl with match (liqueur will ignite). Have cloves prepared so you now have a long orange rind studded with cloves and twisted and held at one end by fork. Hold rind about 2 feet above flaming bowl. Pick up liqueur with ladle and gently let it run down the orange rind back into the bowl. Repeat this procedure 3-4 times. Now pour the coffee into the bowl putting out the flame as you do so. Serve in demitasse cups with pieces of cinnamon sticks in cups.

Serves: 8 to 12

Hugo's Regency Hyatt House
Atlanta, Georgia
Chef: Ludwig Strodel

STRAWBERRY CHEESE PIE

8	ounces cream cheese
1/2	cup sugar
1	cup cooked rice, cold
1 1/2	tablespoons plain gelatin
1/3	cup strawberry juice
1	pound sliced frozen strawberries, thawed and drained
1/2	pint whipping cream, whipped
	9-inch baked pie shell

Mix cream cheese and sugar, whip until fluffy. Gradually add cooked rice, dissolved gelatin, strawberries. Fold in whipped cream last. Put mixture in prebaked pie shell, spread evenly with help of spatula. Garnish with strawberries. Chill before serving.

To prepare rice: stir rice in 2 cups of boiling, lightly salted water. Cover and simmer over low heat for 20 minutes.

To prepare gelatin: soften gelatin in strawberry juice, stir and heat until dissolved. Let cool before adding to the cheese mixture.

Serves: 6

Italian Village
Chicago, Illinois

ZABAGLIONE
(Hot Wine Custard)

8	egg yolks
2	egg whites
1/2	cup sugar
1	cup Marsala

Beat in the top of double boiler 8 egg yolks and 2 egg whites with 1/2 cup sugar. When the mixture is very thick and creamy, add 1 cup Marsala, place the pan over simmering hot water and heat the mixture gradually, never ceasing to beat with a rotary or electric beater. When the zabaglione is very thick and hot, but just before it reaches the boiling point, spoon it into glasses and serve at once.

Serves: 6

Luchow's
New York, New York

PFIRSICH KALTSCHALE

4	large ripe peaches, peeled
	Granulated sugar
2	cups water
1	cup sugar
1/4	cup quick-cooking tapioca
	Juice of 2 large lemons
1	tablespoon Rhine or Moselle wine

Thinly slice 2 of the peaches; cover completely with sugar. Mash and strain remaining 2 peaches; pour over sliced peaches. Combine water, sugar, tapioca and lemon juice; boil 5 minutes. Stir in wine. Pour over peaches. Chill before serving.

Serves: 4

Old Club Restaurant
Alexandria, Virginia
Chef: William Barnes

DEEP DISH APPLE PIE

7	pounds sliced apples
1	pound brown sugar
1	pound granulated white sugar
3	tablespoons nutmeg
3	teaspoons cinnamon
5	ounces flour
1	tablespoon salt
4	ounces apple wine
8	ounces apple juice
4	ounces butter
3	cups pastry flour
4	ounces shortening
1/2	teaspoon salt
1/2	pound butter

Place apples in 15″ x 9″ x 2 1/2″ pan. Blend sugar, nutmeg, cinnamon, flour, salt, apple wine and juice together and pour over apples. Cut butter into thin slices and divide evenly over apples. Mix pie crust with last 4 ingredients and roll out oblong 1/2-inch thick. Cover apples and cut 8 1-inch-long cuts evenly in crust. Bake at 425° for 1 hour. Lower temperature to 325° and continue baking until crust is brown.

Serves: 10

Luchow's
New York, New York

KASTANIEN IN APFELN
(Chestnuts with Apples)

4	cooking apples, peeled, cored and cut in eighths
	Rind and juice of 1 large lemon
1/2	cup water
1/4	cup sugar
1	can (11-ounces) chestnuts, drained and cut in half
2	tablespoons white wine (optional)

Combine apples, lemon rind and juice, water and sugar in medium-size saucepan; simmer gently about 7 minutes or until apples are nearly tender and water becomes syrupy. Stir in chestnuts and wine to taste. Chill.

Serve as garniture for roast game or poultry or as a dessert with sweetened whipped cream.

Serves: 6 to 8

Cork 'N Cleaver Restaurant
Colorado Springs, Colorado
Chef: Jon Oud

HOT WINE ON A COLD NIGHT

1/5	dry red wine
1	cup apple cider
1	cup water
1	cinnamon stick
2	tablespoons sugar
1	tablespoon lemon juice
1/2	teaspoon nutmeg
3	cloves
1	very generous dash bitters

Boil ingredients together 15 minutes and strain.

Serves: 4

Hawaiian Village
Tampa, Florida
Chef: Joe King Sui

SAMOAN TYPHOON

        4   ounces fresh lime juice
        2   ounces fresh orange juice
        2   ounces pineapple juice
        1   ounce honey
        2   ounces passion fruit
        4   ounces Ron Rico dark rum
        1   ounce Meyers rum
        1   ounce 100 proof vodka
        2   pineapple slices
        2   sugared maraschino cherries

Combine the ingredients (do not include the garnish of pineapple slices or maraschino cherries) in a stainless steel mixing cup over shaved ice. Chill. Then place in blender and mix for 30 seconds. Pour the mix into 21-ounce brandy inhalers. Decorate with a pineapple slice and a sugared maraschino cherry.

Serves: 2

Sally's Steak House
Highland Park, New Jersey
Chef: Vilda

SOUTHERN PECAN PIE

       36   eggs
    4 1/2   cups granulated sugar
        7   cups light Karo syrup
        7   cups dark Karo syrup
        8   teaspoons pure vanilla
      3/4   cup melted shortening
        1   teaspoon salt
        6   cups shelled pecan pieces
        4   unbaked 8-inch pie shells

Beat eggs lightly. Add sugar, syrups, vanilla, shortening and salt. Place nuts in pie shells, pour mixture over nuts. Bake in slow oven, 325°-350° approximately 1 hour or until pies puff up.

Serves: 16

INDEX

Recipes

And Finally, Saucery

Restaurants and Locations